Capitalism in Evolution

Capitalism in Evolution

Global Contentions – East and West

Edited by

Geoffrey M. Hodgson

Research Professor, University of Hertfordshire Business School, Hertford, UK

Makoto Itoh

Professor of Economics at Kokugakuin University, Tokyo and Emeritus Professor, University of Tokyo, Japan

Nobuharu Yokokawa

Professor of Economics, Musashi University, Tokyo, Japan

Edward Elgar
Cheltenham, UK • Northampton, MA, USA

Published by
Edward Elgar Publishing Limited
Glensanda House
Montpellier Parade
Cheltenham
Glos GL50 1UA
UK

Edward Elgar Publishing, Inc.
136 West Street
Suite 202
Northampton
Massachusetts 01060
USA

A catalogue record for this book
is available from the British Library

Library of Congress Cataloguing in Publication Data
Capitalism in evolution : global contentions—East and West / edited by Geoffrey M. Hodgson, Makoto Itoh, Nobuharu Yokokawa.
    p. cm.
  Includes bibliographical references and index.
  1. Capitalism. 2. Evolutionary economics. I. Hodgson, Geoffrey Martin, 1946– II. Ito, Makoto, 1936– III. Yokokawa, Nobuharu, 1950–

HB501 .C242454 2001
330.12'2—dc21

2001023588

ISBN 1 85898 860 8

Typeset by Manton Typesetters, Louth, Lincolnshire, UK.
Printed and bound in Great Britain by Bookcraft (Bath) Ltd.

Contents

Figures

Tables

Contributors

Samuel Bowles was born in 1939. He received his PhD from Harvard University, Cambridge, MA where he taught from 1965 to 1973. He is currently Professor of Economics at the University of Massachusetts at Amherst, Director of the Economics Program at the Santa Fe Institute, and cohead of the Research Network on Inequality and Economic Performance. His many publications include *Beyond the Waste Land* (with David Gordon and Thomas Weisskopf, 1984), *Democracy and Capitalism* (with Herbert Gintis, 1986) and *Recasting Egalitarianism* (with Herbert Gintis, 1999). His recent papers are available at http://www-unix.oit.umass.edu/~bowles/.

Robert A. Boyer was born in 1943 in Nice, France. He was educated at the Ecole Polytechnique, Paris I University, Paris VII University, Ecole Nationale des Ponts et Chaussées and Institut d'Etudes Politiques de Paris. Since 1997 he has been a Member of the Council of Economic Analysis, Office of the Prime Minister of France. His recent work includes *States Against Markets* (edited with Daniel Drache, 1996), *Contemporary Capitalism* (edited with J. Rogers Hollingsworth, 1997), *After Fordism* (with J.P. Durand, 1997) and *Japanese Capitalism in Crisis* (edited with Toshio Yamada, 2000).

Herbert M. Gintis was born in 1940. He received his PhD from Harvard University, Cambridge, MA. He is currently Professor of Economics at the State University of Massachusetts at Amherst. His many publications include *Democracy and Capitalism* (with Samuel Bowles, 1986), *Economic Policy after the Conservative Era* (with Gerald Epstein, 1995), *Recasting Egalitarianism* (with Samuel Bowles, 1999) and *Game Theory Evolving* (2000). His website is http://www-unix.oit.umass.edu/~gintis.

Geoffrey M. Hodgson was born in 1946 and educated at the University of Manchester, UK. He is currently a Research Professor at the University of Hertfordshire, Hertford, UK. He was formerly a Reader in Economics at the University of Cambridge, UK. His many publications include *Economics and Institutions* (1998), *Economics and Evolution* (1993), *Economics and Utopia* (1999), *Evolution and Institutions* (1999) and *How Economics Forgot History* (2001). His recent papers are summarized on his website: www.herts.ac.uk/business/esst.Staff/g-hodgson/hodgson. html.

Makoto Itoh was born in 1936 and received his PhD from the University of Tokyo. He is Professor of Economics at Kokugakuin University and Emeritus Professor at the University of Tokyo. He has taught at many universities in the USA, UK, Canada and Australia. He has published widely in both English and Japanese. His books in English include *The Basic Theory of Capitalism* (1988), *The World Economic Crisis and Japanese Capitalism* (1990), *Political Economy for Socialism* (1995) and *Political Economy of Money and Finance* (1999).

Makoto Noguchi was born in 1948. He received his PhD in Economics from the University of Tokyo. He is currently Professor of Economics at Senshu University. His publications in Japanese include *Modern Capitalism and Theories of Effective Demand* (1990) and *Marx Strikes Back* (edited with Nobuharu Yokokawa, 1996).

Ugo Pagano was born in 1951 in Naples. He received his PhD in 1983 from the University of Cambridge, UK, where he later became a University Lecturer and a Fellow of Pembroke College. Currently he is Professor of Economic Policy at the University of Siena and Recurrent Visiting Professor at the Central European University, Budapest. His many publications include the monograph *Work and Welfare in Economic Theory* (1985) and *The Evolution of Economic Diversity* (edited with Antonio Nicita, 2001).

Robert E. Rowthorn was born in 1939 and educated at the University of Oxford, UK. He is currently Professor of Economics at the University of Cambridge, UK. His many publications include *De-industrialization and Foreign Trade* (with John R. Wells, 1987), *The Role of the State in Economic Change* (edited with Ha-Joon Chang, 1995) and *Democracy and Efficiency in the Economic Enterprise* (edited with Ugo Pagano, 1996).

Yoshinori Shiozawa was born in 1943 and educated at Kyoto University. He is currently Professor of Economics in Osaka City University. His many publications in Japanese include *Eutaxy of the Market* (1990), *Introduction to Complexity Economics* (1990), *Consequences of Complexity* (1997) and *Evolution as Method* (2000). His website is http://www.shiozawa.net.

Kiichiro Yagi was born in 1947 and educated in Tokyo University and Nagoya University. He is currently Professor of Economics in Graduate School of Kyoto University. His publications in Japanese include *Studies on the History of Austrian Economic Thought* (1988), *Restitution of Civil Society* (1998) and *Social Economics of Modern Japan* (1999).

Nobuharu Yokokawa was born in 1950 in Kyoto, Japan. He received his PhD from the University of Cambridge, UK in 1983. He is currently Professor of Economics at Musashi University, Japan. His published work in Japanese include *Value, Employment and Crisis* (1989) and *Marx Strikes Back* (edited with Makoto Noguchi, 1996).

1. Introduction

Geoffrey M. Hodgson, Makoto Itoh and Nobuharu Yokokawa

THE PRECARIOUSNESS OF WORLD MARKETS

The chapters in this volume are written in the context of vigorous but potentially unstable developments in the world capitalist system. Especially in the second half of the twentieth century, capitalism has achieved spectacular rates of innovation and growth. But the system is still menaced by financial crises and economic recessions. There is widespread uncertainty about the future. The crash of 1929 is a distant memory. But there was also more recently the collapse of the Bretton Woods agreement in 1971 and the massive and disruptive East Asian and Russian devaluations of 1997. Arguably, furthermore, if the US Federal Reserve Bank had not baled out the Merton–Scholes, Long Term Capital Management hedge fund in 1998, there could have been a world financial collapse. Today, world financial institutions are vulnerable and insufficiently developed to cope with the huge volume of global financial speculation. Many less-developed countries are still burdened by debts that they have little chance of repaying to their rich lenders. Huge trade deficits have piled up in even the richest of nations, defying the dogma of the self-regulating market. At the same time, the doctrinal reliance on unregulated markets inhibits attempts to regulate and stabilize the world financial system.

The spread of world markets has put all national economies in a precarious position. The less-developed economies are particularly vulnerable. The World Bank and the International Monetary Fund have obliged them to enter the global market. Waves of speculative funds flow electronically across national boundaries, in turn boosting expectations and then dashing them again. The possibility of crises depends on little else but a concurrent withdrawal of financial capital, from major economic operations across the world. This can result from a growing and self-reinforcing wave of financial panic, spreading rapidly around the globe. Its likelihood is all the greater because of deregulation. Globalization makes the impact of any crisis more vast.

Many mainstream economists still believe that the unfettered market is the only viable means of economic coordination. For them, free markets are a necessary and perhaps even sufficient condition for the efficient allocation of resources. Typically, any failure of markets to deliver this outcome is often attributed to restrictions and impediments to their free operation. Further deregulation is thus seen as the only possible policy solution. All markets for labour, capital and their products must be free of all regulations and constraints. The doctrine has become self-reinforcing: if the economic system is working then this medicine is clearly doing its job; if the economic system has problems, then a bigger dose of the same medicine is clearly required. As we never actually reach the ideal destination of a wholly pure and free market then it is always possible to call for another dose of deregulation. This argument is clearly circular and non-falsifiable.

However, this view is challengeable on both theoretical and policy grounds. The naive, idealized view of a 'pure' market is untenable. History shows a rich diversity of real, market economies. Markets are themselves institutions, embedded in a social and cultural framework. The alternative view, presented here, is of a historical and geographical diversity of capitalist systems. To understand capitalism in evolution, this diversity must be taken into account. Furthermore, capitalism is always and necessarily impure. The pure, free market system has never existed and can never exist. The analysis of capitalism requires an understanding of the ways in which different economic subsystems are combined. It cannot proceed on the basis of the unrealizable goal of a pure system.

THE AMERICAN MODEL AND ITS RIVALS

From 1917 to 1989, there was rivalry between centrally planned and capitalist solutions to the problems of economic stability and growth. However, with the collapse of the Soviet Union in 1991 and the conversion of China into a market economy, the proponents of market capitalism claimed victory. The collapse of the Soviet system was widely interpreted as a demonstration of the failure of central planning. Furthermore, even Western advocates of a mixture of markets and central planning lost heart. Not only the communist movement but also the social democratic parties of the world were placed in a doctrinal crisis.

In addition, by the early 1990s, the period of rapid growth of the Japanese economy had come to an end. Accordingly, Japanese capitalism was no longer paraded as an alternative 'model' to the American system. The Japanese recession led to similar slowdowns in other, formerly fast-growing, East Asian economies. By the end of the 1990s, the American model of capitalism was seen as the only possible option. Its former challengers – such as Russia and Japan – had substantial difficulties of their own. Soviet-style systems of central planning had collapsed and the Japanese economy had endured a decade of sluggish overall growth. The rivals of Sovietism, on the one hand, and alternative capitalisms, on the other, had withdrawn from the race. The American model was apparently supreme.

Again, this view is challenged in this book. In some chapters the reasons for the Japanese slowdown are dissected. In others it is argued for a plausible variety of capitalist systems. Overall, this book brings together the writings of several global scholars, from different intellectual traditions and geographical locations, to consider the recent and future evolution of the world capitalist system. The authors come from each part of the so called economic 'triad': Europe, East Asia and North America. By representing diverse opinions, from a variety of divergent socioeconomic contexts, this book aims to contribute to the analysis of the modern global economy and to open up critical conversations that may lead to further fruitful research.

MARXIST ECONOMICS AND BEYOND

Perhaps the greatest single analysis of the nature and development of the capitalist system was that by Karl Marx. Although his analysis and predictions have been challenged, his book *Capital* remains one of the greatest works on capitalism and its evolution.

All the authors and editors of the present volume have been influenced to some degree by Marxism. However, among them there is no unanimity of attitude here to Marxist analysis. Some are Marxists: others are not. But what all authors and editors share is an appreciation of Marx's position and a similar concern to reveal the dynamics of capitalist development.

For a brief period in the 1970s, Marxist economics was discussed in the universities of Western Europe and North America. Since 1945, Marxist ideas have been generally more prominent in Japan. In economics, one of the most influential Japanese Marxists was Kozo Uno (1897–1970). He developed a distinctive version of Marxist analysis that remains central to all discussion in this area in Japan.

An understanding of Japanese Marxism requires some knowledge of the works of Uno. However, only a small proportion of his works have been translated or discussed in English (Sekine, 1975; Uno; 1980, Itoh, 1980). Uno's work raises important questions concerning the role of different levels of analysis. It has also fuelled an important theoretical debate on how to deal analytically with the manifest varieties of capitalism of the late twentieth century. For these reasons, a brief discussion of some of his ideas is included below.

Since the 1980s the proportion of academics adhering to Marxism in Japanese universities has declined. Marxism was never so prominent among intellectuals in North America or even Western Europe, as it was in Japan from 1945 to 1980.

Accordingly, in the 1980s and 1990s there has been the growth of alternative (non-mainstream and non-Marxist) approaches to economic analysis in all three parts of the 'triad'. One of the most important of these was the French *régulation* school. In large part this came out of Marxism but soon acquired an identity of its own. As well as Marxism, it also drew on writings in the Post Keynesian tradition. Other post-Marxist groupings formed in North America, for instance the grouping of 'radical economists' at the University of Massachusetts at Amherst. Furthermore, a rival of 'old institutionalist' and 'evolutionary' approaches spread across all three parts of the triad. All these strands of thinking, including Marxism, are represented in this volume.

THE NATURE OF CAPITALISM

Capitalism is defined as a system in which markets and commodity production are pervasive, including a labour market and a capital market. Capitalism is essentially a type of market system involving extensive private property, capital markets and employment contracts. However, markets and private property are necessary but not sufficient features of capitalism: not all market systems are capitalist systems. In short, capitalism is generalized commodity production. Commodities are goods or services that are destined to be objects of market or other contractual exchange. Capitalism is generalized commodity production in a double sense. First, because under capitalism most goods and services are destined for sale on the market, that is, they are commodities. An important example is the existence of a market for capital. Second, because under capitalism one type of item is importantly a commodity: labour power, or the capacity for work. In other words, an important feature of capitalism is the existence of a labour market in which labour is hired by an employer and put to work in a firm according to the terms of an employment contract.

In *Capital*, Marx (1981, p. 1019) clearly identified a 'characteristic trait' of the capitalist mode of production as follows:

> It produces its products as commodities. The fact that it produces commodities does not in itself distinguish it from other modes of production; but that the dominant and determining character of its product is the commodity certainly does so. This means, first of all, that ... labour generally appears as wage-labour ... [and] the relationship of capital to wage-labour determines the whole character of the mode of production.

Under capitalism, wage labour is a key characteristic of capitalist firms and most production takes place in capitalist firms. The 'capitalist firm' was regarded by Marx (1976, pp. 291–2) as an institution where:

1. '[T]he worker works under the control of the capitalist to whom his labour belongs' and
2. 'the product is the property of the capitalist and not that of the worker'.
3. Further, such capitalist firms produce commodities for sale in the pursuit of profit.

Point (1), as Marx elaborated elsewhere in *Capital*, implies an employment relationship between employer and employee. Points (2) and (3) imply the existence of private ownership of the means of production. They are also tied up with the fact that the capitalists, rather than the workers, are the 'residual claimants': they take up the profits and losses from the sale of the products, after all other costs are paid. The definition has formal and legal, as well as cultural and informal, aspects. It entails an employment relationship and excludes cooperatives and one-person firms, as Marx himself made clear on repeated occasions.

THE CONCEPT OF PURE CAPITALISM AND MULTILAYERED ANALYSIS

Both mainstream and Marxist economics have been dominated by notions of an 'ideal' or 'pure' capitalist system. Just as mainstream economists have sometimes posited an ideal or optimal capitalist arrangement, Marxism is also dominated by a primary focus on a single, fundamental capitalist type. One of the theoretical problems discussed in this book is whether or not the analysis of different capitalist systems can proceed from a single model of 'pure' capitalism, and if so, how. This problem can be seen in attempts by Marxists to deal with the post-war diversity and varied dynamics of different forms of capitalism. This problem was acutely obvious in post-war Japan. Did the then dynamic Japanese economy represent an advanced stage of capitalist evolution or was it simply catching up with America or Britain?

Of course, Marx's own writings are of limited use here. British capitalism was the only developed capitalist economy that Marx could observe. Marx saw the system of capitalism in Britain as the most developed form of a model that would spread around the globe. It was widely believed that all capitalist economies would follow in the footsteps of the British capitalism.

This prevailing view among nineteenth-century commentators is very similar to the popular view today of America as the ideal or ultimate model of capitalist development. Then and now, the enduring possibility of a variety of forms of capitalism is downplayed. However, the excuses for this error today are much weaker than those that would apply to the nineteenth century. Today, the variety of different forms of capitalism is manifest (Berger and Dore, 1996; Hollingsworth and Boyer, 1997; Kenworthy, 1995; Whitley, 1999).

Marx did not anticipate the varied historical evolution of capitalist economies and their geographical diversity. His analysis neglected possible divergent forms of capitalist evolution. He focused on capitalism in its British and allegedly most 'pure state'. Hence Marx (1976, p. 90) wrote in the preface to the first edition of *Capital*: 'The physicist ... wherever possible ... makes experiments under conditions which ensure that the process will occur in its pure state. What I have to examine in this work is the capitalist mode of production'.

This idea of examining capitalism in a notional 'pure state' inspired Uno. His work at the first level is largely an attempt to clarify and systematize the conceptual foundations of Marxist economics. He made explicit within Marxism the necessity of different levels of analysis. At the most abstract level, Uno articulated the notion of 'pure theory' and identified a core concept of 'pure capitalism'. As Uno (1980, p. xxii) elaborated in a work originally published in Japanese in 1964:

> [T]he pure theory of capitalism must presuppose the abstract context of a purely capitalist society ... The pure theory, in other words, reproduces a theoretical capitalist society, the self-containedness of which conclusively demonstrates the ability of capitalism to form an historical society.

Like Marx, Uno suggested the idea of a feasible and 'self-contained' capitalist system. This 'purely capitalist society' would have no impurities. An impurity is a partially integrated subsystem of a substantially different structure and type. The family is an example of an impurity, because it is not structured like a capitalist firm and does not work like a capitalist firm; it does not typically employ workers or sell products. Marx believed that the family would change its forms and functions in accord with the historical development of capitalism, but did not much refer to the role of the family in his theoretical system in *Capital*.

Uno took a similar line. Like Marx, he believed in the *theoretical* possibility of a 'pure' capitalist system. Even if it never existed in reality, it was deemed to be theoretically possible. Marx and Uno openly recognized the *empirical* existence of impurities; capitalism historically had never presented itself in a pure form. However, they regarded these impurities as dispensable at a level of research; the impurities had no functional role for the basic system as a whole. The notion of a 'purely capitalist society' involves a denial of the *necessary* role of any impurities at the most basic level of study.

While Marx and Uno recognized the empirical fact of diverse forms of capitalism, at the most abstract level they focused theoretically on a single, pure form. For Marx, the purist form of capitalism had been manifest in England in the nineteenth century. Uno developed this line of thought by arguing that such a free market version of capitalism contained inbuilt tendencies to self-purification. Thus Uno and most of his followers defended the concept of 'pure' capitalism by the argument that 'actual capitalism in its liberal stage of development demonstrated a tendency toward self-perfection, divesting itself more and more of pre-capitalist economic relations' (Sekine, 1975, p. 857). In other words, the theoretical possibility and centrality of 'pure' capitalism was underlined by the supposed tendency of capitalism to purify itself more and more in the process of its ascendance from the previous order. The growth of markets broke down residues of the feudal order and commodified the world.

It was Uno's belief that 'pure capitalism' could be analysed with the theoretical tools outlined by Marx in *Capital*. The most fundamental theoretical picture was of a closed, completely commodified and self-perpetuating 'pure capitalism', where all produced goods and services were sold as commodities on a free market. For Uno, this abstraction was necessary to provide logical and theoretical clarity concerning the essential features of the capitalist system, which were common to all capitalist systems.

However, Uno was sensitive to the fact that different capitalist systems had developed in different ways and exhibited different trajectories of development. Accordingly, he argued that additional levels of analysis were necessary. In an attempt to reconcile Marx's theory with the existence of historical and geographically diverse forms of capitalism, Uno proposed three levels of analysis. The first and most abstract level comprised the basic principles of Marx's theory, developed further where necessary. This was the level of 'pure capitalism' as discussed above.

The next level of analysis embodied an attempt to explain the historical development of the capitalist world system. This intermediate theory involved a 'stages theory of world capitalist development'. This required an examination of the historical development of the globally dominant capitalist systems. At this level, Uno outlined a 'stages theory', arguing that in its evolution, capitalism passes through a number of successive stages. Earlier, 'mercantile' capitalism had been succeeded by the 'liberal', free market capitalism of the nineteenth century. However, within this context of competitive markets, monopolies, cartels and trade unions had emerged. Hence the 'liberal' phase of capitalism had been followed, in the twentieth century, by the less pure, 'finance' and 'imperialist' stages of capitalism.

At the third level of research, the concrete development of individual capitalist countries would be analysed. Each level of analysis must embody the principles of the levels of greater generality and higher abstraction. In other words, analyses at the third level must incorporate the relevant elements of the 'stages theory' at the second level, by embodying the principles pertaining to the actual stage relating to the individual country involved. Furthermore, all analyses at both the third and the second – 'stages theory' – levels must be guided conceptually by the basic principles in performing more concrete studies of capitalist economies at each level. At the same time, each level of analysis had a degree of autonomy, based on the identification of specific properties and degrees of historical concreteness pertaining only to the level in question. These specific properties of research could not be obtained from the other levels of analysis.

VARIETIES OF CAPITALISM AND THE SIGNIFICANCE OF IMPURITIES

Marxists have sometimes debated the possibility of multiple paths of economic development. Towards the end of his life, and inspired by debates about the possibility of a quite different path of capitalist development in Russia, Marx himself showed a belated recognition of path dependence and historical contingency. He wrote in 1877:

> [E]vents strikingly analogous but taking place in different historical surroundings led to totally different results. By studying each of these forms of evolution separately and then comparing them one can easily find the clue to this phenomenon, but one will never arrive there by using as one's master key a general historico-philosophical theory, the supreme virtue of which consists in being super-historical. (Marx, 1977, p. 572)

Nowhere is the concept of path-dependent capitalist development dramatized so acutely as in Japan. Japanese capitalism uniquely combines elements of its relatively recent feudal past with a dynamic organizational and technological impetus. Norms of group identification and loyalty have been harnessed within the modern Japanese corporation.

Although Marxists have often had difficulty in embracing the concept of path dependence, Uno's work arguably contained the possibility of divergent paths of development at the second and the third levels of research. Especially in his stages theory of imperialism, he presented three types of leading economy in the world – namely Germany, the UK and the USA – with each characterized by path-dependent evolution. The particular path dependence of Japanese economic growth cannot be studied adequately with just the basic principles of capitalism. Other levels of analysis are required, informed by the comparative experiences of other latecomers, such as Germany.

Uno's depiction of the 'stages' of capitalist development is arguably incomplete as it was derived from capitalist world history up to 1914. This year marked the end of Britain's imperial hegemony. By 1945 it was not Britain, but the United States that led and provided the emulative model for the world. Furthermore, the age of classical imperialism, through the acquisition of colonies, had all but ended. By the 1960s the British Empire was no more. A fundamentally new era of capitalist development seemed to unfold. It would seem inadequate to react to these changes by treating them as less fundamental, for instance at the second or third levels of Uno's scheme.

The general failure to appreciate the possibility of path-dependent development led to difficult questions concerning the nature of the capitalist system in Japan. For example, regarding the Japanese economy of the 1930s from a Marxist viewpoint, it was very difficult to identify whether it was a capitalist economy or a pre-capitalist economy, since there were many differences from a pure capitalist economy. The 'orthodox' Japanese Marxists – the *Koza-ha* school – asserted that Japanese capitalism was still largely based on feudal agricultural social relations in villages. Another Marxist *Rono-ha* school denied this, and argued that the Japanese society had been basically a capitalist economy since the 'bourgeois revolution' of the Meiji Restoration (Itoh, 1980, pp. 30–37). Uno intended to overcome these one-sided views by introducing an intermediate stages theory, between basic principles and the concrete analysis of (Japanese) capitalism.

As in Germany since the late nineteenth century, Japanese capitalism made use of its remaining peasantry as a source of both agricultural products and as a market for manufactures. Japanese capitalism also made use of the ancient Japanese culture of group identification and workplace loyalty. For much of the twentieth century, Japan made use of these feudal remnants to increase its productivity and strengthen its competitive power. As Thorstein Veblen remarked with amazing prescience in 1915: 'It is in this unique combination of a high-wrought spirit of feudalistic fealty and chivalric honor with the material efficiency given by the modern technology that the strength of the Japanese nation lies' (Veblen, 1934, p. 251).

In contrast, many Marxists in many countries have been restricted by the widespread but mistaken notion that capitalism in all countries must necessarily go through the same sequence of stages of development.

Some authors argue that the concept of pure capitalism and the denial of path-dependent development, go together. The idea of capitalism always being driven towards a pure model implies a universal law of capitalist development in which all countries gravitate to a single path. Their unique cultural and institutional residues, acquired in the specific circumstances of

their own history, have no affect on the final outcome. They may be acknowledged empirically, but ultimately they play no causal role. Others argue that
the notion of 'pure' capitalism is theoretically indispensable. The issue here
is whether the Uno-style view, that capitalism develops towards a pure model,
rules out the possibility of multiple paths of capitalist development. Most of
Uno's followers admit the possibility of different paths of development at
more concrete, second and third levels of research. The question then is how
and why path dependence is admitted at one level and not at another. This is a
problem for further research within a multilayered theoretical analysis.

Notably, even nineteenth-century Britain had an open economy, with many
impurities. It relied upon overseas imports of raw materials and on overseas
markets for manufactured goods. Furthermore, it was a socially integrated
and far from completely commodified economy.

As many writers have argued, there are general limits to the extension of
market and contractual relations within capitalism. Joseph Schumpeter (1976,
p. 139), for example, argued persuasively that such older institutions provide an essential symbiosis with capitalism, and are thus 'an essential
element of the capitalist schema'. Schumpeter's insight was to show that
capitalism depends on norms of loyalty and trust which are in part descended from a former epoch. The spread of market and contractarian
relations can threaten to break up cultural and other enduring bonds from
the past that are necessary for the functioning of the system as a whole. In
particular, as Schumpeter and others emphasize, the state is partly responsible for the bonding of society and the prevention of its dissolution into
atomistic units by the corroding action of market relations. Accordingly,
Polanyi (1944) showed that even in '*laissez-faire*' Victorian Britain the
state was necessarily intimately involved in the formation and subsequent
regulation of markets. Furthermore, he argued that all markets are themselves socially and culturally embedded, and there are many possible different
manifest forms of markets and exchange.

From this perspective, there is no difficulty accepting the idea that coexisting capitalist systems can develop in different ways, especially in different
local circumstances. The evolution of a system depends on both its history
and its context: path dependence is thus acknowledged. It is not even necessary to claim that one impure system is 'more advanced' or 'higher' than
another. After all, what is dynamic or efficient in one context may be less
dynamic or efficient in another.

Once we admit the existence of necessary impurities then arguably no
socioeconomic system can be adequately understood in its 'pure' form alone.
All systems must be understood in terms of a dominant structure along with
necessary impurities. Having established this, the possibility of systemic
varieties and their path-dependent evolution is admitted.

The fact that the need for a dissimilar subsystem can be fulfilled by one or more of a variety of possible subsystems is of theoretical significance. The particular subsystem, the nature of the combination, and the precise boundaries of the demarcation profoundly affect the nature of the specific variety of capitalist system. We are led to acknowledge that an immense variety of forms of any given socioeconomic system could exist. In particular, an infinite variety of forms of capitalism is possible, depending on their historical baggage of impurities.

The response of most Uno inspired Marxists to these arguments is sometimes to admit the necessity of impurities, but then to insist that these are not placed at the most fundamental level of analysis. Then the concept of pure capitalism can remain. Any impurities would be accommodated at a second or higher level of analysis.

From the viewpoint of one of the editors of the present volume, a problem with this response is that the model of pure capitalism is not sustainable in principle. A pure capitalism could not work in reality. Yet recall Uno's (1980, p. xxii) declaration that 'the pure theory of capitalism … reproduces a theoretical capitalist society, the self-containedness of which conclusively demonstrates the ability of capitalism to form an historical society'. However, once it is admitted that a pure capitalist system cannot function, we are unable to reproduce in any 'pure theory' of a 'self-contained' capitalism which demonstrates any historical viability whatsoever. Without the addition of impurities, *at this fundamental level of analysis*, we are unable to construct a viable theoretical conception or ideal type. (See Hodgson (2001) for an extended argument along these lines and a different proposal involving no less than five levels of analysis.) In sum, Uno's own argument suggests that impurities, in so far as they are necessary for capitalist economy to function, must be included at the most fundamental level of analysis. Notably, a group of Uno's followers have abandoned the notion of 'pure capitalism' although in a slightly different context, by emphasizing the notion of world capitalism (Itoh, 1980, p. 44).

As well as neglecting subsystemic impurities in the principles, Uno actually tended to overlook the functional integration of varied socioeconomic systems within the world order. The irony is that the modern development of Japan, from 1868 to the current period, has been overwhelmingly a case of structural interaction with a global system. Much of the dynamic of this interaction has resulted from the combination of the special features of the Japanese system with a contrasting and variegated world.

The Meiji Restoration and Japan's subsequent development was not simply the transcendence of feudalism but the ending of global isolation. The Meiji Restoration was triggered by the arrival of American ships in Tokyo Bay. Japan subsequently imported Western technology and ideas. Post-1945

Japan has depended on its intimate political and trading relationship with the United States, both as a guarantor of political stability and as a huge market for Japanese exports. With increasing globalization in the last third of the twentieth century, Japan played a crucial role in the global development of knowledge-intensive production and high-technology products.

Systematic interdependence at a global level is not confined to Japan. For example, eighteenth-century British capitalism depended on the overseas colonies and the transatlantic slave trade. There is the general possibility that an open system can rely in part on elements of a geographically separate system, as well as dissimilar subsystems within the same social formation. Exogenous influences and events are important.

Accordingly, systems can depend on dissimilar adjacent systems as well as on subsystems. In contrast, most Marxists have traditionally underestimated the importance of exogenous influences, seeing the dynamic forces of economic development as coming largely from within. The emphasis on the 'inner' laws of system development is a corollary of the idea of a 'pure' type. The notion of system purity is upheld by ignoring the importance of influences from outside the system.

A similar criticism can be made of the work of Schumpeter. He defined economic development as involving 'only such changes in economic life as are not forced upon it from without but arise by its own initiative, from within' (Schumpeter, 1934, p. 63). Schumpeter never made a secret of the fact that his theory of capitalist development – with its emphasis on the role of endogenous change – was highly influenced by Marx. Clearly, the importance of endogenous factors such as entrepreneurial activity and technological innovation should not be denied. The point is that Schumpeter should have given due stress to exogenous factors as well. Arguably, in this omission he was misled by Marx.

The global interaction between different national systems has been of significance for hundreds of years. Nevertheless, the globalizing developments in the closing decades of the twentieth century make such issues doubly important. Any resolution of the problem of historical specificity must take global integration into account. We are dealing not simply with national systems or regional blocs, but also with a global system in which the national and regional elements are themselves subsystems. Any taxonomy or periodization of socioeconomic systems must take this factor into account.

THE CONTENTS OF THIS BOOK

This book itself evolved out of a volume originally published in Japanese.[1] Part I offers some general perspectives on the theory of capitalism.

In Chapter 2, 'Contested exchange: a new microeconomics of capitalism', Samuel Bowles and Herbert Gintis explore the nature and limits of
the contractual relation. In neoclassical theory it is usually supposed that:
'Exchanges are solved political problems where contracts are comprehensive and enforceable at no cost to the exchanging parties'. However, many
important commodities, including labour power and money capital, are not
exchanged in such a manner since 'some aspect of the object of exchange is
so complex or difficult to monitor that comprehensive contracts are not
feasible or enforceable by a third party'. In this case 'the de facto terms of
an exchange result in part from the sanctions, surveillance and other enforcement activities adopted by the parties to the exchange themselves'.
They define such a transaction as a contested exchange. They conclude:
'Our conception of power in a competitive economy invites a reconsideration of the boundaries traditionally drawn in liberal political philosophy
between the marketplace, represented as a private arena of voluntary transactions devoid of coercion on the one hand, and the state as public arena
vested with coercive enforcement capacities on the other'. However, 'private enforcement is ubiquitous, particularly in labour and credit markets,
and hence the time-honoured private–public partition is unsustainable'.

In Chapter 3, 'Economic theory and the complexity of capitalism', Yoshinori
Shiozawa develops a theory of continuous economic history, using insights
from complexity theory. Shiozawa argues that existence of concurrent factors
and relations makes it impossible to understand economic systems through
reductionist methods. He argues that 'history is a process of constant change
in which distinct boundaries cannot be identified'. Consequently, an approach to history in which 'the flow of time is appropriately segmented, and
each segment is then held to be a distinctive stage with its own structure' is
invalid. In actual history, where commodities, production methods, and social
processes coexist and intermingle, a continuous vision of history is more
appropriate.

In Chapter 4, 'The development of the market economy and the formation
of voice', Kiichiro Yagi shares an interest with Bowles and Gintis in the
demarcation between public and private coordination. He develops contractual theory from an institutional point of view. Yagi follows Albert Hirschman's
(1970) twin concept of voice and exit. Voice involves an attempt to change
the situation without fleeing from it; this involves mechanisms of political
coordination. Exit means the breaking of the relations with one agent and the
search for other opportunities; this involves market coordination. Yagi argues
that under certain historical conditions it is possible to institutionalize both
market and political coordination, to induce economic development, through
the combination of loyalty and voice. He argues that the post-war system in
Japan is a prime example of this institutionalization. Yagi thus challenges the

view that American capitalism is the only possible institutionalized arrangement.

Part II of this book focuses more directly on the theoretical appreciation of
the coexistence of different types of capitalist system.

In Chapter 5, 'The evolution of capitalism from the perspective of institutional and evolutionary economics', Geoffrey Hodgson criticizes aspects
of Marxist economics and develops an institutional and evolutionary approach. Hodgson criticizes the concept of 'pure capitalism' found in the
works of Marx and Uno. To remedy this defect, Hodgson introduces the
impurity principle. This is the idea 'that every socioeconomic system must
rely on at least one structurally dissimilar subsystem to function. There
must always be a coexistent plurality of modes of production, so that the
social formation as a whole has the requisite structural variety to cope with
change'. This leads to the notion that the capitalist system – like other
economic systems – depends upon this internal variety and could not survive without it. Furthermore: 'Given the potential variety of systemic
combinations, and the reality of path dependency and cumulative causation,
an immense variety of institutions and forms are feasible'. Because a wide
variety of combinations of dissimilars are possible, then a wide variety of
different capitalist socioeconomic formations are feasible, and can in principle coexist.

In Chapter 6, 'Information technology and the "biodiversity" of capitalism', Ugo Pagano develops another approach to the analysis of varieties of
capitalism, focusing particularly on information technology. He argues that
Marxist theory embodies two views which could be named a 'technological
deterministic view' and a 'romantic view' of history. The former view stresses
the influence that the characteristics of productive forces have on property
rights. The latter stresses the influence of property rights and institutions on
the characteristics of the resources that are employed and developed. The
former view is similar to that of American radical economists, while the latter
to that of new institutional economics:

> [I]n the new institutional economics the nature of rights and organizations is
> endogenously and efficiently determined by the characteristics of the resources
> employed in the firm: namely their degree of specificity and their monitoring
> requirements. By contrast, in the radical literature, which has inherited the tradi-
> tion of the Marxian 'romantic view' of history the characteristics of the resources
> employed in the firm are in turn determined by the rights which owners of
> different factors have on the organization.

Pagano sees that these determinations are mutually reinforcing, and he calls
'these self-reinforcing relations between organizational rights and technology
"organizational equilibria"'. He observes that 'multiple organizational

equilibria are still likely to characterize the future of modern economies in the age of information technology'.

In Chapter 7, 'The diversity and future of capitalism, a *"régulationnist"* analysis', Robert Boyer analyses the diversity macroeconomic performance in terms of differences in national modes of regulation. He recognizes four different regulation modes. First, in the United States, 'market forces and countervailing public mechanisms shape and reshape social and economic dynamics'. Second, in Japan, instead of internal markets 'there are mechanisms of corporate *régulation*'. Resources are allocated neither by pure market mechanisms, nor by planning, but by mechanisms operating in between, at the intermediate level. Third, in the Scandinavian countries, Austria and to a lesser extent Germany, negotiation between workers' unions, business associations and public authorities, typically pan out in compromises at the national level. This is the social democratic approach. Fourth, most other European countries, with the exception of the United Kingdom, follow 'a state-led *régulation*'. Boyer argues that: 'One central message is therefore that there is *no single one best* régulation *mode* and that the history and the nature of the political process both constrain and structure the institutional architecture'. However, the breakdown of political alliances in the 1990s within each *régulation* mode has created considerable uncertainty concerning the survival of each type.

Part III addresses the evolution of the global capitalist system as a whole, and the impact of globalization on specific economies.

In Chapter 8, 'Where are the advanced economies going?', Robert Rowthorn addresses deindustrialization and globalization as the most significant developments after the 1980s. Employment growth is the difference between output growth and productivity growth. In the industrial sector, productivity growth surpassed output growth, while in the service sector, output growth surpassed productivity growth. As long as overall economic growth is strong, deindustrialization can occur without increases of unemployment. But poor economic growth has caused deindustrialization with severe increases in unemployment. Regarding recent globalization, Rowthorn emphasizes two new tendencies: intra-industry trade and foreign direct investment. Intra-industry trade 'occurs when countries at the same level of development exchange with each other products which are broadly similar in character – or even identical'. Rowthorn argues that 'Intra-industry trade is mainly an internal phenomenon *within* the large regional blocs' and that it is not a recent phenomenon. It has been well developed in large regional blocs, such as in North America. For Rowthorn: 'The fundamental question is not why do transnational corporations exist, but why does any kind of multi-plant firm exist? And given that multi-plant firms do exist, why was their formation confined within national boundaries for so long?'. He answers: 'Firms initially penetrate new markets, be they in other regions or other countries, by "exporting" from their existing production facilities. When sufficient sales have been achieved in the new market, it becomes feasible to set up local production facilities on a scale large enough to exploit economies of scale'. Thus, there is a natural cycle, whereby firms at first export to new markets and then serve them by local production once exports pass a certain threshold. He concludes that theses two tendencies may lead to regional economic blocs:

> *Within* regional blocs, direct investment and trade are often complementary. Investment may lead to an internal division of labour within the same firm, whereby plants in different countries of a bloc collaborate in producing the same product, or else specialize to produce different goods for export to the entire bloc or beyond. *Between* regional blocs, there is less complementarity, and direct investment may lead to the replacement of trade by local production.

In Chapter 9, 'The evolution of Japanese capitalism under global competition', Makoto Noguchi addresses the relationship between the Japanese economy and the global economic system. He argues that the strength of the Japanese production system in the 1980s and its weakness in the 1990s must be explained by reference to its historical background. In the 1980s, 'a firm's chances of competitive advantage rested on its ability to respond flexibly to the varied and capricious demands of multi-stratified households'. Firms were caught in the dilemma of diversifying their products at the cost of efficiency of mass production. The flexibility of labour management specific to the Japanese system was fitted for these historical conditions. In contrast, in the Anglo-American type of corporate system, specialized workers are employed according to rigid job demarcation. In 1990s, the situation changed, with the emergence of new mass markets, such as for the personal computer. 'The new type of mass production system is based on the intensive use of global networks'. This has put heavy competitive pressure on the differentiated production system in Japan, by force of low prices. In contrast, Anglo-American capitalism is especially suited in these new circumstances. Accordingly, Noguchi offers an explanation of the Japanese economy in terms of the changing nature of global markets and the varying ability of different national production systems to respond to these changes.

In Chapter 10, 'From bureaucratic capitalism to transnational capitalism: an intermediate theory', Nobuharu Yokokawa develops an analysis of the development of twentieth-century capitalism from a Marxist perspective. He attempts to construct an 'intermediate theory', between abstract theory and concrete analysis. Precedents for this kind of analysis include the works of Rudolf Hilferding and Vladimir Illych Lenin, both of whom are seen as applying Marx's 'law of value' to specific phases of capitalist development: 'They developed intermediate-level theories between general theory and concrete historical analysis, examining the specific mechanism of capital accumulation at a particular stage of development of the capitalist world system'. Following this lead, Yokokawa places the evolution of the international monetary system at the centre of his analysis. He analyses the modern global transition from the 'bureaucratic' capitalism of the 1950s and 1960s to the rise of 'transnational' capitalism in the 1990s. He argues that: 'The multilayered nature of transnational enterprises requires global, regional, national and local coordination'.

In Chapter 11, 'The evolutionary spiral of capitalism: globalization and neo-liberalism', Makoto Itoh follows the evolution of capitalist economy in three stages. First: 'The historical evolution of capitalism from mercantilism to Pax-Britannica liberalism, up to the 1870s, clearly showed a trend towards a more and more freely competitive market order'. Second, however, 'for about a century from the late nineteenth century, the capitalist world system took a spiral course and reversed the trend'. Third, from the 1980s, with the wide-ranging impact of the information revolution, 'capitalism reversed gear and began to remove its restrictions on competitive markets'. In two centuries of capitalist history, the system has moved from the freeing of markets, to state regulation, and back to free markets again. However, Itoh argues that capitalist economy retains its essential character. The basic forms of the market economy, 'commodity, money and capital' have remained throughout its long and complex spiral development, although their functions can change. Despite the recent phase of globalization and market liberalization, Itoh argues that the diversity of capitalist economies will remain, and they will not all converge towards a single type of free market economy. Itoh then discusses the future prognosis of capitalism and discusses policies that are appropriate for the current epoch.

NOTE

1. It was published in 1998 by the Keizi Seminar, Tokyo. The editors are very grateful to Paul Twomey for editorial assistance.

REFERENCES

Berger, Suzanne and Ronald Dore (eds) (1996), *National Diversity and Global Capitalism*, Ithaca: Cornell University Press.
Hirschman, Albert O. (1970), *Exit, Voice, and Loyalty: Responses to Decline in Firms, Organizations, and States*, Cambridge, MA: Harvard University Press.
Hodgson, Geoffrey M. (2001), *How Economics Forgot History: The Problem of Historical Specificity in Social Science*, London and New York: Routledge (in press).

Hollingsworth, J. Rogers and Robert Boyer (eds) (1997), *Contemporary Capitalism: The Embeddedness of Institutions* , Cambridge: Cambridge University Press.

Itoh, Makoto (1980), *Value and Crisis*, London: Pluto Press and New York: Monthly Press.

Kenworthy, Lane (1995), *In Search of National Economic Success: Balancing Competition and Cooperation*, Thousand Oaks, CA and London: Sage.

Marx, Karl (1976), *Capital*, vol. 1, translated by Ben Fowkes from the fourth German edition of 1890, Harmondsworth: Pelican.

Marx, Karl (1977), *Karl Marx: Selected Writings*, ed. David McLellan, Oxford: Oxford University Press.

Marx, Karl (1981), *Capital*, vol. 3, translated by David Fernbach from the German edition of 1894, Harmondsworth: Pelican.

Polanyi, Karl (1944), *The Great Transformation*, New York: Rinehart.

Schumpeter, Joseph A. (1976), *Capitalism, Socialism and Democracy*, 5th edn (1st edn. 1942), London: George Allen & Unwin.

Schumpeter, Joseph A. (1934), *The Theory of Economic Development: An Inquiry into Profits, Capital, Credit, Interest, and the Business Cycle*, translated by Redvers Opie from the second German edition of 1926 (1st edn, 1911), Cambridge, MA: Harvard University Press. Reprinted 1989 with a new introduction by John E. Elliott, New Brunswick, NJ: Transaction.

Sekine, Thomas T. (1975), '*Uno-Riron*: a Japanese contribution to Marxian political economy', *Journal of Economic Literature*, **8** (4), December, pp. 847–77.

Uno, Kozo (1980), *Principles of Political Economy: Theory of a Purely Capitalist Society*, translated from the Japanese edition of 1964 by Thomas T. Sekine, Brighton: Harvester.

Veblen, Thorstein B. (1934), *Essays on Our Changing Order*, ed. Leon Ardzrooni, New York: Viking Press.

Whitley, Richard (1999), *Divergent Capitalisms: The Social Structuring and Change of Business Systems*, Oxford and New York: Oxford University Press.

PART I

General Theoretical Perspectives

2. Contested exchange: a new microeconomics of capitalism

Samuel Bowles and Herbert M. Gintis*

INTRODUCTION

In this chapter we develop a new microeconomic foundation for the political economy of capitalism, one that illuminates rather than obscures the exercise of power and which thus is capable of addressing the democratic concerns of the left. To do this we apply recent developments in the microeconomics of incomplete contracts to illuminate themes initially developed by Marx, and particularly his representation of relationships between employers and their workers as *political* as well as *economic*.

In the neoclassical general equilibrium model, each agent maximizes utility subject to a wealth constraint, and prices are set to clear all markets. In competitive equilibrium, moreover, conditions of free entry and exit ensure that for each commodity, including labour and capital, each buyer faces a large number of sellers, each seller faces a large number of buyers. It follows that in equilibrium, if agents A and B engage in an exchange, B's gain exactly equals the gain from his or her next best alternative.

This treatment of exchange views the economy purely as a system of resource allocation and the state as the quintessential system of power. Indeed, the equation of 'politics and power' with the state and 'production and wealth' with the economy is still widely accepted as defining the disciplinary boundary between economics and political science. Among traditional economists the consequent excision of power from economic theory has been a source of celebration. Abba Lerner (1972, p. 259) expresses a common sentiment: 'An economic transaction is a solved political problem ... Economics has gained the title Queen of the Social Sciences by choosing solved political problems as its domain'.

Perhaps the most notable political implication of the neoclassical model, strikingly counterintuitive, is that the location of decision-making authority within the enterprise (its political structure) has neither allocative nor distributive effects in competitive equilibrium, and hence may be considered irrelevant to economic theory. Writing in the early years of this century, Joseph Schumpeter (1934, p. 21) announced this now familiar theme:

> The means of production and the productive process have in general no real leader ... The people who direct business firms only execute what is prescribed for them by wants ... Individuals have influence only in so far as they are consumers ... In no other sense is there a personal direction of production.

Paul Samuelson (1957, p. 894) has expressed the matter more succinctly: 'in a perfectly competitive model', he wrote, 'it really doesn't matter who hires whom; so let labour hire "capital"'.

The apparent power of the 'people who direct business firms' is accordingly said to be illusory, since competition forces those in positions of authority to adopt a unique cost-minimizing solution to production problems determined by given prices and technologies. A relocation of command (for instance from owners to employees) would not alter the decisions made by firms in equilibrium. Moreover the illusory nature of what many would consider a most palpable form of economic power, that of employer over employee, follows directly from the logic of market clearing. If all agents are indifferent between their current transactions and their next best alternative, then Armen Alchian and Harold Demsetz (1972, p. 777) are surely correct: 'Telling an employee to type this letter rather than to file that document is like my telling a grocer to sell me this brand of tuna rather than that brand of bread'.

Exchanges are solved political problems where contracts are comprehensive and enforceable at no cost to the exchanging parties. We use the term *exogenous claim enforcement* to refer to this type of comprehensive and third-party (generally state) enforcement of contracts. Where some aspect of the object of exchange is so complex or difficult to monitor that comprehensive contracts are not feasible or enforceable by a third party, we speak of *endogenous claim enforcement*, and the exchange is *not* a solved political problem. Endogenous claim enforcement is quite general; the two critical exchanges of the capitalist economy – labour and the capital markets – provide, as we shall see, the archetypal examples.

In cases of endogenous claim enforcement we have a *problem of agency*: in an exchange between agents A and B, B can take actions which are harmful or beneficial to A's interests, and which cannot be precluded or guaranteed by contractual agreement. Where a problem of agency exists, the de facto terms of an exchange result in part from the sanctions, surveillance and other enforcement activities adopted by the parties to the exchange themselves.

A transaction characterized by both an agency problem and an endogenous claim enforcement is termed a *contested exchange*. More formally, consider agent A who engages in an exchange with agent B. We call the exchange *contested* when B's good or service possesses an attribute which is valuable to A, is costly for B to provide, yet is not fully specified in a costlessly enforceable contract. Our key claims are that:

- the most important exchanges in a capitalist economy are contested; and
- in contested exchanges, endogenous enforcement gives rise to a well-defined set of power relations among voluntarily participating agents, even in the absence of collusion or other obstacles to 'perfect' competition.[1]

THE LABOUR MARKET AS CONTESTED EXCHANGE

An employment relationship is established when, in return for a wage, the worker agrees to submit to the authority of the employer for a specified period of time. While the employer's promise to pay the wage is legally enforceable, the worker's promise to bestow an adequate level of effort and care upon the tasks assigned, even if offered, is not. At the level of effort expected by management, work is subjectively costly for the worker to provide, valuable to the employer, and costly to measure. The manager–worker relationship is thus a contested exchange.

Let *e* represent the level of work effort provided by employee B. We assume effort is costly for B to provide above some minimal level e_{min}. B's employer A knows that B will choose *e* in response to both the cost of supplying effort and the penalty which employer A imposes if dissatisfied with B's performance. For simplicity we assume the penalty A will impose is the non-renewal of the employment relationship – that is, dismissing the worker. Of course the employer may choose not to terminate the worker's employment if the cost associated with the termination (demoralization or ill-will among fellow workers, a work-to-rule slowdown, a strike, or simply the search and training costs of replacement) are excessive.

In choosing a level of work intensity, the employee must consider both short- and long-term costs and benefits; working less hard now, for example, means more on-the-job leisure now, and a probability of no job and hence less income later. To take into account this time dimension we shall consider the worker's job as an asset, the value of which depends in part on the worker's effort level.

We define the *value of employment* $v(w)$ as the discounted present value of the worker's future utility taking account of the probability that the worker will be dismissed; for obvious reasons it is an increasing function of the current wage rate *w*. We define the employee's *fallback position* z as the present value of future utility for a person whose job is terminated – perhaps the present value of a future stream of unemployment benefits, or the present value of some other job, or more likely a sequence of the two. Then A's threat of dismissal is credible only if $v(w) > z$. We call $v(w) - z$, the difference between the value of employment and the fallback position z, the *employment rent*, or the cost of job loss. Employment rents accorded to workers in labour markets are a particularly important case of the more general category, *enforcement rents*, which arise in all cases of competitively determined contested exchange under conditions of contingent renewal.

Let w_{min} be the wage which equates $v(w)$ and z. This wage rate implies a zero employment rent, and hence induces the worker's freely chosen effort level e_{min}. We term w_{min} the *reservation wage* corresponding to the fallback position z; at any wage less than w_{min} the worker will refuse employment, or will quit if employed. Its level obviously depends on the worker's relative enjoyment of leisure and work, the level and coverage of unemployment benefits, the expected duration of unemployment for a dismissed worker, the loss of seniority associated with moving to a new job, and the availability of other income. In the neoclassical general equilibrium model the equilibrium wage w must equal the reservation wage w_{min}. For if w were greater than w_{min}, then an employed worker would prefer his or her present employment to the next-best alternative, which is impossible in a clearing labour market.

We assume A has a monitoring system such that B's performance will be found adequate with a probability $f(e)$ that depends positively on B's level of effort e.

To elicit greater effort than e_{min}, A is obliged to offer a wage greater than the fallback wage w_{min}, balancing the cost of paying the larger wage against the benefits associated with B's greater effort induced by a higher cost of job loss. For any given wage, the worker will determine how hard to work by trading off the marginal disutility of additional effort against the effect that additional effort has on the probability of retaining the job and thus continuing to receive the employment rent. Noting that the fallback position z is exogenous to the exchange, we may write B's best response to w, which we call the *labour extraction function*, simply as $e = e(w)$. In the neighbourhood of the competitive equilibrium e increases with w, though at a diminishing rate.

The equilibrium wage and effort level is determined as follows. Agent A knows B's best-response schedule $e(w)$. Thus once A selects the wage, the level of effort that will be performed is known. The employer thus chooses the wage w to maximize e/w (that is, work done per unit of wage expended), subject to the worker's best-response schedule $e = e(w)$. The solution to A's optimum problem is to set w such that $e_w = e/w$, or the marginal effect of a wage increase on effort equals the average effort provided per unit of wage cost. This solution yields the equilibrium effort level e^* and wage w^*, shown

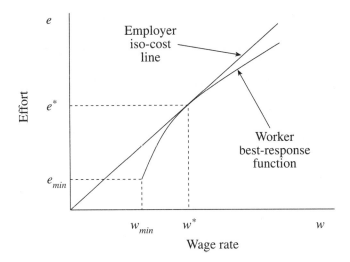

Figure 2.1   The mutual determination of effort and the wage rate

in Figure 2.1. The ray $(e/w)^*$ is one of the employer's iso-labour cost loci; its slope is e^*/w^*. Steeper rays are obviously preferred, while the employer is indifferent to any point on a given ray, as each entails an identical labour cost. The equilibrium effort/wage configuration (e^*, w^*) in this contested exchange results from A optimizing *given the best-response schedule of B*.

Two important results are apparent. First, $e^* > e_{min}$, so B provides a level of effort greater than would have been the case in the absence of the enforcement rent and the employer's monitoring system; and second, $w^* > w_{min}$, so B receives a wage greater than the reservation wage. The first result indicates that A's enforcement strategy is effective; the second indicates that the labour market does not clear in competitive equilibrium: workers holding jobs are not indifferent to losing them, since $w^* > w_{min}$ implies $v(w^*) > z$, and there are identical workers either involuntarily unemployed, or employed in less-desirable positions.

Both results are of course at variance with the neoclassical general equilibrium model, which is a limiting case of contested exchange obtaining either in the absence of a conflict of interest between employer and employee over effort, or when effort is exogenously enforceable.

SHORT-SIDE POWER AND POLITICAL THEORY

Does employer A have power over worker B? As we have seen, in equilibrium there will exist unemployed workers identical to B who would prefer to be employed. Thus A's threat to dismiss B is credible and dismissal is costly to B. Hence A can apply sanctions to B. In addition, A can use these sanctions to elicit a preferred level of effort from B, and thus to further A's interests. Finally, while B may be capable of applying sanctions to A (for example, B may be capable of burning down A's factory), B cannot use this capacity to induce A to choose a different wage, or to refrain from dismissing B should A desire to do so. Should B make A a take-it-or-leave-it offer to work at a higher than equilibrium wage, or should B threaten to apply sanctions unless A offers a higher wage, A would simply reject the offer and hire another worker. Thus A has power over B.

Since an equilibrium exhibits positive enforcement rents, it entails, by definition, involuntary unemployment. The existence of agents without employment (or with less-desirable employment than B), follows from the strict inequality $v(w^*) > z$. This unemployment persists in equilibrium and is not derived from an aggregate demand failure, as in the Keynesian model.

The manager's power flows from having a favourable position in a non-clearing market. We say that the employer A, who can purchase any desired amount of labour and hence is not quantity constrained, is on the *short side* of the market. Where excess supply exists – as in the labour market – the demand side is the short side, and conversely. Suppliers of labour are on the *long side* of the market. When contingent renewal is operative, the principle of *short-side power* holds: agents on the short side of the market have power over agents on the long side with whom they transact. Long-side agents are of two types: those who succeed in finding an employer and receive a rent which constrains them to accept the employer's authority, and those who fail to make a transaction and hence are rationed out of the market.

It might appear that A has expressed a preference for power and has simply traded away some money, the enforcement rent, to gain power. But this is false: A is assumed to be indifferent to the nature of the authority relationship *per se* and is simply maximizing profits.

Moreover, it might be thought that A has intentionally generated the unemployment necessary for the maintenance of short-side power. It is true that the employer's profit-maximizing strategy, when adopted by all other employers, results in the existence of unemployed workers, and that other wage-setting rules would not have this result. But we have assumed that the employer treats the level of unemployment (which figures in the determination of the workers' fallback position, z) as exogenous, for the simple reason that no employer acting singly can determine the level of aggregate employment.

WEALTH AND POWER

What is the connection between the ownership of wealth and the exercise of economic power? The neoclassical general equilibrium model answers that property rights confer no power other than the power to consume or enjoy leisure. Yet where claims are endogenously enforced and short-side power obtains, the connection of wealth to power is both more extensive and less direct. The location of agents to the short and long sides of markets, and hence the locus of short-side power, as well as the division between long-siders who succeed in making transactions and those who fail, is often (but not always) related to ownership: short-siders, as well as those long-siders who receive enforcement rents, are likely to be wealth-owners, while long-siders who are rationed out of the market are not. Access to wealth, through either ownership or favourable location in capital markets, as we shall see, thus not only affords the benefits of purchasing power, but also often confers the advantages of short-side Stackelberg leadership.

The reason for this is straightforward: capital markets are as much arenas of contested exchange as are labour markets. In return for a sum of money from lender A today, borrower B contracts to repay the loan, together with a specified debt service, at some given time in the future. This promise is enforceable in a court of law, however, only if B is solvent at the time the repayment is called for. The borrower's promise to remain solvent is no more amenable to exogenous enforcement than is the employee's promise to supply a particular quality of work.

Just as the employer is not obliged to accept the level of work effort offered by the worker in the absence of the threat of sanctions, so the lender can devise incentives which induce a more favourable level of performance than borrowers would spontaneously exhibit. The lender will generally have an interest to do so, since there is a conflict of interest between lender and borrower concerning the choice of risk: the profits from choosing a high-risk, high-expected-return investment strategy accrue to the borrower, while the costs of such a strategy – an increased chance of default – are borne by the lender. If the borrower's choice among investment projects involving different profiles of risk and rate of return could be contractually specified and effectively third-party enforced, the exchange between lender and borrower would be neoclassical in character. But this is not the case. Not only are the actions of borrowers too subtle to be subjected to effective contractual specifications, but penalties imposed on a reckless borrower are limited by the borrower's exposed assets. Thus capital markets involve contested exchange.

It might be thought that the problem of borrower insolvency can be solved by simply raising the interest rate on risky loans. However, problems of adverse selection and moral hazard limit the effectiveness of the price mechanism in this case. In the adverse selection case, an increase in the interest rate induces borrowers with safe but low-expected-return investment opportunities to drop out of the pool of credit applicants, while those with risky projects remain. Hence the lender's expected return may decline even when the interest rate rises. Moral hazard also obtains, since an increase in the interest rate induces borrowers to take more risks, since only highly favourable outcomes allow positive profits when high interest rates must be paid.

However, there is another enforcement strategy open to the lender – that of requiring the borrower to post collateral. Since this collateral is forfeited if the borrower defaults, the incentive incompatibility between borrower and lender as well as the adverse selection problem are considerably attenuated: a highly collateralized borrower has little incentive to invest in projects involving low expected return or excessive risk. But collateral, by its very nature, must involve the borrower's own wealth, and cannot itself be borrowed without undermining the enforcement effect of the collateral requirement. Furthermore collateral must itself be exogenously enforceable. An agent without tangible property, for example, cannot generally offer claims against future labour earnings as collateral. Thus while a stream of future labour income may be expressed as a present value ('human capital'), and may be indistinguishable in a distributional sense from property, it does not provide the political advantages associated with the ownership of property.

The observed relationship between wealth and command in a capitalist economy thus flows from the fact that only those who possess wealth can post collateral. The wealthy are thus in an advantageous position to make offers characterized by reduced incentive incompatibility. In the next section we shall use a simple model to illustrate this point.

ENDOGENOUS ENFORCEMENT ON CAPITAL MARKETS

Let us now model the lender–borrower exchange, the borrower choosing an investment project in response to a particular level of interest and collateral required by the lender. The borrower's response function will then be taken as a constraint by the lender choosing an optimal interest rate and required levels of equity. The formal structure of the example is thus identical to the previous model of Stackelberg leadership in the labour market.

We make the following simplifications for expositional purposes: all parties are risk neutral, lenders have perfect information concerning the asset position and investment options of potential borrowers, and all loans are fixed-return agreements, so the borrower remains the full residual claimant. We also suppose that borrowers have privileged access to production and investment-related information and skills which are not generally available or easily acquired, and which render them, but not the lenders, capable of exploiting the investment opportunity.

Suppose a potential borrower, one of many seeking a loan in a competitive capital market, has a set of investment opportunities which vary with respect to risk; each requires an outlay 1 today and offers return $1 + r(f)$ at the beginning of the next period where f, the measure of risk, is the probability that the investment project fails. Higher returns are available on riskier projects, so $r' > 0$.

If the project is not successful, the project returns nothing and the original outlay is lost. Suppose also that posting collateral of value k on the loan costs the borrower not only the loss of the collateral in the case of bankruptcy, but some opportunity costs of tying up collateral on one project renders it un-available for other projects or unforeseen contingencies. Moreover, the borrower may be capable of posting only a limited amount of collateral; above this level we take the cost of posting collateral to be infinite.

Consider the case of a single lender facing such a borrower. Like the borrower, the lender is one of many operating under competitive conditions. Suppose the borrower is offered a loan at interest rate i, provided he or she posts collateral k. The lender promises the borrower that the loan will be repeated indefinitely, so long as it is paid back. Then, just as the worker selected a level of labour intensity to maximize the value of the job, the borrower will choose the riskiness of the project to maximize the present value of the project, v, which obviously will vary inversely with the rate of interest and the level of the required collateral k.[2]

The power of the lender over the borrower is based on the exposure of the borrower to two types of losses: the loss of the collateral and the non-renewal of the loan. The present value of the borrower's assets should no loan be secured, k_{res}, is the borrower's *reservation position*: if $v < k_{res}$ the borrower will refuse the loan. When $v \geq k_{res}$ the borrower is willing to accept the loan. The enforcement rent associated with the loan is the difference between the value of the borrower's assets with the loan, v, and the borrower's *fallback position kk*, which is the value of the borrower's assets should the loan be secured, the project then fail, and as a consequence the collateral k be lost. There will be some interest rate i_{max} sufficiently high such that $v = k_{res}$, the minimal present value needed to induce the borrower to post collateral k and accept the loan. If an interest rate $i < i_{max}$ is offered, we term the difference $i - i_{max}$ a *contingent renewal premium*, because only if i is less than i_{max} will the borrower have the incentive to ensure the renewal of the exchange relationship. At interest rate i_{max} there is no contingent renewal premium, and the enforcement rent equals the collateral k, which the lender 'holds hostage' in case of borrower default.

The lender, who knows the options open to the borrower, can thus deter-mine the borrower's probability of default schedule, which is the borrower's best-response schedule $f = f(i, k)$. In general $f_i > 0$; the higher the interest rate charged by the bank, the less will be the value of the project to the borrower, the smaller will be the enforcement rent, and the greater will be the probability of default.

Subject to the borrower's response function, the lender will then choose i and k to maximize the expected return i^e. The lender seeks to select the rate of interest and the level of collateral to maximize the expected return. The solution to this maximum problem is that the borrower sets the interest rate to balance the returns resulting from a high interest rate against the lower probability of repayment induced by the higher rate.

If we assume (for simplicity) that the borrower has a limited amount of collateral k^* which is costless to provide, after which the cost is infinite, we can set aside the choice of the optimal level of k and focus on the choice of an optimal interest rate by the lender.

The resulting equilibrium configuration (i^*, f^*) will generally be such that the optimal interest rate i^* is less than the reservation interest rate i_{max}, yielding a positive enforcement rent. Two characteristics of the equilibrium may be noted. First because $i^* > i_{max}$, the lender may impose an effective sanction on the borrower. Moreover, the positive enforcement rent entailed by $i^* < i_{max}$ implies the existence of capital-rationed agents (analogous to the unemployed) who would prefer to borrow at i^* but cannot. So the lender's threat to terminate the relationship with the borrower is credible. Second, $f^* < f_{max}$, the borrower's most preferred risk level, so the borrower has chosen a response favourable to the lender which would not have been chosen in the absence of the threat of sanctions.

Now consider a lender facing two types of borrowers, the Bs and the Cs, who differ in the amount of collateral they can costlessly provide, the Bs being wealthier than the Cs, so $k_B^* > k_C^*$. The difference in the level of collateral will appear in distinct response functions for the two types of borrowers, the probability of repayment at a given interest rate being greater the larger the collateral provided. Thus B's response function will lie below $C's$ except at point (i_{max}, f_{max}), and the lender will offer loans to all Bs before offering any loans to a C. Some or all of the Cs will thus be capital constrained. This explains why short-side power and wealth are connected even in competitive equilibrium.

The contested exchange emphasis on endogenous enforcement quickly locates the error in this reasoning: 'hiring capital' is precisely 'borrowing' in the sense of this section. In general, lenders maximize profits not only by imposing an enforcement rent on borrowers, but also by requiring borrowers to post a bond in the form of equity or collateral in their investments. Thus access to wealth is a *prerequisite* to access to capital markets, but when ownership is limited, the necessary process of borrowing imposes the possibility of sanctions on the borrower, thus critically limiting the autonomy of managers.

IMPLICATIONS FOR PROGRESSIVE POLICIES

It is well known that capitalism generates a highly unequal distribution of wealth, and as a result, a highly unequal distribution of political power and influence. Our model of contested exchange suggests a third form of inequality: a highly undemocratic exercise of power within the capitalist economy itself. We believe that attempts to ameliorate problems of wealth inequality and the equality of economic power must be addressed *together* if they are to be solved. In particular, attempts to redistribute wealth without taking into account the effects of such redistribution on the exercise of power within the economy have failed in the past and are unlikely to be successful in the future.

A more democratic organization of production may entail a more equal distribution of wealth, for the following reasons. First, if democratic production is indeed efficient, then the costs of redistributing wealth will be low, so we can expect redistributive policies to be more attractive to the citizenry of democratic countries. Second, worker-owners can be expected to save at a higher rate than employees, since saving is a means of reducing the effects of risk exposure on family well-being (Bowles and Gintis, 1993a). Thus the idea of *asset-based redistribution* (Bowles and Gintis, 1999) may become an important form of egalitarian economic policy in years to come.

The future development of capitalism is likely to increase the importance of the distribution of economic power in influencing the distribution of wealth and income. Advanced capitalism is experiencing a continued, and even heightened, shift from agriculture and manufacturing to services. It is in the area of the delivery of services that the types of models developed in this chapter are applied most fruitfully. The productivity of labour in service industries is inherently more difficult to measure than in traditional industrial sectors, and the principal–agent models developed here are likely to become relevant to a larger fraction of total economic activity in the advanced economies over the coming years. Thus the undemocratic character of work is likely to come into ever-greater contrast to the democratic character of the political sphere and an increased degree of egalitarianism in family and community life.

If this is so, then an increasingly important form of egalitarian economic policy may well be that of extending democracy to the workplace, through the development of worker-ownership. Our analysis makes it likely that there are important efficiencies in the organization of production that can flow from worker-ownership, and studies indeed document that this is the case.[3] An important impediment to viable and economically efficient worker-ownership is that the capitalist firm, by vesting ownership in the wealth, who are likely to be close to risk neutral, and by promoting widespread portfolio diversification in stock ownership of firms, solves the problem of risk allocation in a manner not available to worker-owned firms. Pure worker-ownership is thus not likely to be a viable option for many industries.[4] It is our job, as economists interested in furthering a more egalitarian distribution of wealth and power, to devise hybrid forms of residual claimancy and social policy that maintain the efficiencies possible from worker-ownership without exposing workers to excessive, and indeed unsupportable levels of risk (Bardhan et al., 2000).

A number of empirical investigations document a high level of risk aversion on the part of the non-wealthy. Low wealth entails lower return to independent production, for instance, because producers sacrifice expected returns for more secure returns. Rosenzweig and Wolpin (1993) find that low-wealth Indian farmers seeking a means to secure more stable consumption streams, hold bullocks, which are a highly liquid form of capital, instead of buying pumps, which are illiquid but have high expected return. The relevant effects are not small. Rosenzweig and Binswanger (1993) find, for example, that a one standard deviation reduction in weather risk would raise average profits by about a third among farmers in the lowest wealth quartile (p. 75), and virtually not at all for the top wealth-holders. Moreover, they conclude that the demand for weather insurance would come primarily, if not exclusively, from poor farmers. Nerlove and Soedjiana (1996) find a similar effect in Indonesia with respect to sheep.[5]

Thus because of risk aversion, a reassignment of property rights to low-wealth producers might be unsustainable if as a result producers' income streams are subject to high levels of stochastic variation. Carter et al. (1996) and Jarvis (1989) provide a vivid example: in the Central Valley of Chile three-quarters of those families who received an individual assignment of land rights under a land redistribution programme in the 1970s sold their assets within a decade.

However the availability of insurance can lead to increased risk taking and willingness to hold risky assets. But the market for forms of insurance that promote risk taking in production may be imperfect (Atkinson and Stiglitz, 1980). Shiller (1993) provides several contemporary applications, arguing that capital market imperfections even in the most advanced economies lead to the absence of insurance markets for major sources of individual insecurity and inequality. For instance, a major form of wealth insecurity in many families is the capital value of the family home, due to medium- to long-term fluctuations in average housing prices in a region. No insurance for such fluctuations is available, but Shiller suggests that this and other similar insurance markets can be activated through proper financial interventions. Along these same lines, Sinn (1995) argues that the welfare state in the advanced economies can be understood in part as a successful set of policy measures to improve the risk-taking behaviour of the non-wealthy where private 'social insurance' markets fail.

CONCLUSION

In contrast to public choice theory, which models politics as if it *were* an exchange and other variants of modern-day political economy which focus on the relationships *between* politics (the state) and exchange, in this chapter we have modelled the *politics of exchange* itself.

Our project has been to give precise theoretical content to the way institutions involving the production, allocation and distribution of wealth promote certain forms of power, regulate the exercise of this power and establish the conditions for access to positions of power. Additionally we might hope to specify the mechanisms by which this power is (or might be) rendered accountable to individuals and groups in the economy. We thus defend a concept of political economy that has been denied a place in the study of market economies on the grounds that the exercise of power is impossible in competitive equilibrium, and thus no concept of economic power is needed.

Since the logic of competitive price determination and resource allocation involves a system of power relations among economic agents, it follows that political philosophy, which has traditionally limited the study of democratic accountability to the sphere of government, has an important role in analysing economic relationships. We obtain this result by relaxing a single assumption of the neoclassical general equilibrium model: the existence of costless third-party enforcement. Indeed, we have seen that state power and short-side power are in a sense substitutes: the power associated with advantageous market position comes into play precisely where the state cannot be called upon to enforce contracts. It is perhaps ironic that the neoclassical model, so essential to the economic underpinnings of liberal political philosophy, is a limiting case valid only in the context of a state sufficiently powerful and omniscient to enforce all claims arising from exchange.

Our conception of power in a competitive economy invites a reconsideration of the boundaries traditionally drawn in liberal political philosophy between the marketplace, represented as a private arena of voluntary transactions devoid of coercion on the one hand, and the state as public arena vested with coercive enforcement capacities on the other. Upon this partition of spheres is constructed an important conclusion: while liberal precepts of choice apply in both state and economy, the democratic precepts of account-ability of power apply only to the state. But as we have seen, private enforcement is ubiquitous, particularly in labour and credit markets, and hence the time-honoured private–public partition is unsustainable.

NOTES

*   The authors are grateful to the MacArthur Foundation for research support.
1.   We develop these ideas at greater length in Bowles and Gintis (1990, 1993b, 1996, 1999).
2.   To avoid trivial cases, we assume that no borrower chooses to provide full collateral for the loan, and $r(0)$ is so small that it is never profitable to choose the risk-free investment with $f = 0$. We also assume $r'' > 0$.
3.   For more extended analysis of the benefits of team production and ownership by producers, see Bardhan et al. (2000) and Bowles et al. (2000).
4.   Indeed, in advanced market economies, the capital stock per worker required to operate most firms is considerably in excess of the total assets of most working families. In the United States, for example, the value of the capital goods used in production per worker employed averages just under 100,000, while the average net assets of the least wealthy 80 per cent of families including car and home ownership is 64,000. So most working families, even if they sold their house and car could not finance the capital goods to employ even a single family member.
5.   See Hoff (1996) for a discussion of this and related studies.

REFERENCES

Alchian, Armen and Harold Demsetz (1972), 'Production, information costs, and economic organization', *American Economic Review*, **62**, December, 777–95.

Atkinson, Anthony and Joseph Stiglitz (1980), *Lectures on Public Economics*, New York: McGraw-Hill.

Bardhan, Pranab, Samuel Bowles and Herbert Gintis (2000), 'Wealth inequality, credit constraints, and economic performance', in Anthony Atkinson and François Bourguignon (eds), *Handbook of Income Distribution*, Dordrecht: North-Holland.

Bowles, Samuel, Jeffrey Carpenter and Herbert Gintis (2000), 'Mutual monitoring in teams: the importance of residual claimancy and reciprocity', University of Massachusetts at Amherst.

Bowles, Samuel and Herbert Gintis (1990), 'Contested exchange: new microfoundations of the political economy of capitalism', *Politics & Society*, **18** (2), 165–222.

Bowles, Samuel and Herbert Gintis (1993a), 'An economic and political case for the democratic firm', in *The Idea of Democracy*, Cambridge, UK: Cambridge University Press, pp. 375–99.

Bowles, Samuel and Herbert Gintis (1993b), 'The revenge of homo economicus: contested exchange and the revival of political economy', *Journal of Economic Perspectives*, **7** (1), Winter, 83–102.

Bowles, Samuel and Herbert Gintis (1996), 'Efficient redistribution: new rules for markets, states, and communities', *Politics & Society*, **24** (4), December, 307–42.

Bowles, Samuel and Herbert Gintis (1999), *Recasting Egalitarianism: New Rules for Markets, States, and Communities*, London: Verso, edited by Erik Olin Wright.

Carter, Michael, Bradford Barham and Dina Mesbah (1996), 'Agro export booms and the rural poor in Chile, Guatemala and Paraguay', *Latin American Research Review*, **31** (1), 33–66.

Hoff, Karla (1996), 'Comment on "Political economy of alleviating poverty: theory and institutions", by Timothy Besley', *Annual World Bank Conference on Development Economics*, pp. 139–44.

Jarvis, Lovell (1989), 'The unraveling of Chile's agrarian reform, 1973–1986', in William Thiesenhusen (ed.), *Searching for Agrarian Reform in Latin America*, Boston: Unwin-Hyman, pp. 240–65.

Lerner, Abba (1972), 'The economics and politics of consumer sovereignty', *American Economic Review*, **62** (2), May, 258–66.

Nerlove, Marc and Tjeppy D. Soedjiana (1996), 'Slamerans and sheep: savings and small ruminants in semi-subsistence agriculture in Indonesia', Department of Agriculture and Resource Economics, University of Maryland.

Rosenzweig, Mark and Hans P. Binswanger (1993), 'Wealth, weather risk and the composition and profitability of agriculturalinvestments', *Economic Journal*, **103**, January, 56–78.

Rosenzweig, Mark R. and Kenneth I. Wolpin (1993), 'Credit market constraints, consumption smoothing, and the accumulation of durable production assets in low-income countries: investment in bullocks in India', *Journal of Political Economy*, **101** (2), 223–44.

Samuelson, Paul (1957), 'Wages and interests: a modern dissection of Marxian economics', *American Economic Review*, **47**, 884–921.

Schumpeter, Joseph (1934), *The Theory of Economic Development: An Inquiry into Profits, Capital, Credit, Interest and the Business Cycle*, Oxford: Oxford University Press.

Shiller, Robert J. (1993), *Macro Markets: Creating Institutions for Managing Society's Largest Economic Risks*, Oxford: Clarendon Press.

Sinn, Hans-Werner (1995), 'A theory of the welfare state', *Scandinavian Journal of Economics*, **95** (4), 495–526.

3. Economic theory and the complexity of capitalism

Yoshinori Shiozawa

THE RECOGNITION OF COMPLEXITY

An economy is a complex system. Although the term 'complex' has a number of definitions, we shall assume here that there is some level of agreement on the core ideas involved. However, much less consensus exists as to how this complex system should be analysed.

Until the emergence of the so-called 'sciences of complexity', the prevailing scientific method was to understand complex matters as a result of simple rules. Scientists would seek to understand the complexity of a given phenomenon in terms of simple basic rules, or find a simple principle unifying and reshaping several diverse elements into a single system.

But can complex systems be adequately understood through such reductionist or reconstructive methodologies? This question has been raised ever since the surgical scalpels of science were first applied to complex phenomena. Almost everyone debating the proper methodology for the social sciences stressed their differences from the natural sciences. *Geschichtswissenschaft* (the science of history) emphasized the ideographic character of their science, while *Kulturwissenschaft* (the humanities) pointed out the impossibility of reducing cultural factors to universal laws. Hermeneutics suggested the impossibility of formal analysis. Those that worked in these traditions generally claimed that it was impossible to apply a reductionist methodology to these disciplines.

It is not new to say that the economy is complex. However, an effective means of approaching and understanding this complexity has not yet been established. In order to focus on the significance of complexity in economic studies, I posit three aspects of complexity:

1. Complexity of systems and processes as objects of analysis.
2. Complexity of the economy confronted by the active agent.
3. Complexity of the epistemological process.

Much of my own economic research has focused on the second aspect. My main effort has been to understand the behaviour of economic agents in complex environments (Shiozawa, 1990, 1997). But in this chapter, I wish to discuss the third aspect, namely the manner in which complexity intervenes in our epistemological efforts.

The philosopher Wataru Hiromatsu (1980) distinguished between the standpoints of scholars and actors. Although this distinction is necessary to pursue research, in a more fundamental sense, scholars and actors can be described as approaching situations in essentially identical ways. Economic actors can come to be scholars or 'scientists', just as Brian Loasby (1991, pp. 33–6) characterized them after the psychologist George Kelly (1955). While there are differences in degree, scholars and actors both pose hypotheses: they both think and reflect.

Naturally, economic actors do not think matters through exhaustively, systematically use inferences and deductions, or construct tests to prove hypotheses. They are not 'grand scientists'. However, they are 'small-scale scientists' in that they act on the basis of small hypotheses (in other words, knowledge), and their actions are experiments. If economic actors are small-scale scientists then economic scholars are 'grand scientists'. Both economic actors and economists-as-scholars are constrained by the limits of rationality. This has important implications for the formation of economic theories.

CROSS-SECTIONAL ECONOMIC HISTORY

When looking back on economic history, we are accustomed to thinking of time in terms of stages. For example, Marxists see the history of capitalism in terms of successive stages: mercantilist, liberal and then monopoly capital. Viewed over the longer term, history can be divided into the following eras: slavery in ancient times, feudalism in the Middle Ages and modern capitalism. When speaking of economic history, some means of distinguishing between eras is necessary. Indeed, no matter how many history textbooks you examine, you will not find one that does not classify time into historical eras.

One effort to devise a systematic methodological theory to explain the necessity and significance of classifying historical eras was the stages theory of Kozo Uno. Uno divided capitalism into mercantilist, liberal and imperialist stages. He defined the target of contemporary analysis to be the imperialist era. Uno lived from 1897 to 1970, and he saw the imperialist era as still surviving at the time of his death. Although he did not directly connect his theoretical principles to his analysis of present conditions, he argued that it was necessary to distinguish the three eras and to construct theses (or stages theories) to explain their differences.

Although in many ways similar, modern *régulation* theory does not focus on the long-sweep distinction between eras. Its distinctive feature is the premise that capitalist evolution has featured the nineteenth-century British mode of development and the post-1945, Fordist mode of development, with a long transition period between the first and second World Wars. According to leading *régulation* theorist Toshio Yamada (Kitahara et al., 1997, p. 104), modes of development feature 'exchanges' between rise and decline. Yamada calls state monopoly capital theories and the Uno school's historical approach 'three-stage cumulative theories'. He is highly critical of this approach because it implies the following: 'Through this process of development, capitalism has "successively" realized higher stages, so this is a "stages of history perspective" indicating that the present is the final stage'. Yet even in Yamada's *régulationnist* approach, as represented in post-Fordist theory, time periods are clearly marked off, with each period having its own 'accumulation regime' and 'mode of adjustment'. Accordingly, this approach also embraces a stages view of history.

I apply the term 'cross-sectional economic history' to the type of historical time segmentation in which changes of economic structure and institutions or forms are identified at particular points in time. In this approach to history, the flow of time is appropriately segmented, and each segment is then held to be a distinctive stage with its own structure.[1] If the socioeconomic eras are divided by short time periods such as revolutions between which they undergo major changes – that is, if history has a discontinuous structure – then, cross-sectional history is a sound approach. However, if history is a process of constant change in which distinct boundaries cannot be identified, then there will be major weaknesses with the cross-sectional history approach.

HOW DOES HISTORY CHANGE?

Stages of change or continuous change? Marxist thought hypothesized that major discontinuities would give rise to distinctive historical periods. At present, however, this view of history is being reconsidered from many perspectives.

Britain is a country that serves as an indicator for historical division by various Marxist schools, but since the 1960s a great deal of research has been conducted on sixteenth- and seventeenth-century British regions and lifestyles, and it has supported a view of history as continuous. During these centuries, an accumulation of gradual socioeconomic changes, though they may have seemed small when regarded separately, set the stage for the industrial revolution of the eighteenth century.

In her book *Economic Policy and Projects*, Joan Thirsk (1978) has evocatively depicted the changes taking place in everyday life and occupations in the sixteenth century. She demonstrates persuasively that the production of consumer goods was being commercialized, that the variety of goods increased, that this process provided new opportunities for the poor to earn incomes, and that it created new markets as well. This amounted to a procession of minor changes that went largely unnoticed by people at the time, but which over the course of a century generated an astonishing transformation.

In addition, a number of academics have proposed theories of proto-industrialization to explain development in the United States and Germany. These are also basically continuous-history approaches.

When history is divided into eras or stages, political revolutions, wars and other political events often serve as the markers of eras. The use of political events as historical indicators reflects the fact that economic change occurs continuously. Whereas political activities might be viewed as having relatively clear transitional points, economies have no such obvious indicators. Not only do they lack indicators, but one must also understand that there are no dividing points at all. The Meiji Restoration changed the political structure, then it altered incomes and expenditures by abolishing samurai stipends and establishing a new tax regime. It transformed the people's moral ethos as well. But if one examines economic transactions or production processes, it is hard to find any drastic change, because popular customs, consumption patterns and means of production changed only slowly.

If history is regarded as discontinuous, then it consists of what can be termed a structure, and this structure will change at given points in time. Changes that can be called structural often occur in the economic realm. At least, if two points sufficiently separated in time are compared, then the differences between them should be evident. But is it appropriate to identify eras by structural changes that occur in a system as complex as an economy?

There are certain disagreements regarding how economies change over time. Those who regard economic history as a succession of discontinuous stages believe that the economy is 'one' unity. Since the economy is a tightly unified structure, any change that occurs in one part must result in a major change to the entire structure. Those who regard history as a progression of continuous change believe that the economy is, in various meanings and ways, a 'multiplicity': there are various actors, various products, various relationships and a variegated structure. The economy then is a sort of network, whose nodes are loosely connected. The perspective of multiplicity represents the idea that the economy is always in a progression of continuous change. Over the long term, the accumulation of small changes brings large transformations.

A simple calculation will illustrate the point. Let us think of all of the types of goods existing in a given time period. These goods cannot be replaced at a single stroke, but over the long term most of them will have been replaced, to the point that the original product mix can no longer be discerned. For example, suppose that product types are replaced at the rate of a mere 1 per cent a year. One hundred years later, just less than 37 per cent of the original products remain. If the rate of change is 2 per cent in a year, then only 13 per cent of the original products will remain in one hundred years. In the real world, the increase in product range has to be taken into account, but when thinking about consumer products in general, it is hard to imagine that sudden changes or discontinuities occur.

This sort of continuation is regarded as natural in aggregate quantitative areas such as calculating of national income. But there are also many non-aggregate economic areas, including commercial activities, settling accounts, labour practices, production technology, consumption structure and lifestyle modes, in which change occurs only slowly.

Yasusuke Murakami (1996, p. 252) applies the label 'unitary historical perspective' to the approach that he understood as 'revolution-punctuated stages', stating that it is ultimately a perspective according to which 'a large and unique force moves history'. The unitary historical perspective is linked to the linear historical perspective. It also emphasizes a single major causal force. Almost inevitably, it is also linked to the revolutionary perspective, as Murakami emphasizes.

Dividing history into periods may be an easy and easily explained method. However, errors in understanding can arise when this simplicity becomes exaggerated, when understandings of economic change and development become distorted, and when discontinuities are stressed more than is necessary.

Since discussing historical perspectives is not the purpose of this chapter, I shall not discuss their suitability. Still, there is clearly a major divide between the two perspectives, that of history as a continuously variable flow, and that of history as discontinuous stages of development. Which of the two perspectives you adopt marks a branch that alters what you perceive in history. I want to emphasize that this is a serious point to be discussed and should not be treated as a question of convenience.

THE SOCIAL CHANGE THEORY OF KUNIO YANAGITA

The continuous history approach did not develop from European economic history research alone. According to the interpretation of Kazuko Tsurumi (1974), the historical perspective of Kunio Yanagita was thoroughly pluralistic, continuous and anti-elitist. Tsurumi, stimulated by young American scholars and using Yanagita's historical perspective as a clue, advocated the 'icicle model' as a paradigm of social change.[2]

In contrast to the moments of discontinuity emphasized by the Western perspective, Yanagita emphasizes the moments of continuity. With regard to either social or spiritual structure, Yanagita thought that there were no clear distinctions between prehistory, antiquity, the Middle Ages, or modernity, so that prehistorical, ancient, Middle Age and modern human relations, customs and spiritual structures had 'changed little by little and in no remarkable way'. As a result, from the beginning of history up to modernity various social and spiritual structures have coexisted as if in an *irekozaiku*, the Japanese box containing a series of progressively smaller, closely fitting boxes. If we term the cross-sectioning of historical time as used in Western theory a 'stage model', then we can call Yanagita's historical time an 'icicle model' (Tsurumi, 1974, p. 150).

If, following Tsurumi, we regard the Western historical perspective as discontinuous and opposed to that of Yanagita and other Japanese thinkers, then the understanding of history as continuous might seem to originate in the distinctive conditions of Japan. Thinking in a more global perspective, however, might lead us to the following understanding.

Japan has traversed a historical process rather close to that of Europe. Distinctions among ancient slave, Middle Age feudal and modern capitalist systems can be tentatively established for Japan. As Tadao Umezao (1967) and Samir Amin (1973) have pointed out, this pattern of development may have been possible because of Japan's particular situation as an island nation located at the eastern edge of the Eurasian land-mass. Japan has traversed a historical course similar to that of Europe, and has therefore had similarly stratifying historical approaches, most importantly Marxism, applied to it. However, the rigid application of Western-type historical divisions to Japan has often proved difficult and at odds with reality. Yanagita's historical perspective represented an important repudiation of efforts to apply chronological divisions of foreign provenance to Japan, but that does not mean that his viewpoint was distinctively Japanese. In the many countries long dominated by a single social formation best termed a tribute system, applying a stratified historical approach as clear-cut as the West's would be even worse than in Japan's case. As Tsurumi argued, in non-European societies, Yanagita-type continuity models are more easily used than stratification-based Western models premised on discontinuity. Viewed in a global perspective, the revival of the continuous historical approach in Europe may indicate a return to non-European societies as standards.

CONTINUITY AND DISCONTINUITY IN MARX

The debate about continuity and discontinuity is not being battled out in the area of historical approach alone. It is also an issue in disagreements over the practice and nature of economic development.

Joseph Schumpeter argued that innovation was the main motivational force in economic development, and that this process was stimulated by entrepreneurial spirit. As he correctly pointed out, economic development proceeds together with technological progress. However, there are considerable problems in representing technological progress as technological innovation. Nathan Rosenberg (1982, pp. 6–8) emphasizes that cumulative, continuous, small improvements are just as important and effective as technological breakthroughs.

What is interesting here, as Rosenberg notes, is that an argument about technological continuity leads back to Marx. Marx stressed that technological progress reflects the forward movement of tremendous social forces, and he minimized the importance of the individual. As a historian, Marx appears to be a member of the discontinuity school, but as a historian of technological development, he is one of the founding fathers of the continuity school. If Schumpeter's historical vision is regarded as elite orientated, then Marx's is anti-elite and orientated mainly towards the masses. On this point, Yanagita accords with Marx.

The historical perspective of Marxian economics incorporates several schools of scholarly endeavour into a stage-based theory, but in its vision of social forces Marxism also incorporates a very important continuous historical perspective. Within the single person of Marx, the two approaches of continuity and discontinuity were enmeshed in a contradictory, parallel existence.

Marx himself did not notice the contradiction. When two contradictory ideas are enmeshed, and a theoretical ordering takes place, the poles naturally converge towards one idea or the other. It is no coincidence that later Marxist schools all adopted the discontinuity perspective. As Selucky (1983, ch.1) pointed out, there is an irreconcilable contradiction in Marxian thought between the conceptions of political liberation and economic liberation. Just as philosophy was once the handmaiden of theology, Marxian economics is the handmaiden of Marxist political thought, so it was naturally the political concept that triumphed. It was the fate of economics and economic history to be mobilized to demonstrate the inevitability of political revolution and to bring it to realization. As a result, the historical perspective of Marxian economics became incorporated into theories of discontinuity.

COMPETITIVE PARALLEL EXISTENCE

Having discussed Marx, I wish to touch again upon an issue that I have explored in more detail elsewhere (Shiozawa, 1980). It relates to the Marxian expression 'contradiction between productive forces and productive relations'.

There was once a great debate as to which – productive forces or productive relations – should be regarded as primary. However, I feel that it is strange to think that the two are contradictory. There is a sort of category mistake in such a claim. It holds that an increase in productive forces will result in their becoming incompatible with productive relations so that the old structure will have to be swept away and new relations of production introduced. If productive relations become a fetter on the growth of productive forces, then economic stagnation must result. However, I believe that the contradiction is not between productive forces and productive relations, rather contradictions develop among the various types of productive relations.

In recent years, the increasing volume of international commercial activity has generated tremendous interest in the convergence of transaction practices. Each region and country has its own customs for regulating transactions, and if transactions were strictly limited to regional or single-country scales, there would be no particular problem. However, since international transactions have become common, in fact routine, they have created many disputes between traders in different countries. Whatever contract is concluded, in the end traders rely on custom to interpret it, and regions and countries differ on how explicit contracts should be. With the rapid increase in borderless transactions, there has been growing demand for the unification of transaction practices. At present, the United States is leading the call for standardization, and also demanding that its standards become the global standards, a position opposed of course by many other countries. Determining issues such as which set of standards is best will be no easy matter. The advance of standardization itself is giving rise to international disputes.

If transactional institutions are viewed as productive relations, and multiple productive relations are mutually excluded, then a competition to have one's own practices used more widely will normally ensue.

Technology is normally seen as something closely related to productive forces. But, on some occasions, particularly when the choice of techniques cannot be made on the basis of profitability alone, technology can generate a contradiction between productive relations.

A typical example of this sort can be seen in the soda industry. Caustic soda is ordinarily produced by breaking down table salt through electrolysis, which can be performed using either diaphragms, mercury or ion exchange membranes. During the wartime era, the Japanese soda industry produced soda through the Sorbet method, which does not create chlorine as a byproduct. After the war, the development of the petrochemical industry created growing demand for chlorine, leading to the steady adoption of the mercury-based electrolysis method, which produces chlorine as a byproduct, and the displacement of the Sorbet method by the end of the 1950s. However, an environmental crisis erupted in the early 1970s when organic mercury was found to cause Minamata disease, and in 1973 the government decided that the diaphragm method would replace mercury-induced electrolysis. There were found to be problems with quality when diaphragms were used, leading to the development of new methods utilizing ion exchange membranes. This resulted in furious bargaining between the government and business over the deadline for making the shift away from mercury. Technology A was economically efficient but dangerous, and there was strong pressure to adopt the less efficient but safer Technology B; this was a classic case of technological choice becoming subject to social priorities.

Similar contradictions can be seen in the workplace. Consider a situation where Technology A is efficient but dangerous, whereas Technology B is safe but inefficient. The managers prefer to utilize A and the workers demand B, bringing the two sides into conflict. This kind of dispute occurs because there is a social significance to the differences between the two technologies. To be precise, the problem is not a contradiction between productive forces and productive relations, but the choice between the productive relations that would result from Technology A and those that would result from Technology B. With regard to the transaction standard, the nature of the contradiction, or dispute, is different, but there is competition between multiple forms of productive relations.

Let us pursue a somewhat different line of thought to discuss the work of Geoffrey Hodgson (Chapter 5 in this volume) and his 'impurity principle'. Hodgson interprets this notion to mean that: 'The idea is that every socio-economic system must rely on at least one structurally dissimilar subsystem to function. There must always be a coexistent plurality of modes of production, so that the social formation as a whole has the requisite structural variety to cope with change'. If we use his framework, contemporary capitalism includes different sectors such as household production or state structures. Since procreation and childcare are necessary for the reproduction of labour, a legal order maintaining productive relations is necessary, and, needless to say, capitalist economies cannot just be organizations unified in the pursuit of profits. The term 'mode of production' conveys a sense of a system conceived as an entire economy, but if we think instead of the technological and transactional aspects, we can see that this principle has a different significance.

THE LIMITS OF CATEGORIZATION

As an economy is a multifaceted process, comprising multiple competing and intermeshed components and relations, a simple stage-based division cannot possibly encapsulate it. This point is widely understood, but when we want to discuss a particular phenomenon we must have a vocabulary in order to express it. If such verbalization is done on a provisional basis, the phenomenon is named, and we begin to use the name as a concept. Then the name may begin to function as an independent symbol. This is a process of symbolic reification.

In so far as mercantilism, liberalism and imperialism were used to express major characteristics of certain eras concisely, no problems ensued. But if the concept 'liberal stage' ceases to be a provisional concept and comes to be defined as indicating one concrete period, then it creates the impression that it embodies a distinctive structure that was clearly demarcated from other periods of time. When *régulation* theory was introduced to Japan, deciding where to divide Fordism from post-Fordism in Japan was a big problem. I do not make such cut-and-dried distinctions, but those who regard Fordism as a single time period are forced to determine its exact beginning and end.

Fundamentally, the propositional methodology of language has changed little since Aristotle. A given proposition must have an appropriate extension, and the range of this extension must be clear and precise. This means that if one produces a proposition with a given concept as predicate, one can, in principle, discern whether the proposition is true or false. This is 'the law of the excluded middle'. Descartes, the founder of modern philosophy, strengthened this understanding by positing his well-known phrase *'clair et distinct'*. In the present age, scholastic logic has developed into symbolic logic, yet both appeal to the law of the excluded middle.[3]

A few years ago, fuzzy logic became trendy, partly because it is a theory that recognizes vague concepts. However, it is not yet fully appreciated that all scientific terms must allow for a degree of vagueness.

If concern were limited to just two elements in competitive relations, it would be largely a question of how quickly a logistic curve rises. When the rise is very rapid, stage-based arguments are possible. On the other hand, should the occupancy rate of a given element need several decades to change from 20 to 80 per cent, then we must speak in terms of transition periods.

There are many goods whose processes of diffusion trace logistic curves. Therefore, to displace the problem outlined above, the main parameter is the speed of diffusion. It is well understood that a single good, a single lifestyle, or a single means of production involves a long-term process of diffusion. This type of object is often perceived or analysed as something that permeates slowly into the society. So when we speak of other economic phenomena, why do we not adopt this point of view?

The point of stage theory, to return to the earlier discussion, is that an entire economy comprises tightly organized relationships so that when a given part changes, the entire structure must quickly change as well. If logistic curves are traced simultaneously for nearly all aspects and this process of diffusion comes to an abrupt end, the impression of stage-based change is strengthened. If we note that an economy is multifaceted and ordinarily composed of complex contentions, however, we shall be aware that these are forced simplifications.

We have to use language and, in order to conduct theoretical thinking, we have to use clear and distinct concepts. When using such clear-cut concepts, however, it is essential to take care not to distort the nature of the objects.

At the beginning of this chapter, I stated that there are three aspects of complexity in economics. The important point about complexity that I have analysed here is that it is an element that cannot be neglected when we analyse actors' behaviours but also when we want to reflect on the theoretical construction of the economics discipline itself.

NOTES

1. Geographical formations are often composed of many strata separated by exceptionally thin transitional layers. Different strata can usually be perceived through variations in colour. If such structures are found in history, then cross-sectional economic history may be an appropriate methodological approach.
2. This section is also cited in Seiji Tsutsumi (1996, p. 223). The American researcher who 'provoked' Tsurumi was Ronald Morse.
3. However, there are forms of logic, such as intuitive logic and minimal logic, that do not have the law of the excluded middle as a precondition.

REFERENCES

Amin, Samir (1973), *Le Développement Inégal*, Paris: Editions de Minuit.
Hiromatsu, Wataru (1983), *Busshokaron no kozu* (The schema of the theory of reification), Tokyo: Iwanami Shoten.
Kelly, George A. (1955), *The Psychology of Personal Constructs*, 2 vols, New York: Norton.
Kitahara, Isamu, Makoto Itoh and Toshio Yamada (1997), *Gendai shihonshugi o do miru ka* (How to regard contemporary capitalism), Tokyo: Aoki Shoten.
Loasby, Brian (1991), *Equilibrium and Evolution: An Exploration of Connecting Principles in Economics*, Manchester: Manchester University Press.
Murakami, Yasusuke (1996), *Anticlassical Political–Economic Analysis: A Vision for the Next Century*, translated by K. Yamamura from the Japanese edition of 1992, Stanford: Stanford University Press.

Rosenberg, Nathan (1982), *Inside the Black Box: Technology and Economics*, Cambridge: Cambridge University Press.

Selucky, Radoslav (1983), *Marxism, Socialism, Freedom: Towards a General Democratic Theory of Labour-managed Systems*, London and Basingstoke: Macmillan Press.

Shiozawa, Yoshinori (1980), 'Seikatsu no saiseisan to keizaigaku' (Economics and the reproduction of lives), *Shiso no kagaku* (Science of Thought), No. 116 (Cumulated No. 324), March.

Shiozawa, Yoshinori (1990), *Shijo no chitsujogaku* (Eutaxy of the market), Tokyo: Chikuma Shobo.

Shiozawa, Yoshinori (1997), *Fukuzatsusa no kiketsu* (Consequences of complexity), Tokyo: NTT Shuppan.

Thirsk, Joan (1978), *Economic Policy and Projects: The Development of a Consumer Society in Early Modern England*, Oxford: Clarendon Press.

Tsurumi, Kazuko (1974), 'Shakai hendo no paradaimu: Yanagita Kunio no shigoto wo jiku to shite' (The social change paradigm: especially the work of Kunio Yanagita), in Kazuko Tsurumi and Saburo Ichii (eds), *Shiso no boken: Shakai to henka no atarashii paradaimu* (Adventures in thought: new paradigms in social change), Tokyo: Chikuma Shobo.

Tsutsumi, Seiji (1996), *Shohi shakai hihan* (Criticism of consumption society), Tokyo: Iwanami Shoten.

Umezao, Tadao (1967), *Bunmei no seitai shikan* (An ecological history view of civilizations), Tokyo: Chuokoronsha. Reprinted in Tadao Umezao (1989), *Collected Works*, vol. 5, Tokyo: Chuokoron.

4. The development of the market economy and the formation of voice

Kiichiro Yagi

THE SMITHIAN THEORY OF THE DIVISION OF LABOUR

In developing his theory of natural selection, it is well known that Charles Darwin was inspired by Thomas Malthus's *Essay on the Principle of Population* (1798). Darwin extended the necessary struggle for life from Malthusian population theory to the zoological and botanical spheres. But another element of natural selection, the generation of diversity, is missing in Malthusian theory. Accordingly, some researchers seek another inspiration for Darwinian theory in the classical idea of the division of labour. Although there is no evidence of Darwin reading Adam Smith's *Wealth of Nations* (1776), Darwin was acquainted with the idea of 'division of labour' as this idea was familiar to his contemporaries (Hodgson, 1993, ch. 4).

We shall not go into the entangled relations between biology and economics here. But it is possible to regard Smith's theory of the division of labour as an origin for evolutionary economics. Consider Smith's discussion of the diversity of types of dogs in Book I, Chapter 2 of the *Wealth of Nations*. The strength of the mastiff, the swiftness of the greyhound, the sagacity of the spaniel, or the docility of the shepherd dog are almost all the result of artificial crossbreeding and selection in successive generations, to make them suitable for guarding, hunting, petting or shepherding. According to Smith, in the case of the division of labour among men, the difference in the original constitution of the mind and body is rather small. But once they have entered economic life, after being engaged in various occupational activities, men become diversified not only in their skills, but also in their dispositions and habits. Smith argued that this diversity in the division of labour is an unintentional result of the natural development of exchange among people. Since men, by their nature, have a propensity to exchange they can benefit from diversification – dogs cannot.

Modern economists know Smith's analysis by its famous theorem: 'The division of labour is limited by the extent of the market'. For those individuals or firms that are specialized in some particular trade or industry, the market is the place where they purchase goods that they need but do not produce, and the place where they sell their own products. Accordingly, this theorem has a twofold meaning. First, for the emergence of a particular trade or industry the market must already have a complementary structure of other trades or industries. Second, sufficient (potential) demand for the products of the emerging trades or industries must exist beforehand. The complementary relation in trades or industries is by definition the division of labour itself. The demand in the market is in one sense the shadow of the existing division of labour in the sphere of exchange.

The relationship between the division of labour and the market involves circular causation. The division of labour diversifies the market by producing attractive new goods and widens it further by supplying existing goods cheaper than before as a result of increased labour productivity. As a result, the extent and structure of the market that limits the present division of labour itself is the product of the past development of the division of labour. And new emerging trades or industries contain the possibility of restructuring and widening the existing market. Smith's theorem sees economic development as the interaction of the market and the division of labour.

However, Smith also recognized another type of division of labour, not in the overall social allocation of labour but within organizations (firms). This is sometimes called the 'factory division of labour'. This type of division of labour is designed for efficient production by the employer and was analysed by Charles Babbage (1832), a friend of Darwin. The nature of the organization principle of the factory division of labour is 'designed' rather than 'evolutionary'.

It is worth mentioning that Smith explained the emergence of money and capital as the result of the development of the division of labour. The emergence of money is discussed in the fourth chapter following three 'division of labour' chapters, while one must wait till the introduction of the second book to find the necessity of capital.[1] Smith explained the emergence of money as the general means of exchange, saying that in a society with a developed division of labour everyone behaves like a merchant and learns to manage indirect exchanges. It is argued that a stock of materials, tools and wage goods must exist somewhere to start and continue the division of labour, because production and selling take time. This is the necessity of capital. In a market economy, money links the dispersed exchange activities on the market, and capital gives the unit of production (firm). Money and capital are thus two categories that integrate the division of labour in his economic theory.

The deduction of money from the necessity of a general means of exchange follows directly from the theorem cited above. On the other hand, Smith's insight that the division of labour presupposes a preceding accumulation of stock, combines capital theory with the employment of labour. It thus produces the second theorem that supplements the first: 'As the accumulation of stock must, in the nature of things, be previous to the division of labour, so labour can be more and more subdivided in proportion only as stock is previously more and more accumulated' (Book II, Introduction).[2] The division of labour that is generally determined by the first theorem presents itself as the appropriate size of capital stock in the second theorem. Overall, the extent of the market determines the diversification of trades or industries and the necessary size of capital accumulation; the size of capital determines the degree of the division of labour in the factories; the growing productivity of the division of labour in the factories determines the size and structure of the market and thus determines the diversity of trades or industries.

Indirect exchange using money promotes this development. Not only do producers of consumption goods become independent trades or industries, but also producers of intermediary goods are separated in the development of the market. The general exchangeability of money penetrates the structure of the division of labour and imposes such substitutability on its every component. Although the original concept of the division of labour is a complementary relation without substitution, money brings a competitive substitution not only in the selection of consumer goods, but also among production processes and employed workers. In addition to the substitution of goods and workers of the same type, the substitution of heterogeneous goods, technologies and different types of workers, also promotes structural change in industry. Production costs and benefits, and changes in technology and tastes provide the criteria for this substitution. It is no wonder that over a century after Smith's *Wealth of Nations*, Alfred Marshall (1949, p. 597) in his *Principles* interpreted this effect as a limited application of 'the law of the survival of the fittest'.

Smith explained the employment of workers by capitalists by the fact that a previous accumulation of stock has to precede the division of labour. If accumulation of stock should follow the division of labour, workers could accumulate it by themselves. Since the reverse is the case, workers have to depend on the existing stocks offered by others. Hence these stocks assume the nature of capital that is invested in production with the aim of profit.

The division of labour needs capital. In many cases, under the given condition of the technology and the market, a minimum size of capital is necessary to attain the productivity that enables the specialized producer to maintain and develop his business. If this size is too small to employ himself or his family or a few workmen, the division of labour using individuals becomes the unit. Otherwise, the constitutive unit of the division of labour is capital that employs many workers, presenting itself as a firm.

In the first chapter of the *Wealth of Nations*, Smith mentioned three factors leading to higher productivity within a division of labour. First, the increase in the skill and knowledge of workers; second, the reduction of idle time by a closely linked work organization; and third, the invention and introduction of machinery. Smith suggests that the employer or capitalist provides the second and the third factors. Although every business endeavours to use these two, in most cases, their full advantage is realized only by a large-scale production system, in which collective labour is integrated together with improved machinery. However, regarding the first factor concerning the worker's physical and intellectual abilities, some possibility emerges that individual skill and knowledge may develop to reduce the worker's dependence on capital. Today, however, under a highly developed production system, an essential part of the skill and knowledge of individual workers is acquired from continual experience within the workplace and is not always transferable elsewhere.

The skills of workers, the efficient type of work organization, and the introduction of machinery are complementary to one another. To some degree they tend to be fixed by the division of labour in the factory. Productivity grows, on the basis of increasing returns to scale, within this complementary and relatively rigid arrangement.

The existence of these relatively rigid complementarities implies an element of path dependence. Although the division of labour in the factory can be reorganized by the employer at will, there is no guarantee of success. In the case of the division of labour on the market, the employer can rely on the capital and talents of his counterparts, but the lack of a single will in this sphere brings forward the problem of coordination. The historical process of industrial development is composed of some path-dependent inertia. It is a composite development process of markets and organizations, with unintended outcomes.

VOICE AND LOYALTY

In the preceding section we reconsidered Smith's view of the division of labour, together with the concept of capital and employed labour. This suggested that the driving forces of evolutionary development of the economy are found not solely in the sphere of market exchange. In this section we consider further the situation of the employed workers within the system.

The employment relation is an economic exchange between agents with asymmetrical assets and abilities, where one side (the employer) largely determines the conditions of the transaction. Since the result of the transaction depends largely on the selection of the employer, the employees can find themselves discontented with the transaction. Albert Hirschman (1970) provided the twin concepts of voice and exit to describe the action that discontented agents can take in transactions of this type. Voice is defined as the endeavour to change the situation without fleeing from it. It involves an appeal for improvement by request or direct or indirect protest. By contrast, exit involves the breaking-off of relations with the determining principal and the search for another opportunity, perhaps involving another employer. If a relatively attractive alternative opportunity has already been found on the market, the result of exit is certain. By contrast, voice is by nature a political action. The outcome depends on the degree of resistance of the principal and the degree of support of fellow agents.

When mainstream economists talk of the market economy, it is wholly of transactions coordinated by the exit actions, and not the deliberation, dialogue and potential conflict that is associated with the voice option. Indeed, apart from the individual result of the exit action, exit can contribute to the general betterment of the situation. For example, in firms with high labour turnover resulting from discontent with working conditions, managers are pressed to take countervailing measures to mitigate employee dissatisfaction. High labour turnover may not only bring high costs of recruitment but also threaten the productivity and stability of the production system. Economists have interpreted such exit effects in terms of a price mechanism that balances demand and supply of the goods at the market. However, discontent is a multidimensional phenomenon that cannot be reduced to a single dimension of monetary value.

The positive effect of exit depends on various elements. An interesting problem raised by Hirschman is the possibility that exit could undermine the power of voice and as a result the employment situation could be worsened. For example, it is probable that the earliest group of quitters would include those workers with the highest demands, or those who have the greatest possibility of acquiring better conditions under alternative employers. The exit of those workers has the tendency to check the height and diversity of the demands of the remaining workers.

In Hirschman's terms, more important is the attitude of the group expressing 'loyalty'. This group of workers will not choose the immediate option of exit and will continue to be loyal up to some later stage of the situation. In this group, managers can place some trust. However, the loyalty of this group is not unconditional or unlimited. When this group loses trust in its managers, its voice will rapidly become louder. On the other hand, when this group perceives the possibility of exit, the power of voice will rapidly collapse.

Loyalty transcends individualism. To be loyal means to offer service beyond the limit of individual interests. Nevertheless, loyalty is based on a reciprocal expectation of similar services in return. As George Akerlof (1982) pointed out, the employment relationship is partly a social exchange or gift. The basis of this loyalty in industrial relations is the working groups within an integrated division of labour. If loyalty is extended to manage-

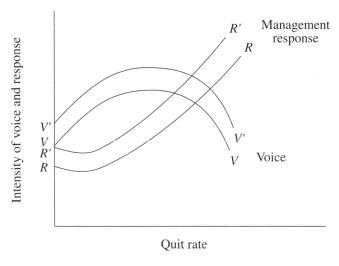

Figure 4.1   Exit, voice and response of management

ment, this will have the feature of a social exchange between capital and labour.

In Figure 4.1, the power of the voice of the workers is shown by the curves VV and $V'V'$.[3] The reason that voice curves have peaks in the middle stage of the quitting rate is explained above. RR and $R'R'$ are the response curves of managers. At low quit rates, managers are insensitive to voice. In a prosperous period when working conditions and wages are good, the voice curve of workers will shift upwards, but the response curve of managers will also shift upwards due to the increased cost of quittance and recruitment Exit moves managers solely in the area where the quit rate exceeds that at the point of intersection. However, in many cases this belongs to the critical, ebbing stage of the firm where the loyal workers begin quitting. The area before the intersection is where the voice of the workers has the possibility of influencing managerial decisions. However, this is also the area where most of the workers remain working, despite a degree of discontent and the managers can make use of the workers' loyalty. Therefore, the subtle relation between loyalty and voice appears at the core of industrial relations.

As Hirschman noticed, loyalty is not a pure 'faith' in others, but is characterized by a 'reasoned calculation' concerning the possibility of influence and gain in the future. Even if it appears as subservience, it has the benefit of avoiding the need to question and express voice. If the adequacy of future compensation is in doubt, the option of voice will be adopted.

The action of the voice extends from an individual revelation of private discontent, to the representatives of small fellow groups, and to action taken in the name of the public interest. As for the effectiveness of such kind of political action, some stress the paralysing possibility of free riders who do not utter voice (Olson, 1965). But we suppose that the loyalty as seen in the industrial relations in modern economies is not a purely individualistic attitude but a collective attitude that is based on the working groups and their interdependence. Accordingly, the voice action of the individual is not always isolated, so long as it is linked successively with the common understanding of the 'loyal' group of the workers.

THE INSTITUTIONALIZATION OF VOICE AND EXIT

In the analysis of unions, labour economists have used Hirschman's twin concepts of voice and exit. Richard Freeman (1980) investigated the influence of the labour unions as the collective voice organization of workers on the quit rate, using US statistics in the 1960s and 1970s. According to him, unions have two functions: first, the monopoly function in the labour market that is aimed at raising wages and other rewards, and second, the voice function that represents the discontents of the workers. He concluded that the effect of the latter, on the reduction of the quit rate and on the lengthening of the employment, exceeds the monopoly function, and that the voice function is statistically verified even in the cases where it does not accompany the monopoly function.

Richard Freeman and James Medoff (1984) further examined union influence on the quit rate. They found two institutional innovations, 'grievance-and-arbitration systems' and 'seniority-based personnel policies', which had been created by unions in the US industrial relations system. These two innovations exhibit a degree of loyalty by a group of workers. The seniority principle directly contradicts the interest of young workers who have only a short history in the workplace. The grievance system is not designed for workers who think it is better to improve their condition by quitting and searching for an alternative employer.

Freeman and Medoff thus showed how US labour unions had institutionalized the voice function. A contrasting investigation into Japanese industrial relations by Tsuru and Morishima (1999) compared the voice function of the unionized and non-unionized firms in the Tokyo metropolitan area. He found institutions for the expression of employee voice even in non-unionized firms. These included not only individual grievance procedures and suggestion systems, but also collective voice systems involving various forms of employee associations and joint consultation. However, Tsuru showed that the range of influence of the voice systems in the non-union firms was more restricted than that of the voice influence in the unionized firms. In particular, in non-unionized firms, voice did not extend to strategic personnel problems or investment policies.*

Freeman and Medoff asked: 'why don't all companies have grievance-and-arbitration systems?' (p. 107). They gave two reasons. First, non-unionized firms are generally orientated to the young, mobile workers who are less interested in that kind of system than are older, more permanent workers. Second, such a system binds managerial decisions and places them within a judicial orbit. Management is often reluctant to share some of their power with well-organized unions, or to encourage union organization by legitimating its presence.

We may then ask why the voice system functions rather well, even in non-unionized Japanese firms. Is the argument of Freeman and Medoff refuted by Tsuru's research? The answer is not straightforward. Analysis of the statistics of Japanese firms shows no significant influence of the voice system, in either unionized or non-unionized firms, on quitting rates. Notably, Japanese unions do not adopt seniority-based policies. Tsuru's results seems to suggest that Japanese unions have different principles of organization from the Americans, which are closely based on the more permanent subgroup of 'loyal' workers. In the case of the grievance-and-arbitration system, Japanese unions try to exert influence and seek a substantial resolution beforehand. Judicial or other outside arbitration is alien to Japanese unions. Collective voice mechanisms, such as employee-friendly societies or councils within the non-unionized firms, can substitute to some degree for the voice function of unions. But the personnel department sustains these non-union representation systems; they are not independent organizations that can fully represent the views of, and form policies for, the diverse employee body.

These two empirical investigations suggest that the nature of the institutionalization of the voice of the employee is one of the axes of the industrial relations. The direction and degree of the development of workers' voice are influenced by the function of the related institutions.

Besides the institutionalization of voice, one can also consider the institutionalization of exit. If members of the loyalty group are forced to make some self-sacrificing efforts, they may generate a hidden desire for exit. Accordingly, if an honourable exit under good terms is institutionalized, the formation of voice is to a certain degree restrained and controlled. Individual promotion out of a workgroup is a sort of institutionalized exit. In cases of mass dismissal, privileged retirement packages are often offered to mitigate employee voice.

In the Japanese political system, the *Amakudari*, or custom of providing former high-ranking state officials with well-paid jobs in private enterprises or semi-public organizations, could also be considered as an example of the institutionalization of exit (Inoki, 1993; Kawamura, 1994). The salary of

Japanese state officials is slightly lower than their university classmates who instead entered large private enterprises. This is despite the fact that the work in ministries is sometimes harder and involves long and irregular hours of work. On the positive side, the promotion of elite bureaucrats is fairly rapid and after two decades almost all find themselves in the position of section chief. However, the competition is fierce and some retire in their late forties. It is an unwritten law of the ministerial bureaucracy that if someone gets to the top position in the ministry every other ministry official who entered ministry service in the same year must quit.

In a classical bureaucracy, job loyalty and good work are demanded in exchange for status and lifelong security. At first sight, the economic compensation of elite bureaucrats in Japan seems to be to the contrary. In reality, lifelong security is replaced by access to outside jobs that are created and controlled by the personnel office of the ministry. High-ranking officials of the Ministry of Finance would often take up the position of director in some private bank. Bureaucrats in the Ministry of Trade and Industry would often receive jobs in manufacturing or distribution companies. Japanese bureaucrats are often criticized because their loyalty is orientated to each ministry rather than to the government or the state as a whole, and struggles between cliques prevail instead of public policy debates. An explanation, from the viewpoint of voice and exit, is because exit is controlled independently by each ministry.

Hirschman (1995) himself found the power of the voice–exit perspective in the process of political change in East Germany up to 1989. He argued that the desire for exit and the formation of voice strengthened each other in an emerging situation in which controlled exit became impossible. When the Berlin Wall was in place, dissident activity was quietened by allowing about ten thousand citizens to leave annually for the West. This checked the formation of voice in the underground. The sudden change in the international relations in mid-1989 ignited the desire for exit, and the restrictive orders of the government brought forth resistance. However, the spontaneously formed voice was not sufficient to guide the following political transition process. There was no intellectual hegemony, and it took only half a year for established West German political parties to dominate politics in East Germany. This was the penalty that East Germany paid for the repressive control of their voice by means of managed exit.

As suggested above, a managed combination of voice and exit is integrated into the politico-economic system of postwar Japan. Japanese industry is partitioned into so many branches as associations (*gyokai*) that are constituted by firms operating in each of their partitions. These partitioned industries have corresponding sections in the ministerial bureaucracy. With the restriction of new entry and of developing new business areas, even the followers have the voice for their survival. At the same time, they are directed to compete against each other for some national goals or technological innovations. As the embarkation on the new business area signifies an exit to the concerning firm, the authority of its permission is an effective means of control in the hands of bureaucracy. While industry-wide associations function as a collective voice organization of the business, the administrative bureaucracy influences the formation of the voice by direct often unofficial contacts with individual firms. This system maintains competition and loyalty at the same time.

As loyalty in employment relations reduces the number of quits and supports the formation of skills, it has made a positive contribution to long-term industrial development in Japan and elsewhere. However, in Japan the control of exit and entry conflicts with the principle of equality and the influences on voice formation undermine collective decisions. The controlling system, which undermines the self-determination of exit and voice, risks a paralysis of the market mechanism as well as the system of political decision making.

CONCLUSION

It has been shown how Smith's twofold division of labour is mediated by a market exchange, while work organization in the factories is subdivided by capital. This Smithian picture was then enhanced by considering the collective organization of labour, and the relationship between economic adjustment and political adjustment using Hirschman's exit–voice framework. The effect of the loyalty group was the focal point. Using Japan as a prime example, it was shown how a politico-economical system could integrate controlling devices over voice formation.

Just as the evolution of the division of labour in a market economy is path dependent, some path dependence also exists in the institutional relations of the politico-economic system as a whole. The productivity of the division of labour depends on complementary relations of worker skill and knowledge, work organization and machinery. This system of complementary components acts as a selection mechanism among variations, and is itself a source of rigidity.

However, through changes in the relations between components, or through the pressure of changing environmental factors, the structure and its functions can change. We cannot exclude the possibility of the creative solution, although it inevitably emerges out of an evolutionary process, by way of a political or collective intellectual decision process. Institutional political economy understands that the evolutionary process of the economy is not solely a spontaneous development on the market, but also a political solution process that is combined with the growth and reorganization of institutions and knowledge. This has effects on both the development of individuals and of society as a whole.

NOTES

1. Nicolas Kaldor (1978, ch. 7) noted that Smith deviated from a dynamic view of the economy after his discussion of money and thus opened the way to equilibrium economics.
2. On this second theorem and its relation to the factory division of labour, see Negishi (1989, p. 98).
3. As the items that influence the attitude of workers are numerous, this graph is not drawn up in accurate, quantitative terms. Seen as a graph of an internal labour market, with wage as a key variable, it reminds us of the concept of 'power theory' in Takata (1995).

REFERENCES

Akerlof, George A. (1982), 'Labour contracts as partial gift exchange', *Quarterly Journal of Economics*, **97**, November, 543–69.
Babbage, Charles (1832), *On the Economy of Machinery and Manufactures*, 1st edn, London: John Murray.
Freeman, Richard B. (1980), 'The exit–voice tradeoff in the labor market: unionism, job tenure, quits, and separations', *Quarterly Journal of Economics*, **94** (4), June, 643–73.
Freeman, Richard B. and James L. Medoff (1984), *What Do Unions Do?*, New York: Basic Books.
Hirschman, Albert O. (1970), *Exit, Voice, and Loyalty: Responses to Decline in Firms, Organizations, and States*, Cambridge, MA: Harvard University Press.
Hirschman, Albert O. (1995), 'Exit, voice and the fate of the German Democratic Republic', in *A Propensity to Self-Subversion*, Cambridge, MA: Harvard University Press.
Hodgson, Geoffrey M. (1993), *Economics and Evolution: Bringing Life Back Into Economics*, Cambridge, UK and Ann Arbor, MI: Polity Press and University of Michigan Press.
Inoki, Takenori (1993), 'Jinteki-Shigen kara mita Sengo-Nihon no Kanryo-Soshiki to Tokushu Hojin' (Bureaucracy and semi-public corporations seen from the viewpoint of human resources), *Nenpo Kindai Nihon Kenkyu* (Yamakawa Shuppansha), No. 15.
Kaldor, Nicholas (1978), *Further Essays on Economic Theory: Collected Economic Essays*, Vol. 5, London: Duckworth.
Kawamura, Yuzo (1994), '"Amakudari" no Kenkyu' (The research on Amakudari), *Sekai* (Iwanami Shoten), July.
Marshall, Alfred ([1949]1961) *The Principles of Economics*, 9th (variorum) edn, with annotations by C.W. Guillebaud, London: Macmillan.
Negishi, Takashi (1989), *History of Economic Theory*, Amsterdam: North-Holland.
Olson, Mancur, Jr (1965), *The Logic of Collective Action*, Cambridge, MA: Harvard University Press.

Smith, Adam (1976), *An Inquiry into the Nature and Causes of the Wealth of Nations*, 2 vols, originally published 1776, edited by R.H. Campbell and A.S. Skinner, London: Methuen.

Takata, Yasuma (1995), *Power Theory of Economics*, translated from the Japanese by Douglas W. Anthony, London and New York: Macmillan and St Martin's.

Tsuru, Tsuyoshi and Motohiro Morishima (1999), 'Nonunion Employee Representation in Japan', *Journal of Labor Research*, **20** (1), Winter, 93–110.

PART II

Theoretical Perspectives on Varieties of
Capitalism

5. The evolution of capitalism from the perspective of institutional and evolutionary economics

Geoffrey M. Hodgson

INTRODUCTION

The terms 'institutional economics' and 'evolutionary economics' are now widely used, each to refer to a variety of theoretical approaches and perspectives.[1] The term 'institutional economics', however, was first applied to the broad approach engineered by American economists such as Thorstein Veblen, John Commons and Wesley Mitchell. Non-Americans such as Karl Polanyi, William Kapp, Gunnar Myrdal and Shigeto Tsuru also came to identify themselves with this institutionalist tradition. Furthermore, this same tradition of institutional economics was the first to adopt the 'evolutionary' label and to argue that ideas from Darwinian evolutionary biology could be usefully transplanted into economic science. Accordingly, it is very appropriate that the term 'institutional and evolutionary economics', or just 'institutional economics', should be applied to this post-Veblenian legacy.

Institutional economics was actually the dominant intellectual approach in America in the first few decades of the twentieth century. However, institutionalism never completed a systematic approach to economic theory of the stature or compass of that of Adam Smith, Karl Marx, Léon Walras or Alfred Marshall. Furthermore, institutionalism itself contained a diversity of approaches and there was a failure to obtain widespread agreement on its definition, boundaries and common core.

Another reason why American institutionalism failed to develop a systematic theory was because it was partially disabled by a combined result of the profound shifts in social science in the 1910–40 period and of the rise of a mathematical style of neoclassical economics in America in the 1930s. Without going into the history of institutionalism here, it is possible to focus on some key ideas in the early institutionalism of Veblen and Commons, and show their relevance to our understanding of capitalism.

For at least four reasons it is useful to compare institutional economics with Marxism. First, especially Veblen and several other institutional economists were profoundly influenced by Marx. Second, Marx has made an enormous contribution to our understanding of the nature of the capitalist system. Third, although institutional economics is distanced from Marxism in several respects, it shares with Marxism a theoretical focus on structurally specific features of socioeconomic formations, rather than building economics on the alleged universal concepts of 'choice', 'scarcity' and 'utility'. Fourth, both institutional economics and Marxism see technology as a major driving force of economic and institutional change. The comparison of institutional economics with Marxism will thus be a major theme of this chapter.

Later sections of this work go beyond elaboration and comparison of the received approach of institutional economics. I shall briefly introduce some of my own ideas concerning the 'impurity principle' and examine their relevance in a general schema for understanding both the variety and evolution of the capitalist system. We shall start, however, with the seminal critique of Marx developed by Veblen.

VEBLEN'S CRITIQUE OF MARX

A central problem in Marx's writings is that human motivations are not explained in any detail: they are assumed to spring in broad and mysterious terms from the relations and forces of the system. When discussing the mechanisms of change at the individual level, Marx was extremely vague. There was frequent reference to 'productive forces', as if technology itself is a driving force, unmediated by individuals. He saw individuals as 'simply embodiments and personifications' (Marx, 1981, pp. 1019–20) of social relations. Thus it was assumed that workers will typically struggle for bigger wages and shorter hours, and capitalists for enhanced profits. But these are little else than expressions of the principles of maximization also common to neoclassical theory. What is missing is an explanation of the historical origin of such calculative behaviour and the mode of its cultural transmission from individual to individual. Marx assumed that values and motives are simply functional to the pursuit of class and economic interests.

Thus Marx believed that the class position of the workers as employees, coupled with the tendency of capitalism to bring workers together in larger and larger firms and cities, would lead to the combination and eventual revolt of the working class against the system. However, this has not happened. Marx's faith that class positions and relations themselves are sufficient to impel action has to be questioned.

Veblen highlighted the analytical gap in Marx's analysis. He noted that it failed to connect the actor with the specific structure and to explain thereby human motivation and action. Veblen's analytical solution to this problem, inspired by Charles Sanders Peirce and the pragmatist philosophers, was based on the key concept of habit.

Veblen saw that Marx's rationalistic concept of action was connected with his meta-historical or naturalistic concept of social labour and the implicit idea that labour can be evaluated according to a global rationality. Veblen identified and rejected the elements of naturalistic thinking in Marx's writings. For instance, the labour theory of value is connected to the proclaimed natural right to full product of labour. Marx presented a modified hedonistic psychology, where rational class interest is substituted for individual self-interest. The explanation of individual action is subsumed within a notion of classes struggling for their own goals and needs.

Veblen rejected Marx's view that if working people reflected rationally upon their situation they would be impelled to criticize and revolt against the capitalist system. In making this assumption, Marx was reflecting a prominent tendency in nineteenth-century thought. As C. Wright Mills (1953, p. 326) has observed: 'both Marxism and Liberalism make the same rationalist assumption that men, given the opportunity, will naturally come to political consciousness of interests, of self, or of class'.

Of course, Marx argued that 'false consciousness' often obscured the truth. Yet his view was that this ephemeral and temporary 'false consciousness' could be readily dissolved in the acid of reason and scientific analysis. What Marx ignored was that *any* form of consciousness, be it 'true' or 'false', is made up of deeply-rooted habits and based on culturally given concepts and values. Reason and science themselves are never entirely culture free; or, at least, if they are stripped of culture they are stripped of meaning.[2]

Veblen rejected Marx's underlying assumption of potential rational transparency and saw how it was connected to a strain of fatalistic and teleological thinking. Stephen Edgell and Jules Townshend (1993, p. 728) have explained this connection clearly:

> Marx's portrayal of humankind as potentially rational also resolves the puzzle as to why Marx could simultaneously entertain the idea of an historical telos, with its deterministic implications, and uphold the voluntaristic and reflexive notions of praxis or practical activity. He assumes that workers – through rational thought, through reflecting on their experience of capitalism, and notably through their increasing immiseration and growing collective strength – will inevitably want and be able to overthrow it.

In Marxism, the process of rational reflection is seen to drive the working class to the same unavoidable outcome. Even if we stress a more open-ended and less deterministic account of capitalist development than the one found in the famous 'Preface' to the *Contribution to the Critique of Political Economy*, 'we are still left with a highly teleological theory of capitalism, with its downfall being the inevitable result of its inner contradictions' (Edgell and Townshend, 1993, p. 729).

Veblen's critique of these rationalistic premises owed a great deal to the pragmatist philosophers. By attacking the rationalistic conception of action, the pragmatist philosophers undermined the foundations of Marx's view. As Commons (1934, p. 150) put it, Peirce dissolved the antinomies of rationalism and empiricism at a stroke, making 'Habit and Custom, instead of intellect and sensations, the foundation of all science'. Habits of thought provide and reproduce the conceptual frameworks through which we understand and attribute meaning to the world. Through the concept of habit, as the pragmatist philosophers realized, thought is linked with action and the Cartesian division of the world between the mental and the physical is dissolved. Peirce had a crucial influence on Veblen and on Commons.

Veblen rejected the continuously calculating, marginally adjusting agent of neoclassical theory and emphasized inertia and habit instead. Institutions were defined by Veblen (1919, p. 239) in 1909 as 'settled habits of thought common to the generality of men'. They are seen as both outgrowths and reinforcers of the routinized thought processes that are shared by a number of persons in a given society. Institutions thereby help sustain habits of action and thought.

Importantly, Veblen also emphasized the importance of novelty and human creativity and distanced himself from cultural or institutional determinism. Furthermore, it was recognized by Veblen and Commons that institutions are not simply constraints. For example, when Commons (1934, p. 73), wrote of the dual presence of 'liberation' and 'control' he clearly sees institutions as a liberating as well as a constraining force.

The importance of institutions in shaping thought and action was implied in Veblen's attack on Marx's 'materialist conception of history'. According to Veblen (1919, p. 314) this 'materialist conception'

> has very little to say regarding the efficient force, the channels, or the methods by which the economic situation is conceived to have its effect upon institutions. What answer the early Marxists gave to this question, of how the economic situation shapes institutions, was to the effect that causal connection lies through the selfish, calculating class interest. But, while class interest may count for much in the outcome, this answer is plainly not a competent one, since, for one thing, institutions by no means change with the alacrity which the sole efficiency of reasoned class interest would require.

Veblen argued that the mere class position of an individual as a wage labourer or a capitalist tells us little about the specific conceptions or habits of thought of the individuals involved. Even if the worker's interests would be served by joining a trade union, or voting for a socialist political party, there is no necessary reason why the worker's position as an employee would necessarily impel him or her to necessarily take such actions. Individual interests, whatever they are, do not necessarily lead to accordant individual actions. In other words, the assumption of a class interest and rational calculation tells us nothing about the habits, concepts and frameworks of thought which are used to appraise reality, or about the mode of calculation used to perceive a supposed optimum.

Contrary to Marx, human agents will not gravitate to a single view of the truth simply on the basis of empirical evidence and rational reflection. As Veblen (1919, p. 442) pointed out, and as sophisticated Marxists such as Antonio Gramsci later emphasized, the members of the working class could perceive their own salvation just as much in terms of patriotism or nationalism as in socialist revolution. The class position of an agent – exploiter or exploited – does not imply that that person will be impelled towards any particular view of reality or any particular pattern of action.[3]

An important case study confirms the point. In his classic study of production workers in the United States, Michael Burawoy (1979) showed that hierarchy and authority on the shop floor are themselves unlikely to lead to the production of socialist ideology or revolt. Burawoy further demonstrated that despite the overriding *de jure* power of the management there was a sphere of autonomy on the shop floor in which a specific subculture survived. It consisted of 'game playing' to maximize production bonuses and the modification of work processes and rules to overcome management inefficiencies.

Such a workplace culture would help to fill the analytical vacuum in Marx's theory. This culture may express the autonomy and even the resistance to authority of the workers. However, detailed examination of its typical features showed that there is no necessary, or even likely, transmission belt from the condition of wage labour to the event of socialist revolution. Contrary to Marx, a given social structure or class system does not imply a tendency towards particular patterns of behaviour.

Such arguments have a wider relevance than Marxism and apply to other calculative or rationalistic conceptions of action. Accordingly, a critique is implied of the optimizing rationality of neoclassical economics. In models of the use of information by rational agents, it is generally assumed that all will interpret the same signals in the same way. In the extreme case of the 'rational expectations hypothesis', it is held that through mere data-gathering, agents will become aware of the basic, underlying structure and mechanisms of the economy. This hypothesis likewise neglects the conceptual framing involved in the perception of data and the theory-bound character of all observation.

In general, neither class interest nor rational reflection upon circumstances will typically lead to a single outcome in terms of either perceptions or actions. For instance, although the capitalists' interests may be best served by striving for ever-greater profits, this tells us little about precise corporate strategy, the mode of management or the precise structure of the firm. In the case of the capitalist the Marxian response to this argument is familiar: capitalist competition will *force* capitalists to follow the more successful route to profit and the accumulation of capital. Lucky or shrewd capitalists will follow this imperative and the others will become marginalized or bankrupt. Thereby the strategy, structure and goals of the firm are uniquely determined by competition. Uncannily, a very similar argument is advanced by the far-from-Marxist, Milton Friedman (1953) in a famous paper, where he argued that competitive 'natural selection' is bound to ensure that most if not all surviving firms are profit maximizing. (See Hodgson, 1994.)

In response, Jim Tomlinson (1982) pointed out that profit cannot act as a simple regulator of the growth or decline of firms. Even if firms are trying to maximize their profits this does not imply a single strategy as to how this maximization is to be achieved. 'Firms like generals have *strategies*, a term which itself implies room for manoeuvre, room for diverse calculations, diverse practices to be brought to bear on the objective' (p. 34, original italic). More concretely, case studies reveal a varied repertoire of strategic responses by firms. Note the study by Richard Whittington (1989) of the varied strategic behaviour of firms enduring a common recession, and the remarks about firm discretionary behaviour made by Richard Nelson (1991). Richard Cyert and James March (1963) and others have argued that firms are generally profit seeking, not strictly profit maximizing. Within limits, and being no longer driven towards a single maximum, a variety of profit-seeking behaviours are possible. This gives scope for varied behaviour by capitalist firms. Conceptions of the sources of greater profit, as well as modes of calculation and appraisal, are always coloured by the cultural context in which firms act. Crucially, institutions and culture vary from firm to firm and from country to country. The objectives of firms are culturally and institutionally specific.

To understand the actual and potential diversity of firm behaviour it is necessary to escape from the straitjacket of equilibrium theorizing. In a dynamic perspective the exclusive focus is no longer on equilibrium outcomes. Out of equilibrium, greater diversity of structure and performance is possible. There can be enormous and sustained variations in productivity between different firms in the same industry. This contrasts with the textbook picture of firms being driven towards the same long-run equilibrium where costs (and revenues) are typically the same across firms. A dynamic and open-ended approach challenges the relevance of a long-run equilibrium and admits an ongoing diversity of outcomes (Eliasson, 1991; Metcalfe, 1988; Penrose, 1959; Steindl, 1952).

Veblen's answer to the Marxian argument that for the firm only one strategic response is possible, and also his rebuff to the neoclassical concept of equilibrium, was his theory of cumulative causation. He saw both the circumstances and temperament of individuals as part of the cumulative processes of change. For Veblen – inspired by Darwin as he was – the idea that all kinds of economic system should converge to one ('natural') type, was as absurd as a presumption that all kinds species should eventually evolve into one.

Directly or indirectly influenced by Veblen, the notion of cumulative causation was developed by Allyn Young (1928), Gunnar Myrdal (1957), K. William Kapp (1976), Nicholas Kaldor (1985) and others. It relates to the modern idea that technologies and economic systems can get 'locked in' – and sometimes as a result of initial accidents – to relatively constrained paths of development (Arthur, 1989, 1990). Hence there is 'path dependency' rather than convergence to a given equilibrium. History matters.

Veblen's concept of cumulative causation is an antidote to both neoclassical and Marxian economic theory. Contrary to the equilibrium analysis of neoclassical economics, Veblen saw the economic system not as a 'self-balancing mechanism' but as a 'cumulatively unfolding process'. As Myrdal and Kaldor argued at length, the processes of cumulative causation suggest that regional and national development is generally divergent rather than convergent. Young and Kaldor suggested that economies of scale imply divergent patterns of corporate growth leading to the domination of a small number of large firms. This contradicted the typical emphasis within neoclassical economic theory on processes of compensating feedback and mutual adjustment, via the price mechanism, leading to greater uniformity and convergence.

Contrary to much Marxist and neoclassical thinking, Veblen argued that multiple futures are possible. Equilibrating forces do not always pull the economy back on to a single track. This exposes a severe weakness in Marx's conception of history. Although Veblen had socialist leanings, he argued against the idea of finality or consummation in economic development. Variety and cumulative causation mean that history has 'no final term' (Veblen, 1919, p. 37). In Marxism the final term is communism or the classless society, but Veblen rejected the teleological concept of a final goal. This means a rejection of the ideas of the 'inevitability' of socialism and of a 'natural' outcome or end-point in capitalist evolution. There is no natural path, or law, governing economic development. Accordingly, and in rejecting any predetermination in capitalist evolution, Veblen accepted the possibility of varieties of capitalism and different paths of capitalist development.

In his *Imperial Germany* (1915) Veblen gave some acute and prescient comments on the nature of the German and Japanese economies. For instance, writing as early as 1915, Veblen (1934, p. 251) wrote: 'It is in this unique combination of a high-wrought spirit of feudalistic fealty and chivalric honor with the material efficiency given by the modern technology that the strength of the Japanese nation lies'. Veblen wrote this well before the rise of modern Japan, but nevertheless saw the root of its future strength. This strength does not lie in technology alone but in its *combination* with conservative and ceremonial institutions 'of feudalistic fealty and chivalric honor'.[4]

Later institutionalists, notably Commons, recognized actual and potential variety within capitalism. Commons argued that the United States was impelled by its own distinct history to evolve organizations and structures quite different from those in Europe. For instance, as Dorothy Ross (1991, p. 203) points out, in his extensive study of US workers 'Commons's central argument was that American labor organization was unique, the product of competitive market conditions and America's unique historical circumstances'.

THE PROBLEM OF NECESSARY IMPURITIES

When analysing the capitalist system Marx assumed away all the non-capitalist elements in that system. This is not merely an initial, simplifying assumption. They are assumed away at the outset, never to be reincorporated at a later stage of the analysis. This is because he believes that commodity exchange and the hiring of labour power in a capitalist firm will become increasingly widespread, displacing all other forms of economic coordination and productive organization. Thus, in the *Communist Manifesto*, Marx and Engels proclaim:

> The bourgeoisie, wherever it has got the upper hand, has put an end to all feudal, patriarchal, idyllic relations ... and has left remaining no other nexus between man and man than naked self-interest, than callous 'cash payment'. ... It has resolved personal worth into exchange value, and ... has set up that single, unconscionable freedom – free trade. ... The bourgeoisie has torn away from the family its sentimental veil, and has reduced the family relation to a mere money relation. (Marx, 1973a, p. 70)

If the family is genuinely 'a mere money relation' then we may analyse money and ignore families in our theory. The statement was clearly an exaggeration for rhetorical purposes, but it attired a more serious analytical belief in the universal, corrosive power of markets and money. Confidence in the all-consuming power of capitalist markets was Marx's justification for ignoring impurities within the capitalist system. Such impurities were regarded as doomed and extraneous hangovers of the feudal past, eventually to be pulverized by the ever-expanding market. Just as capitalism and commodity exchange were assumed to become all-powerful, the Marxian theoretical system was built on these structures and relations alone.

Yet we may question whether a 'pure' capitalism system is theoretically possible. Some crucial subsystems within capitalism can never be organized on a strictly capitalist basis. Consider the family. Contrary to Marx, there are theoretical limitations to the operation of capitalist institutions within that sphere. If the rearing of children were carried out on a capitalist basis then they would be strictly owned as property by the owners of the household 'firm' and eventually sold like slaves on a market. Yet anti-slavery laws within modern capitalism prevent the possession and sale of one citizen by another.[5] Hence within capitalism the household can never be internally organized as a capitalist firm, that is on the basis of markets, individual ownership and profit. Ironically, in both neoclassical and Marxian economics the characteristic features of the family disappear from view. Just as the neoclassical economists treat all human activities as if they took the form of contracted exchange, Marx wrongly assumed that the entire capitalist system can be understood solely on the basis of commodity exchange and the exploitation of hired labour power.[6]

Note that is not an argument about the *empirical* existence of impurities. Marxists freely admit that they exist. The argument here is that it is not possible for capitalism to rid itself of substantial impurities. Accordingly, the *theoretical* notion of a pure capitalist system is flawed. A capitalism that was pure and self-contained would not be able to function.

As many writers have argued, there are general limits to the extension of market and contractual relations within capitalism. Joseph Schumpeter (1976, p. 139), for example, argued persuasively that such older institutions provide an essential symbiosis with capitalism, and are thus 'an essential element of the capitalist schema'. Schumpeter's insight was to show that capitalism depends on norms of loyalty and trust which are in part descended from a former epoch. The spread of market and contractarian relations can threaten to break up cultural and other enduring bonds from the past that are necessary for the functioning of the system as a whole. In particular, as Schumpeter and others emphasize, the state is partly responsible for the bonding of society and the prevention of its dissolution into atomistic units by the corroding action of market relations. Accordingly, Polanyi (1944) showed that even in '*laissez-faire*' Victorian Britain the state was necessarily intimately involved in the formation and subsequent regulation of markets. All markets are themselves socially and culturally embedded, and there are many possible different forms of markets and exchange.

I have used the insights of Polanyi, Schumpeter and others to develop what I call the 'impurity principle'. The 'impurity principle' is proposed as a general idea applicable to all economic systems. The idea is that every socioeconomic system must rely on at least one structurally dissimilar subsystem to function. There must always be a coexistent plurality of modes of production, so that the social formation as a whole has the requisite structural variety to cope with change. Thus if one type of structure is to prevail (for example, central planning), other structures (for example, markets, private corporations) are necessary to enable the system as a whole to work effectively. In particular, neither planning nor markets can become all-embracing systems of socioeconomic regulation. In general, it is not feasible for one mode of production to become so comprehensive that it drives out all the others. Every system relies on its 'impurities'.

Although it cannot be formally proved, part of the justification for this principle can be derived from an analysis of past socioeconomic formations in history. Capitalism today depends on the 'impurities' of the family, household production and the state. The slave mode of production of classical times depended on the military organization of the state as well as trade and an external market. Likewise, feudalism relied on both regulated markets and a powerful church. Finally, without extensive, legal or illegal markets the Soviet-type system of central planning would have ceased to function long before 1989. In each of the four major modes of production after Christ (slavery, feudalism, capitalism and Soviet-type societies) at least one 'impurity', that is, a non-dominant economic structure, has played a functional role in the reproduction of the system as a whole.

What is involved here is more than an empirical observation that different structures and systems have coexisted through history. What is involved is an assertion that some of these economic structures were *necessary* for the socioeconomic system to function over time. Additional and related arguments for the impurity principle can be derived from systems theory (Hodgson, 1984, pp. 106–9; 1988, pp. 257, 303–4).

It should be emphasized that all perceptive Marxian economists have recognized the coexistence of different structures and forms within capitalism and the actuality of different forms of the capitalist mode of production. These are sensible *empirical* statements about the present and past. However, the theoretical recognition of the *necessity* of such a coexistence of structures is absent in the writings of Marx and his followers, a partial exception being the writings of Rosa Luxemburg. The impurity principle is incompatible with orthodox Marxism.

In methodological terms, Marx's analytical procedure involves ignoring the necessary impurities as if they do not exist. Nowhere does Marx indicate any plan to incorporate impurities such as the family into his analysis of the capitalist system (although he did intend to write something on the state). His volume on 'capitalist production' is silent about the role of the household. There is no indication that he intended to rectify this omission.

In much of twentieth-century Marxism, as in *Capital* itself, the over-whelming analytical concentration on commodities and capital, ignoring the role of necessary impurities, has led to many errors and blind alleys. Consider, for example, the work of Kozo Uno (1980). At the most abstract level, Uno and his followers defended the concept of 'pure' capitalism by the argument that 'actual capitalism in its liberal stage of development demonstrated a tendency toward self-perfection, divesting itself more and more of pre-capitalist economic relations' (Sekine, 1975, p. 857). 'Pure capitalism' was not merely a theoretical idea. It was allegedly exemplified by Britain in the nineteenth century. Clearly, the suggestion of such a purified system involves a denial of the role of necessary impurities. Uno saw the subsequent emergence, in the twentieth century, of less pure, 'finance' and 'imperialist' stages of capitalism. For him, precisely because of the corruption of a purer form of capitalism, the system had entered a period of decay and collapse. This argument is thus the negation of the impurity principle: instead of being necessary for the functioning of the system, impurities allegedly undermine the system and threaten its existence.

For these and other reasons, the problem of understanding the nature of modern Japanese capitalism has confounded Marxian economists for decades (Morris-Suzuki, 1989, pp. 103–30). Is modern Japan a highly developed form of capitalism? Or, on the contrary, is it a largely antiquated system in the process of shedding its feudal remnants and moving towards the 'purer' form of modern capitalism found in (say) the United States? Marxists have been unable to resolve these questions among themselves because they have been encumbered by the baggage of the concept (itself implicit in *Capital*) of 'pure capitalism'. Their vision has also been restricted by the notion that capitalism in all countries must necessarily go through the same sequence of stages. In contrast, with the impurity principle, there is no difficulty accepting the idea that coexisting capitalist systems can develop in different ways, especially in different local circumstances, and it is not even necessary to claim that one impure system is 'more advanced' or 'higher' than another. After all, what is dynamic or efficient in one context may be less dynamic or efficient in another.

Another lead provided by the impurity principle is the possibility that developments within a particular economic systems may depend to a significant extent on exogenous as well as endogenous changes. Because all economic systems depend on impurities, there is the possibility that a system can rely in part on a geographically separate system, as well as dissimilar subsystems within the same social formation. For example, eighteenth-century British capitalism depended on the colonies and the slave trade. Modern Japan depends on its intimate political and trading relationship with the United States, both as a guarantor of political stability and as a huge market for

Japanese exports. In contrast, Marxists have traditionally underestimated the importance of exogenous influences, relations and changes, seeing the crucial dynamics of development as coming almost entirely from within.[7]

While the impurity principle contends that different kinds of subsystem are necessary for the system as a whole to function, it does not specify the particular kind of subsystem or the precise boundaries between each subsystem and the system as a whole. Indeed, a variety of types of system and subsystem can feasibly be combined. For example, in many capitalist societies child-rearing is done within the non-capitalist institution of the nuclear family. But, in principle, alternative non-capitalist arrangements are possible for this purpose, such as collective households along the lines of the Israeli *kibbutzim*, or the rearing of children for sale on the market as child slaves. Such arrangements have existed in capitalist societies but they are not themselves capitalist. Up to the American Civil War, an extended system of slavery existed alongside capitalist institutions. Furthermore, in general – as illustrated by the particular case of subsystems of slavery within capitalism – the boundaries between subsystem and dominant system can be highly variable.

These points demarcate the impurity principle from functionalism. Functionalism is typically defined as the notion that the contribution of an entity to the maintenance of a system is sufficient to explain the existence of that entity. In other words, the existence of an entity is fully explained by its function. However, the impurity principle does not purport to explain why any one given mode of production or subsystem exists. To say that the household sustains capitalism does not give an explanation for the existence of the household. As noted above, the capitalist mode of production could be sustained by a system other than the conventional household – child-rearing cooperatives for example. All the impurity principle asserts is that at least one such dissimilar subsystem is necessary for each system to survive. Because it does not purport to explain the existence of any one specific system or subsystem, it is not a case of functionalism.

The fact that the need for a dissimilar subsystem can be fulfilled by one or more of a variety of possible subsystems is of particular significance for the argument here. The particular subsystem, the nature of the combination, and the precise boundaries of the demarcation profoundly affect the nature of the specific variety of capitalist system. *A corollary of the impurity principle is the contention that an immense variety of forms of any given socioeconomic system can exist.* In particular, an infinite variety of forms of capitalism is possible.

Having introduced the impurity principle, it is necessary to briefly respond to Yoshinori Shiozawa's use of it (see Chapter 3 in this volume) to support his idea of 'continuous history'. When I first introduced the impurity principle it was conjoined to another idea: the principle of dominance

(Hodgson, 1984). I have retained this combination of the two principles in later writing (Hodgson, 1988, 2001). The 'principle of dominance' is the notion that although socioeconomic systems are always made up of a plurality of structurally dissimilar subsystems, it is likely that one type of institutional structure, relating to the production and distribution of the requisites of social life, will dominate the rest. This type of institutional structure will dominate, in the sense that the greatest amount of production will take place within institutions of this type. Being the type of institutional domain where the largest portion of production takes place, the values, preoccupations, habits and property distributions connected with this domain will, to some degree, influence and pervade the whole society. In this sense of providing the greatest productive share, capitalist firms dominate modern society. Unlike the impurity principle, the principle of dominance is compatible with Marxism and is expressed by Marx (1973b, pp. 106–7) in his *Grundrisse*.

If the principle of dominance is combined with the impurity principle then Shiozawa's notion of 'continuous history' can be criticized. The principle of dominance makes the segmentation of historical periods possible, according to the dominant structure in each case. Furthermore, if for some reason the transition from one dominant structure to another is disruptive or discontinuous, then the idea of 'continuous history' is placed in question.

VARIETIES OF ACTUALLY EXISTING CAPITALISM

Let us return to the implications of the corollary of the impurity principle, discussed above. Given the potential variety of systemic combinations, and the reality of path dependency and cumulative causation, an immense variety of institutions and forms are feasible. The argument in this work is thus buttressed by the rich evidence of diversity even within modern capitalism. Such evidence encompasses specific institutions such as corporations as well as nations. Nelson (1991) has argued that, even within the same industry, firms typically differ in several respects, including their propensities to commit resources to innovation and imitation, and their success in developing and adopting new products and organizational forms. There is also substantial evidence that profit differentials between firms are quite persistent over time (Mueller, 1986). Differences in productivity are also pronounced in international comparisons (Pavitt and Patel, 1988) and are particularly prevalent in manufacturing sectors (Bernard and Jones, 1996). Similar divergences and path dependency can result from varied corporate or other organizational structures, especially given the persistence and durability of organizational cultures and routines (Binger and Hoffman, 1989; North, 1990).

Charles Sabel and Jonathan Zeitlin (1985) have argued on the basis of historical evidence that in Europe there was an alternative path to industrialization based on small-scale firms and flexible specialization. Also looking at the evolution of the factory system, Maxine Berg (1991) compared explanations based on the supposed dictates of technology with the idea of such an alternative road. She concludes that industrialization could have taken many possible pathways and occurred in different sequences. Broadly in line with this perspective, the literature on the Emilia-Romagna 'industrial districts' of modern Italy addresses an alternative and very different mode of capitalist organization, based on a number of closely networked and highly flexible small firms. These are a significant departure from the presumed capitalist norm of large-scale, mass production (Best, 1990; Brusco, 1982; Piore and Sabel, 1984).

The expanding literature on 'national systems of innovation' (Freeman, 1987, 1995; Lundvall, 1992; Nelson, 1993) is based on the premise that 'basic differences in historical experience, language, and culture will be reflected in national idiosyncrasies' (Lundvall, 1992, p. 13) in the internal organization of firms, the types of interfirm relationship, the role of the public sector, the structure of financial institutions, and the nature, organization and volume of research and development.

One of the most obvious and highly relevant comparisons is between the Anglo-American capitalisms and the capitalist system in Japan. The key to the difference lies in history. Capitalism in Britain emerged after a very long period of gestation. Three hundred years separate the disintegration of classical feudalism in the fifteenth century from the beginning of the industrial revolution in the late eighteenth. Private property relations and an individualistic culture took well over three hundred years to develop. In contrast, the inception of capitalism in Japan was sudden and dramatic. The Meiji Restoration of 1868 marked an abrupt transition from an Asian feudalism to a Western-inspired capitalist society. Hence Japan today still bears the clear hallmarks of its relatively recent feudal past. The Japanese corporation has replaced the feudal estate but codes of loyalty and chivalry are still paramount. Long-standing, Confucian ethical doctrines are now expressed in terms of loyalty both to the capitalist firm and to the nation as a whole.

Western observers sometimes wrongly assume that because the East Asian economies exhibit increasing productivity and growth, then they must be free market economies. It is presumed that only a free market economy could be so successful. In fact, the state has played a quite central role in these economies, and in varied ways, and markets there are generally not as 'free' as is often believed. Typically, state intervention and industrial policy are paramount (Amsden, 1989; Gerlach, 1992).

The recent literature on the emerging economies of post-communist Eastern Europe also confirms that path-dependent and historically contingent processes are leading, not to convergence to a presumed unique 'Western' model, but to historically located and specific varieties of capitalism in each country (Chavance, 1995).

Applied economic analysis gives us a rich picture of diversity. Much economic theory, by contrast, is insensitive to these variations. At the level of its theoretical foundations, economic analysis cannot afford to remain blind to the immense and persistent variety of forms within modern capitalism.

THE SPECTRE OF CONVERGENCE

However, the modern economic system is globally integrated to a degree that has no historical parallel. Transport and communications have evolved and cheapened to the extent that massive international transfers of people, goods, money and information are possible on an hour-to-hour basis. This is leading to some considerable homogenization of languages, ideas, technology, cultures and organizational forms. Does this mean that the arguments concerning the existing and persistent variety within capitalism will be invalidated?

The short answer is no. It has to be accepted that processes of integration and homogenization are likely to persist, and even accelerate. However, this does not mean that convergence will be absolute, or eradicate all important differences between capitalisms. There are several reasons for this judgement. First, and contrary to some pronouncements, the processes of globalization will not eradicate the nation state and supranational unions of states. As Paul Hirst and Grahame Thompson (1996) have argued at length, these arguments do not rest on a solid foundation and there remains substantial scope for national and supranational, political and economic policies.

Second, any socioeconomic system is a *structured combination of partially complementary dissimilars*. Even substantial global forces of organizational convergence are likely to act upon individual elements of the system in different ways, and are unlikely to bring about the required structured combination of complementary institutions. For example, the Japanese system is a 'dual economy', combining large corporations with high productivity rates and enduring labour contracts, with smaller, less-productive, enterprises which are much more flexible in their hiring and firing of labour. Each sector is dependent on the other. When advanced Japanese forms of organization and management spread to other countries they do not always have the adjoining network of smaller and more flexible firms. Furthermore, reigning macroeconomic policies and performance may lead to a climate of slower growth and economic instability in which the Japanese-type corporation does not prosper to the same degree. For instance, it may be less able to shed labour in a recession. As a result, an organizational form which is highly efficient in one national context does not always readily spread with similarly impressive results to another national economic system.

Third, even when convergence occurs, change is often slow and elements of the old system can persist indefinitely. Sometimes this is simply because of a time lag – the time taken to replace one set of reigning habits of thought with another. In other cases it is because elements of the old system are so deeply rooted that it is impossible to change them without endangering the system itself. The paths of convergence may have a narrowing gap, but may never meet. There are instructive examples of this in the natural world. The Eurasian wolf and the Tasmanian wolf are superficially similar in appearance and habit. But the former is a mammal and the latter a marsupial. Thus differences will persist, and will continue to have significant effects. Similar remarks apply to socioeconomic systems.

CONCLUSIONS

Institutional and evolutionary economics addresses the analysis of the evolution of capitalism in terms which in part build upon, but in other ways differ from, the economics of Marx. Shared with Marxism is the acceptance of the need to focus on specific economic systems rather than ahistorical generalities. However, institutional economics differs from Marxism in the following respects:

1. Contrary to the Marxian view of history unfolding itself towards communism, economic development is path dependent and there is no single outcome towards which history is progressing.
2. A huge variety of cultures, institutions, profit levels, levels of productivity and so on, have persisted, and will continue to persist, within capitalism. Despite strong integrative and globalizing pressures, capitalist competition does not automatically produce uniformity. Even if a degree of homogenization emerges, variety cannot be eradicated.
3. This leads to the notion that the capitalist system – like other economic systems – depends upon this internal variety and could not survive without it. This variety, according to the 'impurity principle' includes elements that are dissimilar to the dominant system.
4. A corollary of the impurity principle is to reinforce and extend proposition 2 above. Because a wide variety of combinations of dissimilars are possible, then a wide variety of different capitalist socioeconomic formations are possible, and can in principle coexist.

In this manner, by retaining what is still of value in Marxian economics and rejecting that which is unacceptable, institutional and evolutionary economics can offer a rich approach towards the analysis and understanding of socioeconomic systems.

NOTES

1. In part, this chapter draws on material from Hodgson (1999).
2. It should be emphasized that this paragraph does not necessarily imply a philosophical relativism, where the possibility of objective truth is denied. A single, objective reality can still be assumed and also the possibility of a true account of its essential elements. Although science is never culture free, some versions of science are more adequate in the search for truth than others.
3. This point was sensed by Lenin and an attempt to remedy it – in Marxian terms – was provided by his theory of the energizing and inspirational role of the revolutionary party. However, Lenin's solution was almost entirely in terms of revolutionary agitation and propaganda. By these means the proletariat would be aroused from their conservatism and brought under the banner of socialism. Unlike Veblen, however, Lenin underestimated the longevity of traditional habits of thought and the elusive but powerful role of social culture.
4. Note that Veblen's comment on Japan contradicts the view, argued by Ayres (1944) and others, that Veblen set up a universal dichotomy between 'technology' and 'institutions'. Search through Veblen's writings, however, and such a dichotomy will not be found. See Hodgson (1998).
5. Of course, slavery has existed alongside capitalism, such as in the south of the United States before the Civil War. This involved a combination of slave and capitalist modes of production and the denial of citizenship and other legal rights to blacks. Slavery was incompatible with a universal 'free' labour market and the further development of the capitalist system required the emancipation of the slaves.
6. With the rise of modern feminism in the 1970s, some Marxian theorists attempted to analyse the family as a distinctive entity. Yet the dominant theoretical approach was to subsume this institution within the parameters of the 'labour theory of value' and the guiding prerogatives of the capitalist order, just as neoclassical economists treat the family simply as another contract-based institution within capitalism.
7. The same criticism can be made of the work of Schumpeter. He defined development as involving 'only such changes in economic life as are not forced upon it from without but arise by its own initiative, from within' (Schumpeter, 1934, p. 63). Schumpeter never made a secret of the fact that his theory of capitalist development, with its emphasis on the role of endogenous change, was highly influenced by Marx. Nevertheless, the importance of endogenous factors such as entrepreneurial activity and technological innovation, as stressed by Schumpeter, should not be denied.

REFERENCES

Amsden, Alice H. (1989), *Asia's Next Giant: South Korea and Late Industrialization*, Oxford and New York: Oxford University Press.

Arthur, W. Brian (1989), 'Competing technologies, increasing returns, and lock-in by historical events', *Economic Journal*, **99** (1), March, 116–31.

Arthur, W. Brian (1990), 'Positive feedbacks in the economy', *Scientific American*, **262** (2), February, 80–85.

Ayres, Clarence E. (1944), *The Theory of Economic Progress*, 1st edn, Chapel Hill, NC: University of North Carolina Press.

Berg, Maxine (1991), 'On the origins of capitalist hierarchy', in Bo Gustafsson (ed.), *Power and Economic Institutions: Reinterpretations in Economic History*, Aldershot: Edward Elgar, pp. 173–94.

Bernard, Andrew B. and Charles I. Jones (1996), 'Comparing apples to oranges: productivity convergence and measurement across industries and countries', *American Economic Review*, **86** (5), December, 1216–38.

Best, Michael H. (1990), *The New Competition: Institutions of Industrial Restructuring*, Cambridge: Polity Press.

Binger, Brian R. and Elizabeth Hoffman (1989), 'Institutional persistence and change: the question of efficiency', *Journal of Institutional and Theoretical Economics*, **145** (1), March, 67–84.

Brusco, Sebastiano (1982), 'The Emilian model', *Cambridge Journal of Economics*, **6** (2), June, 167–84.

Burawoy, Michael (1979), *Manufacturing Consent*, Chicago: University of Chicago Press.

Chavance, Bernard (1995), 'Hierarchical forms and coordination problems in socialist systems', *Industrial and Corporate Change*, **4** (1), 271–91.

Commons, John R. (1934), *Institutional Economics – Its Place in Political Economy*, New York: Macmillan.

Cyert, Richard M. and James G. March (1963), *A Behavioral Theory of the Firm*, Engelwood Cliffs, NJ: Prentice-Hall.

Edgell, Stephen and Jules Townshend (1993), 'Marx and Veblen on human nature, history, and capitalism: vive la différence!', *Journal of Economic Issues*, **27** (3), September, 721–39.

Eliasson, Gunnar (1991), 'Deregulation, innovative entry and structural diversity as a source of stable and rapid economic growth', *Journal of Evolutionary Economics*, **1** (1), January, 49–63.

Freeman, Christopher (1987), *Technology Policy and Economic Performance: Lessons from Japan*, London: Pinter.

Freeman, Christopher (1995), 'The "national system of innovation" in historical perspective', *Cambridge Journal of Economics*, **19** (1), February, 5–24.

Friedman, Milton (1953), 'The methodology of positive economics', in *Essays in Positive Economics*, Chicago: University of Chicago Press, 3–43.

Gerlach, Michael L. (1992), *Alliance Capitalism: The Social Organization of Japanese Business*, Berkeley: University of California Press.

Hirst, Paul Q. and Grahame Thompson (1996), *Globalization in Question: The International Economy and the Possibilities of Governance*, Cambridge: Polity Press.

Hodgson, Geoffrey M. (1984), *The Democratic Economy: A New Look at Planning, Markets and Power*, Harmondsworth: Penguin.

Hodgson, Geoffrey M. (1988), *Economics and Institutions: A Manifesto for a Modern Institutional Economics*, Cambridge and Philadelphia: Polity Press and University of Pennsylvania Press.

Hodgson, Geoffrey M. (1994), 'Optimisation and evolution: Winter's critique of Friedman revisited', *Cambridge Journal of Economics*, **18** (4), August, 413–30. Reprinted in Geoffrey M. Hodgson (ed.) (1998), *The Foundations of Evolutionary Economics: 1890–1973*, Cheltenham, Edward Elgar and in Geoffrey M. Hodgson (1999), *Evolution and Institutions: On Evolutionary Economics and the Evolution of Economics*, Cheltenham: Edward Elgar.

Hodgson, Geoffrey M. (1998), 'Dichotimizing the dichotomy: Veblen versus Ayres', in S. Fayazmanesh and M. Tool (eds) (1998), *Institutionalist Method and Value: Essays in Honour of Paul Dale Bush*, vol. 1, Cheltenham: Edward Elgar, pp. 48–73.

Hodgson, Geoffrey M. (1999), *Economics and Utopia: Why the Learning Economy Is Not the End of History*, London and New York: Routledge.

Hodgson, Geoffrey M. (2001), *How Economics Forgot History: The Problem of Historical Specificity in Social Science*, London and New York: Routledge (in press).

Kaldor, Nicholas (1985), *Economics Without Equilibrium*, Cardiff: University College Cardiff Press.

Kapp, K. William (1976), 'The nature and significance of institutional economics', *Kyklos*, **29**, Fasc. 2, 209–32.

Lundvall, Bengt-Åke (ed.) (1992), *National Systems of Innovation: Towards a Theory of Innovation and Interactive Learning*, London: Pinter.

Marx, Karl (1973a), *The Revolutions of 1848: Political Writings*, Vol. 1, edited and introduced by David Fernbach, Harmondsworth: Penguin.

Marx, Karl (1973b), *Grundrisse: Foundations of the Critique of Political Economy*, translated by Martin Nicolaus, Harmondsworth: Penguin.

Marx, Karl (1981), *Capital*, vol. 3, translated by David Fernbach from the German edition of 1894, Harmondsworth: Pelican.

Metcalfe, J. Stanley (1988), 'Evolution and economic change', in Aubrey Silberston (ed.) (1988), *Technology and Economic Progress*, Basingstoke: Macmillan, pp. 54–85.

Mills, C. Wright (1953), *White Collar*, Oxford and New York: Oxford University Press.

Morris-Suzuki, Tessa (1989), *A History of Japanese Economic Thought*, London: Routledge.

Mueller, D. (1986), *Profits in the Long Run*, Cambridge: Cambridge University Press.

Myrdal, Gunnar (1957), *Economic Theory and Underdeveloped Regions*, London: Duckworth.

Nelson, Richard R. (1991), 'Why do firms differ, and how does it matter?', *Strategic Management Journal*, **12**, Special Issue, Winter, 61–74.

Nelson, Richard R. (ed.) (1993), *National Innovation Systems: A Comparative Analysis*, Oxford: Oxford University Press.

North, Douglass C. (1990), *Institutions, Institutional Change and Economic Performance*, Cambridge: Cambridge University Press.

Pavitt, Keith and Pari Patel (1988), 'The international distribution and determinants of technological activities', *Oxford Review of Economic Policy*, **4** (4), 35–55.

Penrose, Edith T. (1959), *The Theory of the Growth of the Firm*, Oxford: Basil Blackwell. Reprinted 1995, Oxford: Oxford University Press.

Piore, Michael J. and Charles F. Sabel (1984), *The Second Industrial Divide*, New York: Basic Books.

Polanyi, Karl (1944), *The Great Transformation*, New York: Rinehart.

Ross, Dorothy (1991), *The Origins of American Social Science*, Cambridge: Cambridge University Press.

Sabel, Charles F. and Jonathan Zeitlin (1985), 'Historical alternatives to mass production: politics, markets and technology in nineteenth century industrialization', *Past and Present*, No. 108, August, 132–76.

Schumpeter, Joseph A. (1934), *The Theory of Economic Development: An Inquiry into Profits, Capital, Credit, Interest, and the Business Cycle*, translated by Redvers

Opie from the second German edition of 1926, first edition 1911, Cambridge, MA: Harvard University Press.

Schumpeter, Joseph A. (1976), *Capitalism, Socialism and Democracy*, 5th edn (1st edn 1942), London: George Allen & Unwin.

Sekine, Thomas T. (1975), '*Uno-Riron:* a Japanese contribution to Marxian political economy', *Journal of Economic Literature*, **8**, 847–77.

Steindl, Joseph (1952), *Maturity and Stagnation in American Capitalism*, Oxford: Blackwell.

Tomlinson, James (1982), *The Unequal Struggle? British Socialism and the Capitalist Enterprise*, London: Methuen.

Uno, Kozo (1980), *Principles of Political Economy*, translated from the Japanese edition of 1964 by Thomas T. Sekine, Brighton: Harvester.

Veblen, Thorstein B. (1915), *Imperial Germany and the Industrial Revolution*, New York: Macmillan. Reprinted 1964 by Augustus Kelley.

Veblen, Thorstein B. (1919), *The Place of Science in Modern Civilisation and Other Essays*, New York: Huebsch.

Veblen, Thorstein B. (1934), *Essays on Our Changing Order*, ed. L. Ardzrooni, New York: Viking Press.

Whittington, Richard C. (1989), *Corporate Strategies in Recession and Recovery: Social Structure and Strategic Choice*, London: Unwin Hyman.

Young, Allyn A. (1928), 'Increasing returns and economic progress', *Economic Journal*, **38** (4), December, 527–42.

6. Information technology and the 'biodiversity' of capitalism

Ugo Pagano*

INTRODUCTION: TECHNOLOGICAL AND INSTITUTIONAL CHANGE IN COASE AND MARX

Ronald Coase, in his 1937 theory of transaction costs, considered the consequences of one of the first massive introductions of modern information technology: telephone lines allowing the transmission of voice among distant sites. He predicted that: 'Changes like the telephone and the telegraph, which tend to reduce the cost of organising spatially, will tend to increase the size of the firm' (Coase, 1937, p. 46).

However in a footnote he also observed that:

> It should be noted that most inventions will change both the cost of organising and the costs of using the price system. In such cases, whether the invention tends to make firms larger or smaller will depend on the relative effect of these two sets of costs. For instance, if the telephone reduces the costs of using the price mechanism more than it reduces the costs of organising, then it will have the effect of reducing the size of the firm. (p. 46, n. 31)

While in this Coasian framework the existence of the firm was explained by referring to market transaction costs, in other writings Coase seemed to believe that competitive market economies were able to produce the optimal institutional mix between markets and firms. In another footnote of the same article he exclaimed that, unlike a centrally planned economy: 'In a competitive market there is an optimum amount of planning!' (p. 37). Coase meant that activities were planned by firms' managers only when this was more efficient than leaving it to the workings of the market. According to Coase an optimization problem was continuously being solved by the competitive system: the optimal mixture of planning and markets was 'recalculated' and 'implemented' each time the technological data changed.

Coase's pioneering analysis of institutional change is very insightful but somewhat contradictory. On the one hand his explanation of the coexistence of different institutions, based on the analysis of their comparative costs, emphasizes that neither markets nor firms can be 'first-best' solutions in the sense that they are both constrained by their own organizational costs. At the same time, Coase sometimes seems to be claiming that an efficient institutional mix, corresponding to the level of development of the technology, is created without relevant organizational costs by a market economy. Consistency would seem to require that the same market transaction and managerial costs, which limit the size of markets and firms, should also limit the efficiency of their institutional mix and constrain the transition from one organization to the other, when technological changes require this.

A transition from market- to firm-type organization must imply transaction costs and/or managerial costs. In a world of positive transaction costs, 'transition costs' must also be positive and the institutional mix cannot simply tend to correspond to the level of technological development but must also be heavily influenced by the pre-existing institutional structure of the economy. In a world of positive market transaction costs, the institution of the centralized firm must be constrained by the inefficiencies of the markets and, vice versa, in a world of positive management costs the disintegration of a firm must be constrained by the inefficiencies of firm-type organization.[1]

Moreover, efficient transitions are also inhibited by the pre-existing institutional arrangements because they imply redistributions of resources that may damage the individuals working under them. For example, under markets, individuals who have developed marketing skills do better than those individuals who have developed management skills (the latter being a more favourable skill in a large firm). Efficient transitions are constrained not only by the degree of organizational efficiency of pre-existing institutions but also by the distributive struggle that they must often imply.

Like much of the new institutional economics, in some respects Coase's work has limitations similar to those of the technologically determinist version of the Marxian theory of history.

Indeed the Marxian theory of history illustrates the tension (and often the ambiguities) of a theory which aims to consider both aspects of the two-way relationship between property rights and technology. One could even say that the Marxian theory embodies two views that could be called a 'technological deterministic view' and a 'romantic view' of history. The former view stresses the influence that the characteristics of productive forces, optimally associated with a certain stage of technological development, have on property rights. The latter stresses the influence of property rights and institutions on the characteristics of the resources that are employed and developed. Marx struggled to melt these two visions in a single interpretation of history but rather ended up having two 'utopia' alternatives to capitalism – each one of them being strictly related to one of his view of history.

Much like Coase, Marx long ago had regarded the firm as an alternative form of organization to the market (Pagano, 1992). Unlike Coase, Marx believed that the increase of efficiency in the organization of production (or the development of the productive forces) would necessarily require an ongoing expansion of the firm-type organization relative to the market-type organization. According to Marx this tendency was already at work under capitalism but it could only be completed under socialism. Socialism (at least in its early stages) was bound to be a single-firm economy where the authority of a chief employer was extended from the firm to the society taken as a whole. In other words, an outcome of the technological deterministic view of history was an authoritarian model of a 'single-firm socialism' corresponding to the alleged needs of the development of productive forces.

At the same time, in Marxian theory, the set of rights characterizing the capitalist firm was not simply an expression of a certain stage of the development of productive forces but was also developing a particular quality of productive forces. De-skilled and detailed jobs, alienated and oppressed workers, machines and organization of production (which complemented more with the workers' stupidity than with their skills) were the productive forces developed by the capitalist firm. Communist rights (at least at a later stage) should have developed productive forces characterized by different qualities. Highly skilled men and women performing interesting and challenging production activities should have become the most important of the productive forces to be developed by the new society. In other words, in Marxian theory, the romantic view of history was somehow related to an 'anti-capitalist firm model of communism' (Pagano, 1985) where the quality of the development of productive forces would finally correspond to the needs of people as producers.

The relationship between property rights and the characteristics of productive forces, which created so many interesting problems and contradictions (as well as so many wrong 'predictions') in the Marxian approach became a non-issue in neoclassical theory. In a market economy, workers' or capitalists' ownership should have no effect on the characteristics of the resources (or of the productive forces) employed by the firm. At the same time, the characteristics of the resources employed in the firm have no implications whatsoever on the form of ownership which characterizes the organization. This point of view was well expressed by Samuelson (1957, p. 894) when he argued that: 'In a perfectly competitive economy it doesn't really matter who hires whom'.

Since Coase's path-breaking contribution, both the new institutional and radical economists have reconsidered the interaction between rights and technology. However, their relationship is still very controversial. As in Marxian theory, in these two streams of the literature the direction of causality runs in opposite directions. Following Coase's insights, in the new institutional economics the nature of rights and organizations is endogenously and efficiently determined by the characteristics of the resources employed in the firm: namely their degree of specificity and their monitoring requirements. By contrast, in the radical literature, which has inherited the tradition of the Marxian romantic view of history, the characteristics of the resources employed in the firm are in turn determined by the rights which owners of different factors have on the organization.

There is little doubt that we are experiencing a third industrial revolution: changes in information technology are having very deep effects on the rights that individuals have on the organization of production. The new institutional literature has helped to clarify the mechanisms by which this may happen. However, it can be seriously misleading to consider only the direction of causality running from the fast-changing characteristics of resources employed in production to the rights of the agents over these resources and, in general, the institutional mix that tends to prevail in modern economies. One must also consider the opposite direction of causality running from the nature of institutions to the resources employed in production. In the following sections of this chapter we shall claim that this dual relation between the nature of the resources employed in production and the characteristics of the organization of production results in mechanisms of cumulative causation that may help to understand the diversity of organizations that exists in spite of some common features of the information revolution. We shall call these self-reinforcing relations between organizational rights and technology 'organizational equilibria' and we shall maintain that multiple organizational equilibria are still likely to characterize the future of modern economies in the age of information technology.

INFORMATION TECHNOLOGY AS THE CAUSE OF THE REDISTRIBUTION OF ASYMMETRIC INFORMATION

One of the main arguments that underlies the idea that information technology causes a change in property relations and, in general, in the structure of the organizations prevailing under capitalism, is that it brings about a dramatic change in the distribution of the information that must be available to the producers. Since Hayek's (1935) famous contribution, economists have considered the influence of the distribution of private information on the distribution of property rights. If information is distributed among various agents and it can only be transmitted at a very high (sometimes infinite) cost, the distribution of decision-making power generally needs to follow a similar pattern. Otherwise, the members of society will not be making an efficient use of the knowledge distributed among them.

In Hayek's view, centralized planning failed because of the difficulty in obtaining the private information of agents. A socialist economy required an extremely costly and even unfeasible transmission of information from the periphery to the centre. However, as Coase had pointed out, markets also require the costly gathering and processing of information. Indeed, information costs are largely overlapping with market transaction costs (Engelbrecht, 1997) and modern economic theories have clarified how, in situations of asymmetric information, adverse selection and moral hazard may threaten the very existence of markets.

In their famous article, Alchian and Demsetz (1972) argued that, in situations of team work – when each worker finds it costly to gather information about the other workers – specialized centralized monitoring is necessary to avoid a situation of generalized free riding. According to them the emergence of the capitalist firm is due to the fact that, in many cases, efficiency can be greatly increased by giving hiring and firing rights to an entrepreneur who can easily monitor assembly-line types of workers and terminate the employment contract of those workers who do not work satisfactorily. Moreover the entrepreneur should also own that part of the physical capital that is difficult to monitor, in the sense that measuring its user-induced depreciation is very costly and rental arrangements are prohibitively expensive. Alchian and Demsetz observed that, unlike the case for unskilled workers, in 'artistic' or 'professional' work watching a man's activities is not a good clue to what he is actually thinking or doing with his mind. In this case the distribution of information is different and ownership arrangements are likely to follow a different pattern; forms of decentralized workers' ownership replace the centralized monitoring solution of the capitalist firm.

According to new institutional theory, besides the distribution of private information, information technology can also change the degree of specificity of the resources employed in production. Also these characteristics can cause changes in ownership relations and organizational arrangements. Specific resources cannot be easily employed in alternative uses. For these reasons the owners of specific resources will work for organizations where they have no rights (or, at least, safeguards against unfair termination) only at a premium that compensates them for the 'illiquidity' of their investments. By contrast, this premium is not necessary for the owners of general-purpose resources because they can easily find alternative employment. Whenever the distribution of specificity characteristics is not matched by the distribution of rights and safeguards, efficiency may be increased by shifting them from the owners of the general-purpose resources to the owners of specific resources. An important corollary of this argument is that, whenever this is possible, co-specific resources should be owned together to avoid the hold-up risks that separate ownership would otherwise involve. Thus a high degree of cospecificity of physical capital must necessarily involve a high degree of concentration of ownership.

Coupled with the original Coasian analysis, the monitoring and specificity arguments provide a powerful mechanism by which new institutional theory and the new property rights approach (Brynyolfsson, 1994; Hart, 1995) can help to explain the impact of information technology on institutional change.

Information technology favours disintegration in smaller firms and greater incentives to the workers (often in the form of ownership of small firms) as long as:

1. The more recent novelties in information technology reduce the cost of decentralized coordination occurring in the market more than the cost of centralized coordination within firms (unlike the case of the Coasian telephone and telegraph lines). The impact of information technology on the development of electronic markets, where many agents interact with other agents, may be greater than its impact on the development of electronic hierarchies where a centralization and a simplification of these interactions has already been carried out (Malone et al. 1994). The shift to market relations is likely to occur when the introduction of centralized hierarchies has reduced coordination costs at the expense of production efficiency. In this case information technology, reducing the relative impact of all types of coordination costs, may imply that total costs (the sum of coordination and production costs) become relatively lower under market arrangements.
2. Machines become easily re-programmable and, therefore, less co-specific to other machines. Decentralized ownership does not cause any hold-up problem and allows an efficient flexible reallocation of machines to their changing best uses. Moreover information technology may make it less expensive to check cases of misuse of equipment and make it relatively cheaper to arrange rental contracts or financial support for worker-owned firms.
3. Re-programming machines and handling the massive amount of information that becomes available with information technology involves many skilled tasks. Thus, information technology requires that workers acquire a lot of valuable knowledge to perform their tasks. The monitoring characteristic of their work becomes more similar to those features of artistic and professional work mentioned by Alchian and Demsetz than to those of the easily observable assembly-line workers. Moreover, relative to assembly-line workers who could easily be reallocated to other tasks, their ability may become more specific to the problems involved by some production activities. Because of the changes in the monitoring and specificity characteristics of their jobs, workers should be given

high-powered incentives for their daily effort and adequate safeguards for their investment in specific human capital. Both changes may be provided to a relatively larger number of workers–entrepreneurs if, thanks to the effects of information technology considered under the preceding two points, small organizations become not only feasible but even more efficient than large firms.[2]

By contrast, information technology will favour firm-type hierarchical organization as long as:

1. It facilitates the monitoring of the other agents. Here, an Orwellian 'big brother is watching you' world becomes cheaper or more feasible: because of information technology, agents who could not easily be observed under the traditional technology become 'easy-to-monitor factors'. In this case, asymmetric information can be redistributed and concentrated and some features of the traditional Fordist model can be extended beyond its traditional boundaries. Among the numerous possible examples one is particularly striking: truck drivers were once considered hard-to-monitor workers who, in the absence of self-employment and truck ownership, would take long breaks and little care of their trucks. Satellite control and black boxes now allow employers to get very cheap, detailed information about truck drivers. Both the recent French strike and the UPS strike in America seem to indicate that this sector is experiencing not only the organization but also the labour relations typical of Fordist relations.

2. It increases the extent of economies of scale and complementarities both in the gathering and the use of information. Economies of scale and complementarities have always characterized these two processes. Each piece of information is more useful and often makes sense only in the context of other information. Moreover each piece of information can be used many times without additional costs. These characteristics of information can make the concentration of much information in one or a few persons very productive. Each individual is characterized by bounded rationality or, in other words, by a bounded capacity to gather and process information. However, information technology can relax these constraints on bounded rationality allowing a single individual to exploit, to a larger extent, the economies of scale and the complementarities that characterize information. As long as this occurs, the ownership of assets should follow a similar pattern. Asset owners who do not hold the information relevant for their best use should bargain with the individuals who hold this information. Thus, in the world of incomplete contracts considered by Hart (1995) and Brynyolfsson (1994), these agents have a

lower incentive to invest than those agents who control both the physical assets and the relevant information. In other words, information technology, which makes it convenient to concentrate information in the hands of a few, should also lead to a concentration of assets.[3]

According to Hart (1995), Brynyolfsson (1994) and Barca (1994), the first set of effects prevails on the second set of effects and, therefore, information technology tends to cause greater disintegration and forms of dispersed ownership.[4] However, this conclusion is dubious for two reasons. In the first place we have seen that, in principle, information technology can push the distribution of information and physical assets in both directions. When we consider the case of countries different from the United States, the impact of information technology is ambiguous (Carnoy, 1997). Second, the distribution of assets cannot only be seen as a consequence of an 'optimal' distribution of information corresponding to the state of technology. The distribution of assets may influence the distribution of information by making it more convenient to apply information technology in a particular direction. We shall see that this may lead to a diversity of configurations that we have called 'organizational equilibria'.

DISTRIBUTION OF ASSETS AND DISTRIBUTION OF INFORMATION: A TWO-WAY RELATION

The relation of causality considered in the preceding section is surprisingly similar to the 'deterministic' view of history contained in Marxian theory. Some 'radical' authors, appealing to the 'romantic' view of history that is also contained in Marx, have argued that technological parameters, such as the distribution of information and specificity characteristics, are themselves influenced by the prevailing property rights.

According to Braverman (1974), the approach of 'scientific management', which was started by Taylor at the beginning of this century, has had a lasting impact on the development of the organization of work under capitalism. Taylor realized that the traditional system of management was badly suited to increasing workers' effort. Traditional management relied upon the knowledge of the workers, in the sense that the managers believed that the workers knew better than they did how to perform their jobs. Under traditional management, the workers could work below par by maintaining that a certain time was required to perform a certain job. The situation of 'asymmetric information', existing under traditional management, implied that the managers had no means of challenging this sort of statement. Taylor's solution to this problem was straightforward: the managers (and not the workers) should know how the jobs could be best performed, plan how they should be executed, and give the workers detailed instructions about their execution.[5] It was only by gaining control of the labour process that the managers could invert this situation of asymmetric information and control workers' effort. In spite of some considerable limitations of his analysis, Braverman has the merit of providing an example of causation opposite to standard economic theories where the exogenously given distribution of information is used to determine endogenously the most efficient incentive structure or the distribution of assets that can best solve the agency problem. In Braverman the distribution of assets is exogenously given and, according to him, Taylorism tried to determine endogenously the best distribution of information for a given distribution of assets. When, under a certain ownership system, because of asymmetric information, the use of a technology is particularly costly, there will be attempts to devise technologies that imply a distribution of information that better fits that system.

In Braverman's analysis, under capitalist ownership relations, there is a tendency to devise technologies that, inverting pre-existing information asymmetries, make labour an easy-to-monitor factor. A similar process occurs for the specificity of assets. Taylorism also implies that much of the specific knowledge used by the workers is made redundant by introducing a technology under which the workers are ordered to perform homogeneous tasks requiring only generic skills.[6]

According to the new institutional view, assembly-line workers do not have rights in their organizations because the current technology requires that they do not hold relevant 'hidden' information or specific skills. However, according to the radical view, the opposite is true: the workers do not have relevant information or specific skills because, under the current system of property rights, workers with these characteristics are very costly. Only a property right regime where workers have adequate incentives to identify with their organization can make their hidden information and their specific skills cheaper and change the nature of the human resources employed in production.

Thus the new institutional and the radical approaches have emphasized two different directions of causality. However this does not make their approaches contradictory. Indeed the main thrust of my own work on 'organizational equilibria' (Pagano, 1993) is that the self-sustaining nature of economic institutions can be properly understood only by unifying these two approaches. The fact that (a) causes (b) and (b) causes (a) are not mutually incompatible; rather, they imply that (a) can reinforce itself via (b) and (b) can reinforce itself via (a). When this occurs, the new institutional and radical mechanisms taken together imply that an institution of production such as the Tayloristic firm is characterized by a self-reinforcing mechanism that may give it a remarkable degree of institutional stability. The small information and specific skill content of workers' jobs imply that very small amounts of agency costs would be saved by giving them rights in the organization at the expense of high agency cost capital and management. At the same time these rights feed back on the characteristics of technology in a self-reinforcing manner, creating incentive conditions under which it is not convenient that the workers hold hidden information or invest in specific skills. Again this reinforces the pre-existing rights and so on. In other words, the nature of rights and of the technology reinforce each other, creating situations of organizational equilibrium which are characterized by institutional stability in the sense of being resistant to 'weak' property rights and technology shocks. Indeed, Pagano and Rowthorn (1996) have shown how organizational equilibria have an intrinsic resistance to 'efficient' alternative owners. Alternative owners are efficient because they allow a great saving of agency costs that would otherwise be paid if they were employed by the current owners; but exactly for this reason they tend to be substituted by the latter and the conditions under which switching ownership becomes convenient may never come about. Moreover, since network externalities exist among both property rights and the technological characteristics of resources (David, 1994) the nature of organizational equilibria implies that the tendency to homogenize technological standards brings about a tendency to homogenize property right standards and vice versa. Multiple institutionally stable economic systems are therefore likely to exist and it may be impossible for a single firm to move to a new organizational equilibrium even if this could be advantageous if all the firms were undergoing this change.

ORGANIZATIONAL EQUILIBRIA AND SPECIES OF CAPITALISM

The self-reinforcing characteristics of organizational equilibria may explain some puzzling features of the dynamics of capitalism. These include the coexistence of different 'national' forms that occurs in spite of common technological innovations, such as those associated with information technology. Also, 'new organizational species', whose success is often related to these new technological opportunities, often tend to emerge in countries that are different from those that were successful in the preceding phase of capitalist development.[7]

Chandler (1990) pointed out how the managerial revolution (which later would also lead to the development of Taylor's 'scientific management') was paradoxically inhibited in England by its prominence in the first industrial revolution.

In the first industrial revolution, where textiles allowed successful small-scale production, family-controlled firms were adequate. In this framework, while family members had an incentive to make firm-specific investments and could also, without serious organizational costs, oversee difficult-to-monitor factors, the same was not true for non-family-member managers. These managers were trapped in an 'organizational equilibrium' that was a vicious circle for them: because of the family system, weak managerial rights implied an unfavourable distribution of asymmetric information and of specific skills which, in turn, implied that the case for managerial rights remained very weak. In England this organizational equilibrium resisted the pressure of the 'second industrial revolution' where the changes associated with the development of railways pushed in the direction of the development of sophisticated managerial hierarchies. Thus, the self-reinforcing aspects of organizational equilibria can explain why the new species of managerial capitalism, together with the full strength of the second industrial revolution, blossomed with much greater intensity in the United States and Germany than in England. Still, the new species of capitalism coexisted with the original species and no country was purely characterized by a single organizational form.

Under 'managerial capitalism', often independently of their ownership entitlements, managers acquired considerable rights in the firm and accumulated large amounts of hidden information and specific skills. By contrast, the development of 'scientific management' implied that the large majority of workers were 'expropriated' of hidden information and of all the specific skills that had survived the first industrial revolution. Workers' weak rights in the organization were associated with an unfavourable distribution of asymmetric information and specific skills causing the self-sustaining organizational equilibrium that characterized Taylorism.

Also, in the case of the 'Tayloristic organizational equilibrium', one of the most important challenges to this vicious circle did not originate in the centre of the system in the United States where the competition among the numerous members of the 'Tayloristic' species was strongest. Rather, it came about in defeated, post-war Japan contributing in an impressive way to the exceptional development of that economy which, for a while, seemed even to challenge the supremacy of American capitalism.[8]

Besides its peripheral location, the new species did not emerge 'spontaneously' as the exclusive outcome of the workings of market forces. By contrast, the strong 'institutional shocks', which characterized the years following military defeat and the American occupation of Japan, had a fundamental, and very often unintended role, in the complex delivery of the new organizational equilibrium. While a comparison with American capitalism can easily be used to emphasize the numerous elements of continuity within the history of Japanese capitalism, the discontinuity between the *zaibatsu* and the *keiretsu* systems is striking, and cannot convincingly be explained without referring to the institutional shocks that characterized that period.[9]

The American expropriation of the *zaibatsu* families and the compulsory retirement of senior managers was coupled with an initial period of strong union rights. These factors helped the birth of a new organizational equilibrium where the workers acquired strong rights in their organization. These rights favoured the accumulation of job-specific and difficult-to-monitor skills.[10] That, in turn, reinforced the rights of the workers. In other words, the institutional shocks created the conditions for a new self-sustaining organizational equilibrium (Pagano, 2000) characterized by a distribution of asymmetric information and of specificity characteristics that was in sharp contrast with the theory and practice of Taylorism.

Similar self-reinforcing mechanisms characterize other modes of production such as Italian districts, 'German corporatism',[11] and the enormous varieties of organizational forms that are emerging in the ex-socialist countries.[12] As in the case of the second industrial revolution, the 'third industrial revolution' will have a great impact in reassessing the relative merits of these organizational forms and some may turn out not to be viable. However, also in this case, the diversity of organizational forms is unlikely to be narrowed. While we have seen the influence of informational technology to be far from bringing about unidirectional transformations, pre-existing property rights will somehow continue to shape technology (including information technology).

A possible argument, predicting a reduction in the 'biodiversity' of capitalism, could be based on the observation that information technology favours the process of globalization of the world economy and that, in a 'globalized world', imitation and other factors may bring about an increase of organizational homogenization. However, in a globalized world the existing different forms of national capitalism may more effectively exploit their 'comparative institutional advantage' in different sectors of the economy and some new viable forms of capitalism may even emerge in this process. In this sense, globalization allows the specialization of the economies in those sectors where they have or develop a comparative institutional advantage related to their own particular organizational equilibrium and may even favour the diversity of the forms of capitalism. Thus, there is no reason to believe that the biodiversity of capitalism is bound to decrease. By contrast, at least in this particular sense, we are far from reaching an 'end of history'.[13]

CONCLUSION

A diversity of organizational equilibria is possible. Both 'political' shocks on property rights and 'technological' shocks can threaten the institutional stability of a system and bring about a new type of organizational equilibrium. The shocks of information technology are not likely to destroy this diversity of organizations for at least three reasons.

In the first place the nature of the shocks induced by information technology is ambiguous and it can mean either more decentralized ownership and decision making or more concentration of both.

In the second place, organizational change is not simply characterized by the transfer of given bundles of rights but more often by an 'unbundling' and redistribution of them. For instance, the institution of life employment 'unbundles' shareholders' right to use their machines with the employees that they prefer from other ownership rights (such as the right to sell their machines) and gives the workers the right to work with the machines for a certain length of time. Rights can be bundled, unbundled and redistributed in numerous ways. A remarkable diversity of organizational equilibria is therefore possible and does, indeed, exist in reality.

Finally, either because of the ambiguity of shocks induced by information technology or because of the diversity of the possible organizational arrangements, political shocks on property and control rights are likely to continue to have a crucial importance in selecting one of the self-reinforcing mechanisms defining organizational equilibria.

Information technology, redefining the distribution of information and the specificity characteristics required by many jobs, has a serious impact on the rights on physical assets. However, the latter also have an important influence on the former and may determine which one is going to be the particular way in which information technology may be applied. In principle, information technology may favour both the 'concentration' and decentralization of information (Zuboff, 1988); the particular organizations and 'bundles' of property rights prevailing in the economy may reinforce one of these two effects. The impact of information technology should be studied neither with a 'deterministic' nor with a 'romantic' approach but it should be analysed with an open mind towards both the directions of causality emphasized in these two views. Information technology should make us increasingly aware of the strong complementarity existing between the distribution of information and the distribution of assets. A democratic society, where most people have access to important pieces of information, tends to be egalitarian. On the other hand, an egalitarian society, where many people have rights on physical assets, can help to create the conditions under which many people acquire relevant information or, in other words, the conditions for a full-blown democracy.

NOTES

*   The author is grateful to Ministero dell'Università e Della Ricerca Scientifica for financial support.

1.   In this sense the Coasian approach must necessarily lead to some form of 'evolutionary' economics where the institutional starting point is necessarily relevant for the explanation of the final outcome. Coase (1988 p. 13) notes that the 'so-called Coase theorem' has derived implications from his writings that ignore the fundamental importance of positive transactions costs. The many versions of this 'theorem' in the literature assume either zero transaction costs or a zero transaction cost institutional environment. One could assume that the Coase theorem involves also some 'efficient' bargaining on the relevant institutions, but the efficiency of these institutions depends, in turn, on the fact that they are negotiated in a zero transaction cost institutional environment. This generates an infinite logical regress. If one wants to avoid the 'Nirvana fallacy' of a zero transaction world one must specify the organizational costs of the initial institutional set-up; or, in other words, one must move towards some sort of history-dependent evolutionary economics. On a related issue, see Anderlini and Felli (1998).

2.   In other words, according to this view, information technology would push in the direction of 'flexible specialization' and small-scale production. Sabel and Zeitlin (1997) show how the two systems have always coexisted and only a unilateral view of history could see it as a constant expansion of mass and large-scale production. For instance, Poni (1997) observes that while, in the case of cotton, the industrial revolution was typically associated with these characteristics, at the same time the silk industry was characterized by flexible specialization and small-scale production.

3.   This effect may be so strong as to induce some form of retreat in sectors that used to be leading cases of small-scale production and flexible specialization. Capecchi (1997) observes how this type of retreat from flexible specialization to a wide but relatively fixed menu of product can be observed in the case of the Bologna automatic packing machinery production that was one of the most successful cases of small-scale production and flexible specialization. The key element seems to be the importance of the economies to scale and complementarities that characterize modern information technology and, in particular, electronic engineering which entails a fundamental role for top-down science-based innovations.

4.   Moreover, according to Barca (1994), information technology tends to make ownership a less-efficient incentive system because, while many individuals need high-powered incentives, ownership can give incentives to only a few of them.

5.   In this way 'scientific management' not only challenged the traditional craftsman apprenticeship system but also the traditional forms of 'family capitalism' where the members of the 'family dynasty' could govern the firm without acquiring the relevant managerial skills. In this sense, Taylorism was also associated with the managerial revolution and with the growth of managerial hierarchies. The rights of the members of the family dynasty could seriously inhibit the growth of these hierarchies and the system of competence-based promotion rights that were associated with them.

6.   Both factors are evident when we consider the three fundamental principles of Taylorism as they are summarized by Braverman (1974): (1) dissociation of the labour process from the skills of the workers. (2) separation of conception from execution. (3) use of this monopoly over knowledge to control each step of the labour process and its mode of execution. According to Braverman the first principle is implicit in the following quotation from Taylor: 'The managers assume ... the burden of gathering together all the traditional knowledge which in the past has been possessed by the workmen and then classifying, tabulating, and reducing this knowledge to rules, laws, and formulae' (F. Taylor, quoted in Braverman, 1974, p. 112). The second principle can be found in Taylor's statement: 'All possible brain work should be removed from the shop and centred in the planning or laying-out department' (F. Taylor, quoted in Braverman, 1974, p. 113). Finally, according to Braverman, the third principle is clearly pointed out by Taylor when

he states that, unlike under traditional types of management, under scientific management the managers should give the workers detailed instructions about each task to be performed and these tasks should specify 'not only what is to be done, but how it is to be done and the exact time allowed for doing it' (F. Taylor, quoted in Braverman, 1974, p. 118).

7. In other words the evolution of capitalism seems to be characterized by forms of 'allopatric speciation' in the sense that new forms of capitalism often tend to emerge in countries different from those where the preceding forms had had a successful development. Pagano (2001) considers the problems related to the origin of new species in biology and some common law of structure and change that characterize the formation of new organizational species; in particular, the emergence of American and German managerial forms of capitalism are considered in the framework of the theories of allopatric speciation developed in evolutionary biology.

8. Another challenge came from West Germany and its system of 'unionized' capitalism based on occupational markets. In this case, employers' associations and the trade unions with the help of the state used to agree on a common division of labour within each firm that allowed the creation of 'flexible' occupational markets characterized by the fact that workers could move from one firm to another without wasting much organizational specific knowledge. Observe how this flexibility was strictly associated with the internal rigidity of the firm that must be characterized by a common type of division of labour and related professional competencies. On these issues, see Pagano (1991 and 1993).

9. The discontinuity between pre-war and post-war Japanese capitalism and the relevance of the post-war institutional shocks can be clearly understood by considering an alternative (and perhaps more appropriate) comparison with Italian capitalism. While the policies of the Allied Powers reinforced the Italian system of family capitalism, the American occupation terminated its Japanese version. The 'institutional bifurcation' that was created had long-lasting consequences and shaped the development of the two countries (Barca et al., 1999).

10. In particular teamwork, which often replaced the assembly line in Japanese organizations, was necessarily characterized by the specificity of the skills (each skill becoming specific to those of the other team members) and by the difficulty of monitoring the workers (it is difficult for an outsider to disentangle the contribution of a single worker from those of the other members of the team).

11. In many respects the Japanese species of capitalism represented a 'mixture' of rigidities and flexibility opposite to those of the German system. In the German system the rigidity of the internal division of labour allows the external flexibility of occupational markets; by contrast, in the case of the Japanese system, the flexibility of the internal organization of the firm implies that often no equivalent 'slots' for the skills of its workers could be found in other organizations. In this sense the 'internal flexibility' of Japanese firms is somehow associated with their 'external rigidity'. Thus, given the two different associated technologies, the German system could be regarded as a system of self-sustaining 'occupational rights' and the Japanese could be regarded as a system of self-sustaining 'organizational rights' (Pagano, 1997).

12. This multiplicity of feasible organizations is very important for economic policy and, in particular, for the problems related to the transformation of the former socialist countries (Aoki, 1995; Pagano, 2000). A comparative institutional analysis is required to consider the self-reinforcing mechanisms or the complementarities (Aoki, 1996) that characterize each one of the feasible alternatives.

13. Other reasons for which this is a very unlikely outcome are given in Hodgson (1999, p. 153) who points out how the idea of the 'end of history' is 'deeply connected to an Enlightenment principle. This is the idea of a universal history: the notion of an universal destination, underpinned by absolute rational principles'.

REFERENCES

Alchian, A. and H. Demsetz (1972), 'Production, information costs and economic organization', *American Economic Review*, **62**, 777–95.

Anderlini, L. and L. Felli (1998), 'Costly Coasian contracts', Mimeo, Cambridge.

Aoki, M. (1995), 'Controlling insider control: issues of corporate governance in transition economies', in M. Aoki and H. Kim (eds) (1995), *Corporate Governance in Transitional Economies: Insider Control and the Role of Banks*, Economic Development Institute Development Studies, Washington, DC: World Bank, pp. 3–30.

Aoki M. (1996), 'Towards a comparative institutional analysis: motivations and some tentative theorising', *Japanese Economic Review*, **7** (1), 1–19.

Barca, F. (1994), *Imprese in cerca di padrone. Proprietà e controllo nel capitalismo italiano* (Firms in Search of a Master. Ownership and Control under Italian Capitalism), Bari: Laterza.

Barca, F., K. Iwai, U. Pagano and S. Trento (1999), 'The divergence of the Italian and Japanese corporate governance models: the role of the institutional shocks', *Economic Systems*, **1**, 35–61.

Braverman, H. (1974), *Labour and Monopoly Capital*, New York: Monthly Review Press.

Brynyolfsson, E. (1994), 'Information assets, technology and organization', *Management Science*, **40** (12), 1645–62.

Capecchi, V. (1997), 'In search of flexibility: the Bologna metalworking industry 1900–1992', in C.F. Sabel and F. Zeitlin (eds), *World of Possibilities. Flexibility and Mass Production in Western Industrialization*, Cambridge: Cambridge University Press, pp. 381–418.

Carnoy, M. (1997), 'The new information technology – international diffusion and its impact on employment and skills. A review of the literature', *International Journal of Manpower*, **18** (1/2), 119–59.

Chandler, A.D. (1990), *Scale and Scope. The Dynamics of Industrial Capitalism*, Cambridge, MA: Harvard University Press.

Coase, R.H. (1937), 'The nature of the firm', *Economica*, **4**, 386–405.

Coase, R.H. (1988), *The Firm, the Market and the Law*, Chicago: University of Chicago Press.

David, P.A. (1994), 'Why are institutions the "carriers of history"? Path dependence and the evolution of conventions, organisations and institutions', *Structural Change and Economic Dynamics*, **5** (2), 205–21.

Engelbrecht, H. (1997), 'A comparison and critical assessment of Porat and Rubin's information economy and Wallis and North's transaction sector', *Information Economics and Policy*, **9**, 271–90.

Hart, O. (1995), *Firms, Contracts, and Financial Structure*, Oxford: Clarendon Press.

Hayek, F.A. (1935), *Collectivist Economic Planning*, London: Routledge.

Hodgson, G.M. (1999), *Economics and Utopia: Why the Learning Economy Is Not the End of History*, London: Routledge.

Malone, T.W., J. Yates and R.J. Benjamin (1994), 'Electronic markets and electronic hierarchies', in T.J. Allen and M.S. Scott Morton, *Information Technology and the Corporation of the 1990s*, Oxford: Oxford University Press, pp. 61–83.

Pagano, U. (1985), *Work and Welfare in Economic Theory*, Oxford: Basil Blackwell.

Pagano, U. (1991), 'Property rights, asset specificity, and the division of labour under alternative capitalist relations', *Cambridge Journal of Economics*, **15** (3), 315–42.

Reprinted in G.M. Hodgson (1993), *The Economics of Institutions*, Cheltenham, UK: Edward Elgar.

Pagano, U. (1992), 'Authority, co-ordination and disequilibrium: an explanation of the co-existence of markets and firms', *Economic Dynamics and Structural Change*, June, 53–76. Reprinted in G.M. Hodgson (1993), *The Economics of Institutions*, Cheltenham, UK: Edward Elgar.

Pagano, U. (1993), 'Organizational equilibria and institutional stability', in S. Bowles, H. Gintis and B. Gustafsson (eds) (1993), *Markets and Democracy: Participation, Accountability and Efficiency*, Cambridge: Cambridge University Press, pp. 86–115.

Pagano, U. (1997), 'Workers' rights and economic flexibility', in P. Arestis, G. Palma and G. Sawyer, *Markets, Unemployment and Economic Policy*, London: Routledge, pp. 354–63.

Pagano, U. (2000), *Transition and the Speciation of the Transition of the Japanese Model*, London: Macmillan, pp. 198–236.

Pagano, U. (2001), 'The origin of organizational species', in A. Nicita and U. Pagano (eds), *The Evolution of Economic Diversity*, London: Routledge, pp. 21–47.

Pagano, U. and R. Rowthorn (1996), 'The competitive selection of democratic firms in a world of self-sustaining institutions', in Pagano and Rowthorn (eds), *Democracy and Efficiency in the Economic Enterprise*, London: Routledge, pp. 116–45.

Poni, C. (1997), 'Fashion as flexible production: the strategies of the Lyons silk merchants in the eighteenth century', in C.F. Sabel and F. Zeitlin (eds), *World of Possibilities. Flexibility and Mass Production in Western Industrialization*, Cambridge: Cambridge University Press, pp. 37–74.

Sabel, C.F. and F. Zeitlin (1997), 'Stories, strategies, structures: rethinking historical alternatives to mass production', in Sabel and Zeitlin (eds), *World of Possibilities. Flexibility and Mass Production in Western Industrialization*, Cambridge: Cambridge University Press, pp. 1–36.

Samuelson, P. (1957), 'Wage and interest: a modern dissection of Marxian economic models', *American Economic Review*, **47**, 884–912.

Zuboff, S. (1988), *In the Age of the Smart Machine: The Future of Work and Power*, New York: Basic Books.

7. The diversity and future of capitalisms: a *régulationnist* analysis

Robert A. Boyer

INTRODUCTION

As we entered the new millennium, many economists celebrated the apparent victory of the market. They pointed to the collapse of Soviet-type economies, the major difficulties experienced by social democratic countries and the seemingly irreversible decay of state-led strategies. The long and steady boom of the American economy during the 1990s was contrasted with sluggish European economic growth and job creation. Some political philosophers have even argued that history has come to an end, since no alternative to the market economy and the democratic polity seems viable. We find the modern Dr Pangloss, proclaiming that this is the best of all possible worlds. All will be well, it is said, as long as governments give markets free rein and let entrepreneurs prosper. Both Marx and Keynes are dead and buried: their visions of an unstable and crisis-prone capitalism are both seemingly obsolete.

The *régulation* school challenges this erroneous consensus. It has built a conceptual and theoretical framework to analyse the long-run process of structural change within capitalism. The interpretation of contemporary transformations is different from both the Marxist tradition, which stresses the irreversible evolution towards a final crisis, and the Panglossian vision put forward by the neoclassical fundamentalists who believe in the self-equilibrating property of a market economy. By contrast, the *régulation* research agenda is to provide some understanding of the strains and contradictions that permeate contemporary societies and international relations, especially in reaction to some quite surprising developments since the end of the Second World War. These include the exceptionally fast and stable growth of developed countries during the 1960s, followed by the demise of economic optimism in the 1970s. Also addressed is the diversity of trajectories followed by the United States, the European countries and Japan during the 1990s, and the uncertain prospects concerning the global financial system. This chapter reviews the contribution of *régulation* theory to our understanding of these phenomena.

CONSTRAINTS IMPOSED BY THE POLITY: THE HIDDEN ORIGIN OF THE GOLDEN AGE

The prevailing wisdom is that governments who wish to promote growth and job creation must pursue privatization, deregulation and 'return to the market' strategies. They are obliged to maintain the neutrality of the public budget and the independence of the Central Bank. However, in the face of these opinions, it is useful to recall some major and seemingly paradoxical findings.[1]

The exceptional dynamism and stability of economic growth, which was observed in the United States, Europe and Japan after the Second World War, was not triggered by the implementation of free market mechanisms. On the contrary, it resulted from strong constraints imposed upon economic activity by social and political action. For the first time in history, the rights of wage earners were widely recognized, both in the political arena, due to the strengthening of democracy and citizenship, and in the economic domain by a genuine capital–labour accord. Mass production blossomed in response to this new accord. Although its form differed from one country to another, it addressed the needs and functions of the members of the wage-earner class from the cradle to the grave. Sharing the fruits of higher productivity made possible mass consumption in response to mass production. Basic human needs were addressed by social security systems.

Contrary to much orthodox Marxist theory, the state was not so much the state of monopoly capital but rather a 'wage-earner state'.[2] Much of the surge in public spending was due to the growth of social security provision rather than subsidies to monopolies or large firms. Establishing this point, *régulation* theory investigated the prevailing institutional regime, known as Fordism. Built at the international level upon a Pax Americana, at home it meant the adoption of modern mass production techniques, moderate and organized competition among national firms, and the enhanced role of credit money. Last but not least, it meant an interventionist state, in charge of investment in collective infrastructures and the fine tuning of economic activity, aiming to prevent unemployment as well as inflation (Figure 7.1). This virtuous process lasted three decades, which, in retrospect, was called the 'Golden Age' (1947–76) (Marglin and Schor, 1990). But it came to an end during the 'two painful decades' (1977–97).[3] This drastic shift has to be explained.

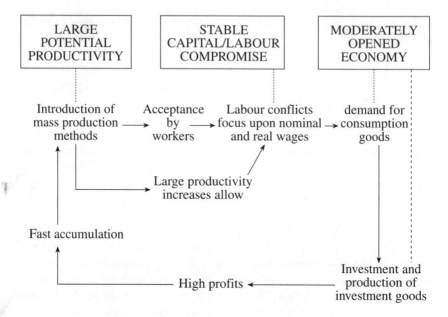

Figure 7.1   The Fordist regime and its three conditions

INTERNATIONALIZATION, FINANCIAL GLOBALIZATION AND THE EROSION OF THE POST-WAR FORDIST REGIME

This remarkable Fordist accumulation regime and sociopolitical configuration was finally destabilized by its very success. Full employment increased the bargaining strength of wage earners, and propitiated inflation as an outcome. A period of instability ensued, with an economic slowdown and growing mass unemployment. The economic imbalances and social contradictions of the 1980s and 1990s took a form very different from those of the Great Depression of the 1930s.

For example, in the United States, the ossification of Fordist methods led to an enduring productivity slowdown (see Table 7.2, below). In response, by the 1990s, a new accumulation regime emerged. This new regime is at odds with the previous Fordist one, built upon permanent productivity increases and the diffusion of a typical lifestyle. Ongoing increases in standards of living are now associated more with increases in working hours, rather than advances in productivity (Schor, 1991). A widening of social inequalities has promoted a strong differentiation of life styles, thus further threatening social cohesion (Boyer and Juillard, 1995).

Similar structural transformations, long unnoticed, have taken place in other advanced capitalist economies, first in response to the two oil shocks and second after the diffusion of financial deregulation and globalization.

A second structural change relates to the dynamism of internationalization via trade, investment and ultimately finance. The search for increasing returns to scale, associated with the division of labour typical of Fordism, first benefited from the dynamism of domestic markets. But after a while, they became too narrow and the pursuit of the same strategy called for an international expansion. The accumulation regime became less governed by domestic consumption and became export led.

The fatal sickness of the Fordist regime in the United States was thus transmitted to the majority of other developed countries, via the interdependence of world trade and the growth of world markets. The variability of exchange rates and the dynamism of financial markets exacerbated the affliction.

At the same time, contemporary capitalism has a renewed impetus to conquer new regions and sectors, due to the resilience and flexibility of market relations. From this point of view, the current wave of internationalization is in accord with some long-run trends which have been observed since the emergence of merchant capitalism. Nevertheless, the contemporary evolution has brought new countries and geographical zones into the global capitalist system (Hirst and Thompson, 1996; Boyer, 1997). Since the 1980s, foreign direct investment has tended to be far more dynamic than trade itself. Financial flows are increasing rapidly, and exerting a major role in the redeployment of productive capital.

The demise of the Fordist accumulation regime has brought a slowdown in growth, which in turn has reduced employment and job creation. This contrasts greatly with the labour scarcity that prevailed during the Golden Age. The rise of employment, statistically recognized or hidden, has eroded the bargaining power of workers and unions. Now unrestrained by union power or the Soviet threat, and challenged by new global economic forces, employers have torn up the post-war accord between capital and labour. This has taken place even in social democratic countries such as Sweden, and in state-led countries such as France.

Reforms have now been undertaken in order to slim down and 'rationalize' social security systems, which have become more and more difficult to finance given the economic slowdown and shrinking tax base. These structural transformations have even finally affected the strongest economies of the 1980s, such as Germany, Japan and more recently South Korea.

Orthodox Marxists may conclude that contemporary capitalism is again stricken by iron laws of long-run development: both at the national and international levels, the poor become poorer and the rich become richer;

every country is fighting an economic war against its neighbours; finance capital is gaining power and imposing its governance over large firms and national governments. However, for *régulation* theory, contemporary economies are very different from those of the nineteenth century, or even the 1920s and 1930s.

Consider, for example, the role of public influence and opinion. First, the principles of responsibility and solidarity embedded into national social security systems still shape the expectations of the workers and citizens, who may rebel against budgetary cuts in social spending, which are perceived as unfair and breaking the core citizen–state compromise. Second, elections still provide an opportunity for citizens to challenge government economic policies. Although governments are often tempted to oblige the international financial community rather than domestic public opinion, they have experienced many difficulties in proposing new compromises that attempt to deal with the conditions of the 1990s. Under these circumstances, democracy and markets can conflict. This is largely unrecognized in conventional Marxist analyses, elaborated in an epoch when workers had a more limited political voice.

Thus, for *régulation* theory, the so-called 'long waves', suggested by Kondratief, may well be an illusion, since capitalism is not running with the regularity of a 'Schumpeterian clock'. On the contrary, the very contradictions of this economic system give birth to new configurations, which in turn support unprecedented accumulation regimes that finally enter into structural crises. There is no cycle; never the repetition of a single pattern. For instance, the Fordist capital–labour accord reconciled intensive accumulation with effective demand by enhancing the living standards of the wage earners. But, as a result, this compromise triggers inflation, internationalization and financial fragility. Any relevant analysis has to take into account the strong historicity and path dependence of accumulation regimes. It is especially important to disentangle recurring and unprecedented factors at work during the 1990s.

CONTRASTING POLITICAL COMPROMISES SHAPE THE DIVERSITY OF CAPITALISM

Recent *régulationnist* research has pointed out another major result. Very different national trajectories can be observed within developed economies, even if they share some common features concerning production and consumption (Bruno et al., 1997; Baslé et al., 1994). Each national territory exhibits highly specific political compromises that inform and govern the related accumulation regimes and *régulation* modes (Table 7.1). Consider the following examples.

- In the *United States*, market forces and countervailing public mechanisms shape and reshape social and economic dynamics. For instance, during the 1960s, the Fordist wage–labour nexus was closely related to union bargaining power within some leading sectors, such as the car industry. When productivity slowed down and unemployment increased, the workers accepted wage cuts, part-time employment, low-skilled jobs, and greater geographical and occupational mobility. High-tech and sunrise industries now coexist with a surge of new tertiary jobs and surviving traditional industries. Given the highly selective nature of the social benefits and the reform of the tax system, social and economic inequalities are increasing, but unemployment has been kept at a lower level than in Europe. Clearly, the Fordist growth regime is dead! It has been replaced by a totally different configuration, where multiple jobs within the same family and long working hours are the only methods for sustaining the growth of household consumption (Mishel et al., 1997). Credit expansion and financial speculation complement the strategy for maintaining the ongoing increases in standards in living. The United States is a good example of an extensive accumulation regime, largely inward looking, and associated with deepening inequalities. The United Kingdom is another example of a market-led economy.

- *Japanese capitalism* follows a quite different trajectory. It is largely shaped by the strategy of large conglomerate firms, the *keiretsu*. These organize and distribute within their affiliates' capital, knowledge and worker and managerial skills, according to mechanisms which are largely substitutes to the markets of credit, labour, managers and professionals observed in market-led capitalism. Instead of internal markets there are mechanisms of corporate *régulation*. The allocation of resources derives not from pure market mechanisms, or from state planning, or strong public intervention, but is run by mechanisms operating at intermediate levels. This institutional setting has been quite effective in governing Japan's adoption of modern technology. It is good for enhancing the competitiveness of industries that require substantial coordination between interdependent suppliers, such as the car industry and consumer electronics. As a result of the crises of the 1970s, a competitive shift was required from reducing costs of standardized goods to differentiation by quality, servicing and innovation. To these requirements, Japan was highly adaptable, and this sustained its growth during much of the 1980s. As a result, the Japanese economy built up a large and lasting trade surplus, which first triggered a strong appreciation of the yen with respect to the dollar. These events led to international pressures for the opening up and reform of the financial system and for the opening up of Japanese domestic markets to foreign imports. Clearly, the distinctiveness of this

Table 7.1 *Capitalist systems: four distinctive* régulation *modes*

Régulation

	Market led	Corporate	Social democratic	State led
1. Core logic and hierarchical principles	Market mechanisms govern most if not all institutional forms	The large corporation is the central locus for sharing risks, economic benefits and social solidarity	Social partners constantly negotiate compromises and institutional reforms required by a wide insertion into the world economy	The whole economic circuit is shaped by public interventions for production, demand, price formation and institutional codification
2. Consequences for institutional forms: Wage–labour nexus	Wage negotiations are largely decentralized, wage systems are individualized and labour markets segmented	Highly differentiated capital–labour accords within the large firms but synchronization of wage increases at the national level	Traditionally, centralization of collective bargaining, under a strong constraint of competition	Strong institutionalization by law or decree about employment, work duration, average wage, wage hierarchy and welfare
Competition	Law and jurisprudence periodically try to restrict concentration. During the last 20 years, shift from one oligopolistic form to another	Relatively open competition between conglomerates present over many interdependent product markets	Small number of big multinational corporations inserted into international competition	Usually moderate, due to public regulations, professional associations or, more recently, large concentration
Monetary and financial regime	Sophisticated financial markets, many financial innovations, large role of stock market in the governance of large corporations, usually an independent Central Bank	The main bank allocates capital across all the firms belonging to the *Keiretsu*. Until the early 1990s, strong control by public authorities (Ministry of Finance), including upon the Central Bank	The banking system is more important than the stock market and is instrumental in the management of the manufacturing sector	Until the mid-1990s, strong control by Ministry of Finance of the banking system, the Central Bank and many nationalized commercial banks

State	Fragmented into a series of independent agencies in charge of controlling the players upon each market. Competition among politicians	Limited size but active role of the state, which provides the coordination of expectations and the collective goods that cannot be supplied by corporations	Extensive public interventions, organizing important transfers between sectors, regions. individuals. Until the early 1990s, strong influence of state regulations and collective agreements	Important size of the public budget and welfare-related redistribution, via national-ized firms, banks, public spending, collective infrastructures, and legislation
Insertion into the international regime	Political strategy promoting free trade, even if some legislation is designed in order to protect from unfair competition (some differences between US and UK)	The external trade strategy and the rules governing imports are aimed at the technological and economic performance of domestic firms	Clear acceptance of the competitiveness principle and incentives to technological, social and organizational innovations	Traditionally, strong control by the state over tariffs, quotas, technical norms. Has been extended to the European level over the last two decades
3. Main features of the *régulation* mode	Dominance of market-led mechanisms, with adequate public control by jurisprudence and legislation	Many economic and social adjustments take place within the large firms, and they largely structure the rest of the economy	Tripartite negotiations between business associations, workers unions and state define institutional arrangements and thus macroeconomic adjustments	The state plays a central role in most if not all macroeconomic adjustments and firms respond to the changing rules of the game (i.e. currently privatization)

accumulation regime, mainly export led, explains first the success, then the trade frictions with the United States, and finally the severity of its structural crisis of the 1990s.

- *Social democratic* or *negotiated economies* represent a third approach. It is a method for overcoming the contradictions that does not give primacy to market mechanisms, or the state, or the large corporation. It is based on *negotiated compromises* between social groups, that is, workers' unions, business associations and public authorities, in most cases at the national level. The Scandinavian countries, Austria and to a lesser extent Germany, are good examples of such a capitalism. *Social democratic capitalism* used to exhibit, at least until the mid-1980s, an ability to respond to the evolution of the international system, as well as to the innovations associated with the new productive paradigm. The related accumulation regime was built upon a clear acceptance by social part-ners of an export-led growth, built upon quality, servicing and innovation much more than on low prices for standardized products. These coun-tries exhibited strong social mechanisms for redistributing income and creating public employment in the sectors linked to health, education, training and retraining of workers. In contrast with the market-led capi-talism, inequalities were kept within much narrower limits. Nevertheless, some of these economies experienced severe crises during the 1990s. It is a general rule that no *régulation* mode may prosper for ever, without major transformation.

- *State-led régulation* is the fourth approach. Public interventions have been notable in countries where market competition is not universally accepted, where business associations and workers' unions are weak and antagonistic, and where the business class is unable to facilitate strong economic and social spillover effects upon the rest of the economy. Many European countries – with the prominent exception of the United Kingdom – seem to follow such a state-led *régulation*. France is the foremost example of such an accumulation regime, where the state intervenes in many spheres of economic activity. During the Golden Age, the state was active in production, via the nationalized sector, but also in demand formation, via public spending on infra-structures, transport, health, education and so on. The state had a role in price formation, for the public sector and agricultural products. Furthermore, the state was highly active in the legal codification and enactment of many institutional forms, from the wage-labour nexus to the nature of competition and the monetary regime. Again this pattern has run into major difficulties during the 1990s, but they differ significantly from the problems experienced within other *régulation* modes.

One central message is therefore that there is *no single one best* régulation *mode* and that the history and the nature of the political process both constrain and structure the institutional architecture. This is an important departure from mainstream economic theory, which generally assumes that economic adjustments and institutional requirements apply universally, without regard for historical time or geographical location.

IS THERE A GRESHAM'S LAW FOR CAPITALISMS? THE TURNING POINT OF THE 1990S

Going back to the end of the 1980s, each one of these brands of capitalism exhibited both strong features and underlying weaknesses. But the distribution of these costs and benefits was such that, given the limited volatility of the international system, all of them could coexist and prosper without major strains.

- *Market-led régulation* propitiates fast adjustments to exogenous shocks and innovations, since a clear definition and enforcement of property rights is an incentive to entrepreneurship and technological innovation. The sophistication of financial markets helps the selection of efficient projects, at least as far as short-term returns are considered. But the other side of the coin is precisely that countries such as the United States and the United Kingdom usually suffer from short-termism and an underinvestment in public infrastructures. Another drawback of such market-led regimes is their propensity for rising inequalities of income and wealth.
- *Corporate régulation* is very effective during the process of technological catch-up. This mode facilitates learning by doing, firm-specific competence building, and cumulative incremental innovations in product quality and differentiation. But this *régulation* mode has its own drawbacks. In times of enduring economic stagnation – as with Japan in the 1990s – the job security that is at the core of the capital–labour compromise restricts layoffs and undermines profits. Investment and growth are thus threatened. Similarly, the close and long-term links between the banks and industry can lead to an imperfect screening of investment decisions.
- *Social democratic régulation* has advantages in the organization of rapid technological innovation. It has tackled fundamental social problems such as health care, urban organization and provision for the elderly. It has helped to maintain social cohesion, by limiting economic inequalities. This system has also been strong in diffusing

education and professional retraining for the workers affected by the decline of mature industries. Nevertheless, social democratic *régulation* is not without its costs. It needs large-scale public intervention, thus maintaining full employment by a continuous rise in public employment. It may rest upon a banking system quite different from the market-led financial systems that now dominate the globe.

- *State-led régulation* is quite effective when an economy has to catch up along a well-defined technological paradigm, and within sectors where significant indivisibility and externalities make market mechanisms relatively inefficient. Such externalities exist in health and education, for example. But this state-led *régulation* is not without major problems. The high degree of bureaucratization may impede major structural change. The centralization of decision making is unsuited to issues of product quality, product differentiation and innovation.

As long as stable political alliances within these countries have endured, and the international environment has not greatly constrained national choices, these four brands of capitalism have proved to be more complementary than competing. Each type of capitalism has succeeded in developing its own legacy of institutional resources into sources of international competitiveness (Amable et al., 1997). But the situation seems to have changed drastically during the 1990s. Japanese growth has halted and unemployment in Europe has surged. In contrast, the US economy has enjoyed sustained expansion in the 1990s. Consequently, the competitive positions of the various brands of capitalism have diverged.

In both Europe and Japan, the institutional architecture of the Golden Age has been put under strain. In Japan, institutional arrangements governing the capital–labour accord have been slow to adjust (see Boyer and Juillard, 2000). Similarly, the system of cross-shareholding between the main bank and the different firms belonging to the *keiretsu* has changed only marginally (Loulmet, 1998). The consequence of this institutional rigidity is a decline in the profit rate, preventing the recovery of investment. The present threat to social democratic *régulation* modes or state-led *régulation* is even more severe. In Europe, as a result of demographic and other changes, it has become more and more difficult to sustain extended social security systems. Many governments have been adopting vigorous financial liberalization measures, more or less ambitious social security reforms and a slimming down of labour laws that used to monitor the Fordist wage labour nexus. Market-led capitalism is emulated. By importing most of its typical economic institutions many governments hope to reduce unemployment and stimulate innovation and growth. Furthermore, international organizations such as the International Monetary Fund, the

Capitalism against capitalism under the pressure of internationalization

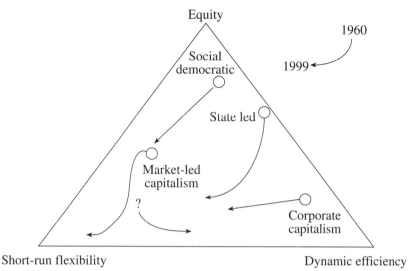

Note: This diagram assumes that the full pursuit of the three objectives is not possible or at least very difficult. The historical evidence and international comparisons do not contradict this hypothesis. A capitalism reconciling totally the three objectives is still to be invented.

Figure 7.2   A general evolution towards short-run efficiency at the cost of long-run performance and social justice?

World Trade Organization and the Organization for Economic Cooperation and Development have been quite active in advocating market liberalization and a scaling-down of public interventions.

The breakdown of the political alliances that were the keystone of world economic growth since 1945 gives the final blow to the outlived institutional architectures (Figure 7.2).

- *During the Golden Age*, the most successful capitalisms exploited a synergy between *social justice* and *dynamic efficiency*. They reduced inequality to share out the 'dividend of progress', thus diffusing mass consumption and boosting product innovation. When recessions were milder, only *limited* short-run flexibility was required. In the 1960s, many American scholars visited Europe and Asia to investigate the French, Italian, German and Japanese 'miracles'. Market capitalism was frequently perceived as inferior to the so-called 'organized capitalisms', operating in Europe and in some Asian countries.

- *During the 1990s*, the economic and intellectual scenery changed dramatically. Internationalization and the diffusion of technological and financial innovations have generated new uncertainty and quite large economic perturbations, which call for *greater* short-run flexibility. In this new context, market-led capitalisms show some superiority, since they can react faster and implement some radical innovations more easily. Structural adjustments come at the cost of 'creative destruction'. By contrast, the other three brands of capitalism experience many difficulties in coping with this new environment. Thus the economic and political elite in Europe and Japan looks towards market-led countries, especially the United States, in order to reform their ailing economies. Thus many governments promote venture capital, pension funds, a slim state, flexible labour markets, privatization and a wide opening to foreign capital. Social justice and dynamic efficiency – which used to be the trump cards for social democratic, state-led and even corporate capitalism – are now perceived as irrelevant and defining obstacles to economic performance. The requirements of short-run flexibility give a large premium to market-led capitalism.

However, while most experts and governments tend to view market mechanisms favourably, empirical evidence does not confirm such an absolute superiority (Table 7.2). On the contrary, social democratic or state-led economies seem to exhibit higher profit rates than a market-led economy such as the UK, whereas the unemployment rate is rather low in the USA and the UK but quite large in Europe. In spite of its impressive scientific and technological resources, the American economy has not yet matched the total factor productivity increases which were observed during the 1960s: other brands of capitalism are performing as well or even better. In any case, a major problem concerns inequalities. These have soared in all market-led economies. But they have increased more modestly in Japan, and even decreased in Germany – a hybrid of state-led and social democratic capitalisms. Clearly, there is no single brand of capitalism that is superior with respect to all major economic objectives.

This analysis casts some doubts upon the naive hypothesis according to which the selection of the various brands of capitalism is governed by an efficiency principle, and that the dynamism of growth is automatically promoting a reduction of social inequalities. There could well be a Gresham's law for capitalisms: the bad systems may drive out the good. Such a conclusion would differ significantly from both conventional Marxist theory and mainstream economic thought.

Table 7.2 The performances of the four capitalisms compared

	Firm's performance		Employment performance			Consumption and welfare redistribution		Social justice Ratio of the 9th to the 1st decile (men's wage)		
	Profit rate 1997 (%)	Total factor productivity increases (annual average) 1979–97	Work duration (hours per year) 1996	Activity rate 1998 (%)	Unemployment rate 1998 (%)	Private consumption increases (annual average) 1990–97 (%)	Share of public and social spending/GDP (%)	1979	1995	Average annual rate of increase (%)
Market led										
• United States	nd	0.6	1904	77.5	4.6	2.4	31.6	3.18	4.35	+2.7
• United Kingdom	10.4	1.2	1769	75.2	6.5	1.8	41.0	2.45	3.31	+2.0
Corporate										
• Japan	12.8	1.2	1993	78.1	4.3	2.0	35.2	2.59	2.77	+1.2
Social democratic										
• Sweden	12.3	1.2	1784	74.5	6.5	0.6	62.3	2.11	2.20	0.8
• Austria	14.8	1.0	nd	66.9	6.1	1.7	49.8	2.61	2.77	0.9
State led										
• Germany	14.5	0.6	1643	68.2	11.2	1.8	47.9	2.38	2.25	−1.3
• France	15.9	1.3	1763	67.3	11.8	1.1	54.2	3.39	3.43	+0.2
	(1)	(2)	(3)	(4)	(5)	(6)	(7)	(8)	(9)	(10)

Sources: Columns (1), (2), (4), (5), (7): OECD (*Economic Outlook*, December 1998) (computed from the statistical appendix); (3): Asahi Shimbun, Japan Almanach (1999, p. 107) and Freeman (1998); (6), (8), (9), (10): Freeman (1998, p. 44).

RÉGULATION THEORY: DISTINCTIVE FEATURES AMONG THE INSTITUTIONALIST RESEARCH PROGRAMME

This is one of the specific feature of this theoretical approach, which is built upon a precise set of hypotheses about the origin, the role and evolution of the institutions of capitalism (Figure 7.3).

- The first distinctive feature deals with the criteria according to which *institutions are evolving and selected*. For many economic theories, efficiency is the key criteria for assessing the emergence, viability and eventual decay of any institution. Theoreticians apply the same basic principle: competition. That which is assumed to govern the allocation of products, processes and investment, is also assumed to govern the creation and selection of organizational forms and economic institutions. By contrast, some institutional economists stress the crucial role of *collective action* in the emergence of organizational and institutional forms: the political arena is regarded as essential in shaping socioeconomic coordination mechanisms.[4] Thus *régulation* theory considers that institutional forms emerge through resolution of social conflict (for instance via collective agreement), which in turn calls for political intervention and recognition by decree, law or even constitutional change.[5] The viability of an emerging institutional architecture can only be fully assessed *ex post*, since any innovation, especially if it is overarching, usually triggers unintended outcomes. In this respect, *régulation* theory is close to the older American institutionalism, and it has some homology with some theories of law and jurisprudence.
- Major capitalist institutions do not emerge out of the aggregation of purely local and isolated compromises: they derive from systemic processes. Many crucial institutional forms, from the framework of labour contracting to the laws of trade, are organized under the aegis of the state. Whereas neoclassical economic theories have searched for micro foundations to macroeconomic regularities, *régulation* theory looks for *macro social and political foundations* to the strategies and behaviours of individual economic actors. For instance, the organizational forms adopted by firms are largely related to the general institutional context, which defines not only property rights but also forms of competition, credit and monetary regimes or the style of industrial relations. *Régulation* theory is thus close to some approaches found in political science (among the vast literature: Zysman et al., 1997; Hall, 1997), in economic history (Greif, 1997; North, 1990), and in some theories of law (Trubek et al., 1994). From a methodological standpoint, this approach belongs to a

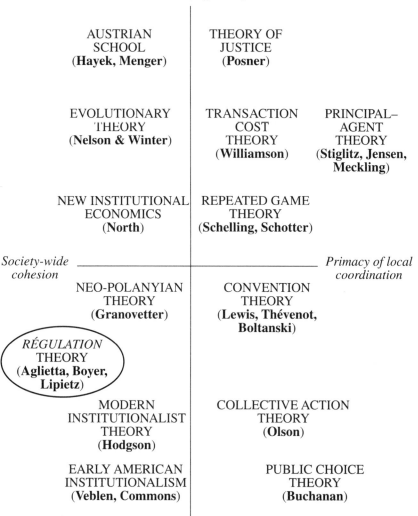

Selection by efficiency

AUSTRIAN
SCHOOL
(**Hayek, Menger**)

THEORY OF
JUSTICE
(**Posner**)

EVOLUTIONARY
THEORY
(**Nelson & Winter**)

TRANSACTION
COST
THEORY
(**Williamson**)

PRINCIPAL–
AGENT
THEORY
(**Stiglitz, Jensen,
Meckling**)

NEW INSTITUTIONAL
ECONOMICS
(**North**)

REPEATED GAME
THEORY
(**Schelling, Schotter**)

*Society-wide
cohesion* ——————————————— *Primacy of local
coordination*

NEO-POLANYIAN
THEORY
(**Granovetter**)

CONVENTION
THEORY
(**Lewis, Thévenot,
Boltanski**)

RÉGULATION
THEORY
(**Aglietta, Boyer,
Lipietz**)

MODERN
INSTITUTIONALIST
THEORY
(**Hodgson**)

COLLECTIVE ACTION
THEORY
(**Olson**)

EARLY AMERICAN
INSTITUTIONALISM
(**Veblen, Commons**)

PUBLIC CHOICE
THEORY
(**Buchanan**)

*Selection by
collective action*

Source: Freely adapted from Villeval (1995, p. 485).

Figure 7.3   How does régulation *theory relate to contemporary institutional
research?*

brand of 'hol-individualism', that is, a framework where actors behave according to what they believe is their best interests, but within institutional forms that have been constructed by past collective action. This architecture, which is inherited, cannot be challenged every day. There is a strong dichotomy between, on the one hand, playing within a given set of rules of the game, which may deliver a *stable régulation* mode, and on the other hand, redesigning new rules of a game – after a structural crisis or as a result of recurring conflicts – the aim of which is no less than *changing régulation* mode itself.

- Among a vast contemporary institutional literature, a third feature is emphasized by *régulation* theory: social contradictions, political conflicts and economic unbalances are always present and eventually manifest themselves through crises during which the acceptance and viability of past institutional compromises are challenged. We now know that even dynamic models with rational expectations may have chaotic outcomes. In *régulation* theory, actors have no real capability for forecasting and thus overcoming structural crises, since these crises basically derive from the complex interactions of individual actions operating in distinctive fields. The Fordist growth regime was initially perceived as stable. Nevertheless, the contradictions of capital accumulation have finally surfaced. Thus, it is likely that the current *régulation* modes could experience such a destabilization during the coming decades: the historical record does suggest that no growth regime lasts for ever.[6]

Thus, *régulation* theory sheds some light upon contemporary evolutions and puts forward some original hypotheses and prognoses.

EMERGING CONTRADICTIONS AND STRUCTURAL CRISES WITHIN CONTEMPORARY CAPITALISMS

Most macroeconomists praise the American authorities for having tutored a totally new growth regime, which would appear to be immune from the ills that plagued the Fordist era. Fast, stable and non-inflationary growth and near full employment can be created, it is claimed, by the adoption of information technologies, market deregulation, sophisticated financial instruments and the adhesion to the principle of globalization. *Régulation* theory casts some serious doubts on this claim.

- Financial innovations have been so diverse, strong and globally pervasive that the *financial and credit regime* has imposed its own institutional logic on firm reorganization, the redeployment of public interventions, and even the wage–labour nexus. Consequently, the speculative motive is overcoming the careful evaluation of the long-term rate of return of productive investment, whereas paradoxically, the illusion that financial markets are basically self-equilibrating has become widely accepted. Financial and currency crises in Japan (since 1992), Mexico (1994), South-East Asia (1997), Russia (1998) and Brazil (1999) have retaught a major lesson from economic history: any speculative bubble finally bursts. Part of the *régulationnist* research agenda is to examine the potential for instability in the contemporary international financial system (Aglietta, 1995, 1998).

- But the potential crises are not limited to the financial sphere, since the credit and monetary regime is having a strong influence on the redesign of the governance mode of large corporations, affecting the nature of competition and the structuring of international relations. Also the wage–labour nexus is itself affected by the dominant role of the finance motive. The search for high rates of return for financial capital is putting strong pressures upon industry concentration, and thus price formation. Simultaneously, firms try to engineer quick responses to the external environment by using more flexible hiring and firing mechanisms. They also promote a form of risk sharing, such as profit sharing, or the buying of shares in the firm by its workers. Consequently, a totally new *finance-led accumulation regime* has the potential to replace the Fordist one (Figure 7.4).

- Given these distinctive novel developments, the sources of fragility and structural crisis are also likely to be new. As noted above, in the *Fordist regime*, the strength of the institutionalization of the wage–labour nexus in conditions of near full employment eventually triggered a decline in the profit rate. Profits were structurally too low with respect to the evolution of demand. In the *new finance-led regime*, the risk is quite different. Financial institutions closely monitor the level and stability of profitability, by saving on fixed capital and controlling the wage bill. Easy credit, buoyant stock markets and higher profits sustain effective demand. Nowadays the profit rate is relatively high compared with the underlying trends in effective demand (Figure 7.5).

- *Structural crises are recurrent but do not necessarily resemble one another*. Unlike the interwar crisis, the crisis of Fordism has not been deflationary but inflationary.[7] This is the direct consequence of the institutionalization of wage formation, the shift towards oligopolistic competition, and the importance of income redistribution via the welfare and tax systems. A repetition in form of the 1929–32 major depression is very unlikely, even if there are some similarities between

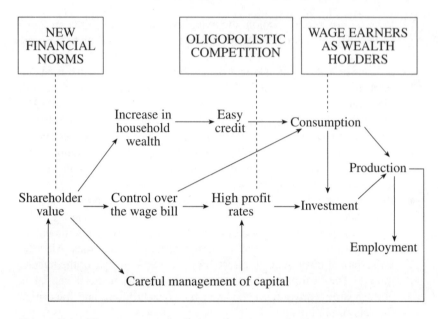

Figure 7.4   The contours of a finance-led accumulation regime

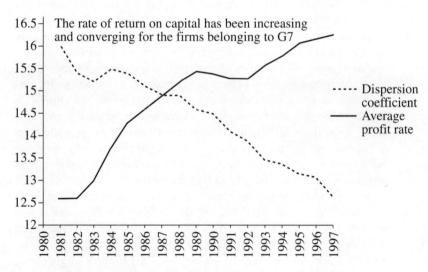

Sources: OECD (Economic Outlook, No. 61, June, 1997), UNCTAD/DTR/17, p. 96.

Figure 7.5   Profit rates in national accumulation regimes

the two episodes, such as the dominance of financial capital, unbalances in the world system, and the weakness of worker organizations. Policy responses also differ from the 1930s. For instance, during the summer of 1998, the Federal Reserve Board was aware of a systemic risk of financial collapse and acted accordingly. The whole institutional architectures are different. No capitalist economy goes twice through the same structural crisis. The understanding of the potential structural world crises is at the top of the *régulationnist* research agenda.

• Lastly, the 1990s have exacerbated tensions between the extension of markets and the democratic imperative, between economic forces and the sovereignty of the political arena. Accordingly, a new regime, which might seem viable from a purely economic standpoint, might well be blocked by a widespread political reaction. Social movements may arise against large inequalities and the erosion of national solidarity. On the other hand, the success of such movements may bring a transformation of the national institutional forms in a way that conflicts with the requirements of internationally mobile financial capital, with its strong discipline over political, economic and institutional innovations. This is why the most recent advances in regulation theory have addressed the mutual links between polity and economy in the era of globalization.[8]

In sum, major uncertainties affect the capitalisms of the new century. We find a lack of coherence between processes of capital accumulation that are operating more and more at the multinational level and political decision making in the national arena. National governments experience difficulties in building coordination and solidarity mechanisms at the relevant level, be it regional, national, continental or global. The very near future may be full of surprises, including major crises with no historical precedent. The ambition of *régulation* theory is to provide a relevant diagnosis of such episodes. Let us hope that other economists and social scientists will share this project.

NOTES

1. Among a large literature, see Aglietta (1976, 1998); Lipietz (1983); Boyer (1986); Boyer and Saillard (1995).
2. This concept was coined by Bruno Théret (1992).
3. In French, the 'Golden Age' is called 'les trente glorieuses' by contrast with the subsequent period 'les vingt douloureuses'.
4. See the special issue of *L'Année de la Régulation 1999* on the topic of state and economic policy.
5. Chartres (1995) has argued that many structural crises in the past have been resolved by the emergence of new political coalitions, promoting genuine compromises and the bases for new institutional forms.

6. This is the major finding of long-run historical research about American capitalism (Aglietta, 1998; Juillard, 1993), as well as the French one (Boyer and Mistral, 1982). The same results are true for the Japanese trajectory (Boyer and Yamada, 2000).
7. For most detail about a comparison of the 1929 and 1967–73 crises, see Boyer and Mistral (1982).
8. See the various contributions to *L'Année de la Regulation 1999* (Boyer, 1999); (Jobert, 1999); (Palombarini, 1999); (Théret, 1999); (Lordon, 1999).

REFERENCES

Aglietta, Michel (1976), *Régulation et Crises du Capitalisme*, Paris: Calmann-Lévy, 2nd edn 1982.

Aglietta, Michel (1995), *Macroéconomie financière*, Collection Repères, Paris: La Découverte.

Aglietta, Michel (1998), Commentaire sur 'Instabilité du système financier international', *Rapport du Conseil d'Analyse Economique*, no. 14, La Documentation Française, Paris, pp. 133–8.

Amable, Bruno, Rémi Barré and Robert Boyer (1997), *Les systèmes d'innovation à l'ère de la globalisation*, Paris: OST-Economica.

Baslé, Maurice, Jacques Mazier and Jean-François Vidal (1994), *Quand les crises durent ...*, 1st edn, Paris: Economica.

Boyer, Robert (1986), *La Théorie de la Régulation: Une analyse critique*, Paris: La Découverte, Agalma.

Boyer, Robert (1997), 'Les mots et les réalités', in *Mondialisation au-dela des Mythes*, Paris: La Découverte 'Les dossiers de l'Etats du Monde', pp. 13–56.

Boyer, Robert (1999), 'Le politique à l'ère de la mondialisation et de la finance: Le point sur quelques recherches régulationnistes', *L'Année de la Régulation 1999*, vol. 3, Paris: La Découverte, pp. 13–75.

Boyer, Robert and Michel Juillard (1995), 'Les Etats-Unis: adieu au fordisme!', in Boyer and Saillard (eds) (1995), pp. 378–88.

Boyer, Robert and Michel Juillard (2000), 'Japan in the 90's: a crisis of a whole "*régulation*" mode not so much the archaism of the wage–labour nexus', in Boyer and Toshio Yamada (eds) (2000).

Boyer, Robert and Jacques Mistral (1978, 1982), *Accumulation, Inflation, Crises*, Paris: Presses Universitaires de France.

Boyer, Robert and Yves Saillard (eds) (1995), *Théorie de la régulation: L'état des savoirs*, Paris: La Découverte.

Boyer, Robert and Toshio Yamada (eds) (2000), *Japanese Capitalism in Crisis*, London: Routledge. Japanese edition (1999), Tokyo: Fujiwara Shoten.

Chartres, Jacques André (1995), 'Le changement de modes de régulation. Apports et limites de la formalisation', in Boyer and Saillard (eds) (1995), pp. 273–81.

Freeman, Richard (1998), 'Le modèle économique américain à l'épreuve de la comparaison', *Actes de la Recherche en Sciences Sociales*, no. 124, September.

Greif, Avner (1997), 'Microtheory and recent developments in the study of economic institutions through economic history', in David M. Kreps and K.F. Wallis (eds) (1997), *Advances in Economics and Econometrics: Theory and Applications*, vol. 2, Cambridge: Cambridge Unversity Press, pp. 79–113.

Hirst, Paul and Grahame Thompson (1996), *Globalization in Question*, Cambridge: Polity Press-Blackwell.

Jobert, Bruno (1999), 'Des États en interactions', *L'Année de la Régulation 1999*, vol. 3, Paris: La Découverte, pp. 77–96.

Juillard, Michel (1993), *Un schéma de reproduction pour l'économie des Etats-Unis: 1948–1980*, Bern: Peter Lang.

L'Année de la Régulation 1999 (1999), vol. 3, Paris: La Découverte.

Lipietz, Alain (1983), *Le monde enchanté. De la valeur à l'envol inflationniste*, Paris: La Découverte.

Lordon, Frédéric (1999), 'Croyances économiques et pouvoir symbolique', *L'Année de la Régulation 1999*, vol. 3, Paris: La Découverte, pp. 171–211.

Loulmet, Laurence (1998), 'Le modèle des Keiretsu en question. L'invariance des principes de coordination', Université des Sciences sociales de Toulouse, January.

Marglin, Steven A. and Juliet Schor (eds) (1990), *The Golden Age of Capitalism*, Oxford: Clarendon Press.

Mishel, Lawrence, Jared Bernstein and John Schmidt (1997), *The State of Working America 1996–97*, Economic Policy Institute, Armonk, NY: ME Sharpe.

North, Douglass (1990), *Institutions, Institutional Change and Economic Performance*, Cambridge and New York: Cambridge University Press.

Organization for Economic Cooperation and Development (OECD) (1997, 1998), *Economic Outlook*, various issues, Paris: OECD.

Palombarini, Stefano (1999), 'Vers une théorie régulationniste de la politique économique', *L'Année de la Régulation 1999*, vol. 3, Paris: La Découverte, pp. 99–128.

Schor, Juliet B. (1991), *The Overworked American. The Unexpected Decline of Leisure*, New York: Basic Books.

Théret, Bruno (1992), *Régimes économiques de l'ordre politique. Esquisse d'une théorie régulationniste des limites de l'etat*, 'Economie en liberté', Paris: Presses Universitaires de France.

Théret, Bruno (1999), 'Vers une théorie régulationniste de la politique économique', *L'Année de la Régulation 1999*, vol. 3, Paris: La Découverte, pp. 129–70.

Trubek, David M., Yves Dezalay, Ruth Buchanan and John R. Davis (1994), 'Global restructuring and the law: studies of the internationalization of legal fields and the creation of transnational arenas', *Law Review*, **44** (2), Winter, Case Western Reserve University.

Villeval, Marie-Claire (1995), 'Une théorie économique des institutions?', in Boyer and Saillard (eds) (1995), pp. 479–89.

Zysman John, Eileen Doherty and Andrew Schwartz (1997), 'Tales from the "global" economy: Cross-national production networks and the reorganization of the European economy', *Structural Change and Economic Dynamics*, **8** (1), March.

PART III

Global Paths of Capitalist Development

8. Where are the advanced economies going?

Robert E. Rowthorn

INTRODUCTION

This chapter examines some of the major trends now affecting advanced economies.[1] It deals with the rise and fall of manufacturing employment, the continued importance of manufacturing production in advanced economies, emerging trade patterns and the rise of transnational corporations. Because of limited space the policy implications of these developments are considered only very briefly at the end.

ECONOMIC DEVELOPMENT AND STRUCTURAL CHANGE[2]

In the course of economic development, the structure of employment undergoes the following changes. There is initially a phase of 'industrialization' during which the share of agriculture in national employment falls rapidly, and the labour thereby released is absorbed into the service sector and into industrial activities such as manufacturing, mining and construction. As growth proceeds, the service sector continues to expand and agriculture continues to shrink. However, after its initial increase, the share of industrial employment stabilizes and then starts to fall back again. This new phase is known as 'deindustrialization'. Most advanced economies reached this turning point during the 1960s, and they have been joined more recently by East Asian countries, such as Korea and Taiwan, where the share of manufacturing has been falling quite fast during the past decade (Figure 8.1).

Explanations for the declining employment share of manufacturing in advanced economies can be classified under the following headings:

- demand;
- productivity growth;

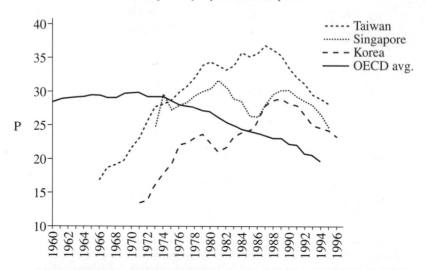

Figure 8.1　Employment share of manufacturing in selected countries

- statistical illusion; and
- the international division of labour.

Let us consider these in turn.

Demand

Early theorists of post-industrial society, such as Daniel Bell, assumed that the pattern of employment is a direct reflection of the pattern of demand. They argued that every society goes through three stages in the course of economic development: agrarian, industrial and post-industrial. In agrarian society, the bulk of the population work on the land, few manufactured goods are utilized and consumption consists largely of food. As per capita incomes rise, the demand for food stabilizes, while the demand for manufactured goods rises rapidly. To produce these goods requires a massive increase in employment in manufacturing and the industries which supply it with energy and raw materials. Thus, society enters the industrial era. However, this is only a passing phase and at very high levels of per capita income the composition of demand shifts yet again. People become satiated with manufactures, just as they did earlier with food, and their demand shifts towards services such as health, restaurants, entertainment and the like. To meet this exploding demand for services, labour must be withdrawn from manufacturing and allied industries where output is stagnating for lack of demand. Thus, according to this theory the declining employment share of manufacturing in advanced economies is due to the fact that people are satiated with manufactures and their main desire is for more services.

Casual observation should make us reject this theory in the extreme form just stated. Almost every conceivable economic activity in modern society makes use of manufactured goods. Many of the expanding service industries use large amounts of equipment and a few of them, such as air transportation and telecommunications, are highly capital intensive. The personal consumption of manufactured goods such as computers, video recorders and the like, has been rising strongly as a trip down any high street or shopping mall will confirm. Even so, there has been a shift towards services, and as Table 8.1 shows, official statistics indicate that the production of services in advanced economies is now growing faster than that of manufactured goods.

Table 8.1   Output and employment in the OECD, 1960–1990 (% growth rates)

	1960–73	1973–90
Output		
Manufacturing	6.3	2.5
Services	4.9	3.1
Difference	1.3	–0.6
Output/person employed		
Manufacturing	4.9	2.8
Services	2.6	0.8
Difference	2.3	2.0
Employment		
Manufacturing	1.4	–0.3
Services	2.4	2.3
Difference	–1.0	–2.6

Note: The table refers to the period 1960–90. Satisfactory figures for later years are not available because of boundary changes and the entry of new countries into the OECD.

Source: OECD Historical Statistics.

Table 8.2   Manufacturing employment share (%)

	Taiwan	Korea	Singapore	Hong Kong	OECD
1960	–	–	–	–	27.3
1961	–	–	–	–	27.7
1962	–	–	–	–	27.9
1963	–	–	–	–	28.0
1964	–	–	–	–	28.1
1965	–	–	–	–	28.3
1966	16.4	–	–	–	28.2
1967	18.2	–	–	–	27.9
1968	18.6	–	–	–	27.9
1969	19.2	–	–	–	28.5
1970	20.9	–	–	–	28.7
1971	22.2	13.3	–	–	28.6
1972	24.6	13.7	–	–	28.1
1973	26.6	15.9	23.7	–	28.0
1974	27.0	17.4	28.4	–	28.1
1975	27.5	18.6	26.2		27.5
1976	28.7	21.3	26.9	–	26.9
1977	29.6	21.6	27.2	–	26.8
1978	30.7	22.4	28.2	44.4	26.5
1979	32.4	22.9	28.8	43.3	26.1
1980	32.9	21.6	29.2	42.1	25.9
1981	32.4	20.4	30.4	39.0	25.2
1982	31.8	21.1	29.5	37.5	24.6
1983	32.4	22.5	27.8	36.3	24.0
1984	34.2	23.2	27.4	37.0	23.6
1985	33.7	23.4	25.4	36.1	23.3
1986	34.1	24.7	25.2	35.0	23.1
1987	35.2	27.0	26.7	34.2	22.7
1988	34.6	27.7	28.5	32.0	22.4
1989	33.9	27.8	29.0	29.7	22.3
1990	32.0	27.2	29.1	27.7	21.5
1991	30.8	26.8	28.2	26.0	21.4
1992	30.0	25.5	27.5	23.8	20.3
1993	28.4	24.2	27.0	21.3	20.0
1994	27.8	23.7	25.6	19.6	19.2
1995	27.1	23.4	24.0	18.4	–
1996	–	22.5	–	16.0	–

Sources: Employment from *ILO Yearbook of Labour Statistics* except for Taiwan, which is from *Republic of China Yearbook of Statistics*.

Productivity Growth

Table 8.2 also highlights another fact that is important for employment in the advanced economies. For some decades, labour productivity in manufacturing has grown at about 2 per cent faster a year than in the average service activity. Even allowing for possible measurement errors, this is a very large gap. From a theoretical point of view, the impact of productivity growth on the level of employment in a particular sector is ambiguous. On the one hand, it means lower costs and hence lower prices, thereby stimulating demand and leading to greater output in the sector concerned. On the other hand, higher productivity implies that less labour is required to produce any given volume of output. What happens to employment depends on which of these forces is greater. In the case of manufactured goods, empirical estimates suggest that in the advanced economies the demand-creating effects of productivity growth are much weaker than its labour-saving effects, so its net impact on employment is negative.[3] Higher productivity has reduced costs dramatically in the manufacturing sector, and the resulting fall in the relative price of manufactured goods has helped to boost an otherwise flagging demand for such goods. However, this boost has not been sufficient to maintain employment in the sector.

Statistical Illusion

In his analysis of the structure of advanced economies Blades (1987, p. 164) observes:

> It has frequently been noted that a significant part of the 'decline' of manufacturing, as measured by its falling share in total value-added or employment is due to formerly 'in-house services' – security, cleaning, recruitment and data processing for example – being contracted out to specialist service producers. The value-added of these activities, when they are provided by specialist producers, swells the recorded contribution of services to total value-added and diminishes that of manufacturing firms which previously provided these services for themselves. It is argued that their apparent decline in 'goods' output and employment, and the concomitant increase in 'services', is a statistical illusion which reflects merely greater specialisation rather than a fundamental change in the mix of output.

Following Blades's approach, I have made some rough calculations to indicate the degree to which the service sector in advanced economies is tied in with the production of material goods (see Rowthorn, 1997). Services can be divided into two main categories: 'free standing' and 'goods related'. The former are services which are useful in their own right. They include personal services such as tourism, hairdressing and the like, together with government services such as defence, health and those aspects of education which are concerned primarily with personal development. Goods-related services are those which derive their utility because of their connection with the supply and allocation of material goods. Some of these are what Blades calls 'services directly linked to goods production' (p. 164), and are mostly provided by commercial enterprises, although some are provided by the government and non-profit-making agencies. They include wholesale and retail distribution, transportation of material goods, most technical education, together with a substantial part of finance, insurance and other business services. The remaining goods-related services are concerned with the allocation and enforcement of personal property rights over material goods. Included under this heading are financial and insurance services to individuals, many legal and protective services, and public administration concerned with taxation and welfare benefits.

Table 8.3 presents some estimates of what happened between 1970 and 1990. Over this period, the share of the OECD civilian workforce who were

Table 8.3   Goods and services in OECD economies 1970–1990 (% of civil employment)

		1970	1990
1.	Goods	51	37
2.	Goods-related services	25	32
	Directly linked to goods production		
	(a) market services	17	21
	(b) non-market services	3	4
	Other goods-related services		
	(c) market services	2	3
	(d) non-market services	3	4
3.	Total goods and goods-related services	76	69
4.	Free-standing services	24	31
5.	Grand total	100	100

Notes and sources: This table is based on Blades (1987). Rows (1) and (2a) use Blades's own definitions; row (2c) consists of financial, insurance and business services purchased by households; row (2b) consists of items such as publicly financed education and training in connection with goods production and goods-related services; row (2d) consists of public activities in connection with the assignment and policing of property rights and running the goods-related economy; row (4) consists of all services not elsewhere included. Row (a) is from *OECD Labour Force Statistics*. Rows (2b) and (2d) are each assumed to account for 6 per cent of total service employment. Rows (2a) and (2c) are based on estimates by Blades for the period 1980–84; they account for 35 and 5 per cent, respectively, of total service employment.

employed in the goods-producing sectors (agriculture, mining, manufacturing, construction, electricity and gas) declined from 51 to 37 per cent. When goods-related services are included, the figures are 76 and 69 per cent, respectively. Thus, the employment increase in goods-related services did not completely offset the very large fall in the conventional goods-producing sectors. The estimates shown in Table 8.3 are very crude and the classification system is somewhat arbitrary, but nevertheless the overall picture they present must be fairly accurate. Goods production is still generating, directly and indirectly, about two-thirds of all employment in the typical advanced economy, and despite all the talk of a post-industrial era, these economies are still primarily devoted to the production, distribution and allocation of material goods. However, this picture is slowly changing as employment in free-standing services expands.

The International Division of Labour

The decline in manufacturing employment in advanced economies is often ascribed to shifts in the international division of labour. Richard Brown and De Anne Julius (1994) claim that advanced economies are abandoning the production of manufactured goods and specializing in the production of services. They argue that the advanced economies are still consuming large quantities of manufactured goods, but these are increasingly being imported from poorer countries, and to pay for them the advanced economies are providing poorer countries with sophisticated services such as banking and consultancy. They predict that manufacturing production in the advanced economies will shrink rapidly in the future, and that these economies will become specialized service producers supplying the rest of the world with services in return for manufactured goods. Thus, the shift to post-industrial society is seen as part of a wider shift in the international division of labour whereby manufacturing industry migrates to poorer countries, while rich countries specialize in services.

There is little evidence to support this claim. Imports of manufactured goods from poorer countries are certainly rising, but so are exports of manufactured goods in the opposite direction, and the advanced economies remain major producers and exporters of manufactured goods. However, this does not imply that nothing has changed in the relationship between rich and poor countries. Brown and Julius are right to argue that there has been a major shift in the international division of labour, but they are wrong about its nature. This shift is not from manufacturing to services, but *within* the manufacturing sector itself. Many labour-intensive manufacturing activities in advanced economies, such as clothing or routine assembly, have been put out of business by rising imports from developing countries with a resulting loss of employment in areas concerned. However, these manufactured imports have not been financed by the export of services, as Brown and Julius claim, but by the export of other manufactures, especially capital goods and inter-mediate products such as chemicals. The result is an emerging international division of labour in which developing countries of the South specialize in types of manufacturing which utilize their abundant supplies of cheap and less-qualified labour, while the advanced countries of the North specialize in areas of manufacturing where they have a comparative advantage because of their superior endowment of capital stock, R&D facilities and qualified labour.

Adrian Wood (1994) considers this trend to be the most important factor behind what has happened to manufacturing employment in advanced econo-mies. The migration of low value-added, labour-intensive production to poorer countries has destroyed many jobs for unqualified workers in the advanced economies. This type of production has been replaced by capital- or knowl-edge-intensive export industries, whose value-added per worker is very high and the quantity of new employment they provide is therefore quite small. Thus, a large number of jobs for unqualified labour has been replaced by a much smaller number of jobs for skilled or highly educated workers. Wood argues that this development has greatly reduced overall employment in manufacturing and seriously harmed uneducated workers in the advanced economies. It helps to explain why unemployment is so high among workers of this type and why their relative earnings have fallen in many countries in recent years.

Wood estimates that North–South trade has caused a net loss of 24 million manufacturing jobs, or 7 per cent of total employment in the advanced economies. Most economists would dispute this finding and many believe that the true figure is quite small. My own estimates suggest that the net loss of manufacturing jobs resulting from North–South trade is about 6 million or 2 per cent of total employment (see Rowthorn and Ramaswamy, 1999). This is less than one-fifth of the manufacturing jobs lost since 1970 and amounts to less than 0.1 per cent of total employment per year. Such a loss may pose serious problems for certain individuals and regions, but it is not the main factor behind either high unemployment or the marked increase in wage inequality in recent times in many advanced economies.

INTERNATIONAL TRADE

This section explores in greater depth some of the major issues raised in the preceding discussion.

Trade and Resources

The advanced economies have already undergone major structural changes arising from their trade with developing countries. Labour-intensive manufacturing industries such as clothing have been run down in the face of cheap imports, and new activities have arisen to replace them, although the social cost has been considerable and the scars still remain. This process has not yet run its course, but as labour-intensive manufacturing disappears the scope for further upheavals from this source will decline. The countries which in the near future are likely to be most affected by competition from poor countries are the newly industrialized economies of East Asia, such as Korea and Taiwan, which are now shedding their labour-intensive industries and specializing in more sophisticated products. As industrialization spreads to other countries, this story is likely to be repeated many times in the future, and we shall see industries like clothing and toy-making migrate from country to country in search of low wages – or even from region to region within the same country.

Trade Between Equals

Trade patterns reflect differences in national endowments of natural resources, capital and qualified labour. But this is not the only factor. In the modern world a great deal of trade takes place between countries with similar endowments of human and material resources, and for purely historical reasons countries may end up specializing in different kinds of economic activity. Britain, for example, has a trade surplus in chemicals and financial services, but a deficit in consumer electronics. Within the same broad industrial category, countries may specialize in the production of particular items. For example, France may produce more of one type of chemical and Germany more of another. Or they may produce differentiated versions of the same product, such as motor cars and export them to each other. They may even trade with each other in identical products, such as basic steels.

There are many reasons why such trade may develop and why it may eventually decline. Of these, economies of scale are probably the most important. In some cases, economies of scale make it profitable to concentrate production in a single country and serve foreign markets by exporting. Many so-called 'niche' products are in this category, since the global or regional market for them is quite small and does not justify the establishment of plants in several countries. The same may also be true in the early phase of development of a potential mass product. The firm which first develops such a product may initially serve foreign markets entirely through exporting. However, this may be merely a transitory phase, and as foreign sales expand, the point may eventually be reached where economies of scale make it profitable to set up production facilities abroad. Even where the innovating firm does not follow this route, exports may eventually be lost because foreign firms develop rival products of their own. Whoever is responsible for overseas production – the innovating firm or foreign rivals – its effect may be to reduce trade in the product concerned.

Intra-industry Trade and the Formation of Blocs

The modern literature on trade stresses the alleged importance and novelty of so-called 'intra-industry' trade. This occurs when countries at the same level of development exchange with each other products which are broadly similar in character – or even identical. It is often said that intra-industry trade is the characteristic form of manufacturing trade in the modern world.

This claim is misleading for a number of reasons. First, it ignores the rapid growth of North–South trade which is based on large differences in national endowments of human and physical capital, and involves the exchange of very different kinds of product. Second, it ignores the role of resource endowments in trade between countries at the same level of development. Finally, it ignores the regional dimension of trade between advanced economies. The bulk of intra-industry trade between countries occurs within Western Europe, and its recent growth is a peculiar feature of European economic integration, not a pointer to the future pattern of world trade in general.

The apparent novelty of intra-industry trade is an illusion caused by the fact that world trade statistics record trade between countries, but not between regions within the same. If the individual states of the USA or the *Länder* of Germany were reclassified as countries, we should find that intra-industry trade is not in the least new and is a normal feature of market unification. Until recent times the unification of markets has mostly taken place within national frontiers, and international trade has not been of the intra-industry variety. There was some move towards market integration in Western Europe before the First World War, but this was disrupted by conflict and the inter-war crisis, and it only resumed again in the 1960s. Since then integration has accelerated dramatically and the West European market is now approaching the same degree of unification as the internal US market.

In 1960, imports into the typical West European country accounted for about 5 per cent of total expenditure on manufactured goods. By 1990 this figure had risen to 40 per cent in the larger countries and well over 50 per cent in the smaller ones, and is still rising. Of these imports, three-quarters come from other European countries. For sophisticated products the proportion is even higher. In 1992, some 83 per cent of all chemical imports into West European countries came from other West European countries, and for machinery and transport equipment the proportion was 73 per cent. Conversely, 70 per cent of West European manufactured exports go to other West European countries, and most of the rest go to developing countries. Less than 10 per cent of manufactured exports from the average West European country go to North America and Japan combined.

Intra-industry trade is mainly an internal phenomenon *within* the large regional blocs. It is extensive within Western Europe and within North America. It is just beginning to develop between Japan and its more advanced neighbours such as South Korea and Taiwan. The extent of manufacturing trade between the large regional blocs is quite limited, and most of this is not of the intra-industry variety. Japan, for example, imports few manufactured goods of any kind from other countries. The total value of manufactured imports into Japan in 1992 was equivalent to just 2.8 per cent of GDP or about 6 per cent of total expenditure on manufactures. Of these a significant fraction came from the more advanced parts of Asia.

A striking feature of Japanese trade is its asymmetrical nature. Exports from Japan to Western Europe and the United States are much greater than imports. In the case of manufactured goods, they exceed imports from Western Europe by a ratio of 3.5 to 1, while for the USA the ratio is about 4 to 1. Despite all the publicity surrounding Japanese exports, the total amounts involved are not very large, although they can be significant in particular industries such as motor cars. In 1992, manufactured imports from Japan amounted to just 0.74 per cent of West European GDP and 1.51 per cent of American GDP.

American trade across the Atlantic is less of a one-sided affair and there is more intra-industry trade than in the case of Japan. Even so, the quantities are relatively small. In 1992, total manufactured imports from Western Europe were only 1.2 per cent of American GDP and at most 3 per cent of US expenditure on manufactures. American manufactured exports in the other direction were only 0.8 per cent of European GDP and about 2 per cent of European expenditure on manufactures. There is an interesting contrast here with Canada. On a per capita basis, manufacturing trade with the US is more than six times as large for Canada as it is for Western Europe. This indicates both the degree of integration between the US and Canada and the lack of integration between the US and Western Europe.

We may summarize this discussion as follows. Intra-industry trade is largely an intra-regional affair. It is extensive within Western Europe and between Canada and the USA. There is little intra-industry trade between Japan and other developed countries, since Japan imports few manufactures of any kind from these countries. There is some intra-industry trade across the Atlantic, but this is not very large in relation to the huge size of the economies concerned. The developed world is now mostly divided into three blocs comprising North America, Western Europe and Japan. These blocs are largely self-contained in sophisticated manufactured goods and most of their trade in these items is internal to the bloc. In the case of Japan, the country still forms a bloc in itself. Imports of sophisticated manufactures from its neighbours are rising, but they are still quite small. In 1992, Japan's total manufactured imports from the whole of Asia, including China and the Middle East, were less than 1 per cent of Japanese GDP. Of these about two-thirds were of the labour-intensive variety, and the combined figure for imported chemicals, machinery and transport equipment from Asia was 0.3 per cent of GDP. These tiny figures indicate how little integration of the European or North American type, or indeed any other type, has yet occurred between Japan and its more advanced neighbours. For all the talk of an emerging East Asian bloc, economic integration in the region is still in its infancy.

TRANSNATIONAL CORPORATIONS

It was mentioned in the preceding section how international investment can influence the pattern of trade and economic activity. This section explores the issue at greater length. We shall focus on what is called 'foreign direct investment', by which is meant the acquisition or establishment of production and allied facilities in other countries. These need not be wholly owned, but the parent company must have a substantial stake in them.

Foreign direct investment (FDI) in the manufacturing sector has a long and chequered history. There was a surge of investment abroad by German companies before the First World War, but many were forced to relinquish their assets during the war. Japanese firms invested in Manchuria and Korea but they lost most of these investments after the defeat of Japan in the Second World War. American companies invested in Europe and elsewhere during the earlier part of this century, and many of the operations they established are still around today. British companies invested quite heavily abroad, especially in the Empire, and there was also a fair amount of investment abroad by other European countries. The outward thrust of direct investment from the advanced economies was blunted during the disruption and uncertainties of the 1930s and the Second World War, but it resumed when peace was established and has been accelerating ever since.

The Dynamics of International Investment

Considerable energy has been spent in seeking to explain why firms invest overseas. However, this is a misleading way to approach the issue. By its nature, the capitalist system is dynamic and universal. Capital has an inherent tendency to expand over boundaries of all kinds, be they local or national, and the formation of transnational corporations is just an extension of the same process which originally gave rise to national corporations – or to multi-plant firms of any kind. Once we can explain why firms should establish production facilities in more than one locality, even within the same country or region, we understand the basic forces which cause them to expand overseas.

The fundamental question is not why do transnational corporations exist, but why does any kind of multi-plant firm exist? And given that multi-plant firms do exist, why was their formation confined within national boundaries for so long? Why was their outward thrust confined to exports rather than overseas production? The reason for rephrasing the question in this way is not mere sophistry, but to challenge a particular mind-set which takes the national firm as a point of reference and regards overseas investment as a departure from normality requiring special explanation. This mind-set leads to an underestimation of the forces driving firms to invest overseas and a failure to appreciate the precarious nature of exports. A better starting point would be to regard global production as the norm and then look for the special, often transitory, reasons why firms may choose to export instead of producing overseas.[4]

This was the approach which Stephen Hymer and I took in our early analysis of the dynamics of international investment (Hymer and Rowthorn, 1970). We took as our paradigm the idea that firms develop in stages from local producers to global corporations. First they serve a purely local market in some particular region of the national economy. Then they extend outwards within the same country by exporting from their local base. After a time they establish production facilities elsewhere in the same country until they eventually become an integrated national corporation. The same logic then drives them to expand overseas, at first by exporting and then ultimately by establishing overseas plants. The two decisive elements in this process are firm size and market penetration. Firms initially penetrate new markets, be they in other regions or other countries, by 'exporting' from their existing production facilities. When sufficient sales have been achieved in the new market, it becomes feasible to set up local production facilities on a scale large enough to exploit economies of scale. Thus, there is a natural cycle, whereby firms at first export to new markets and then serve them by local production once exports pass a certain threshold. Since large firms tend to have larger exports and more capital at their disposal, they will normally do most of the investing. Moreover, as poorer countries develop, both their firms and their exports increase in scale, and these firms also lose the advantage of cheap labour because their wage costs rise. As a result, some of these firms begin to invest overseas and become transnational.

Our work was a response to Servan-Schreiber's *Le Défi Americain* (1967), which articulated widespread fears concerning the scale of US direct investment in Europe at the time. We argued that this was a perfectly normal phenomenon and that it would eventually be matched by European investment in the United States. At the time European firms were growing rapidly and their exports to the United States were increasing. We predicted that once a significant foothold had been established in American markets through exporting, the larger European firms would start to invest on a large scale in the United States. Events have proved the accuracy of this prediction. In a separate work I extended the same reasoning to Japan, arguing that

> wage costs in Europe and Japan are rising rapidly, so the advantage of cheap labour is being lost. Continental and Japanese firms have established markets for many of their products by exporting. Mergers and high rates of accumulation have strengthened them to the point where many can now afford to build efficient-sized plants overseas and can finance the promotion of their products where necessary ... The overseas expansion of big European and Japanese firms will increasingly take the form of direct investment in other countries, including the United States itself. Exports will, however, continue to be important for small firms and certain products. (Rowthorn, 1971, pp. 44–5)

At the time, Japanese investment overseas was negligible, but since then it has mushroomed and the events foreseen in the above quotation have come to pass, although on a less extreme scale than I predicted.

Despite the spectacular growth in FDI in recent years, there are still few truly global companies. Most large OECD economies, and even some of the smaller ones, are still dominated by firms which produce most of their output within the national boundaries. Of the world's top 100 transnational corporations in 1996, only 41 had more than 50 per cent of their total employment abroad (Dicken, 1998, Table 6.2). Many of the latter corporations were based on very small countries such as the Netherlands or Switzerland. Only eight American, three Japanese and two German companies in the list had more than 50 per cent of their workforce abroad.

Towards the Formation of Regional Blocs?

We have already seen in the discussion of foreign trade how there is a tendency towards the formation of regional blocs among the advanced countries. There is relatively little trade between these blocs and a great deal within them. The tendency towards regionalization is also reflected in direct investment, although in rather a complex way. Within Western Europe, the process of mergers, acquisitions and greenfield investment is leading to the formation of European-wide firms, but this is a gradual process which still has a long way to go. The same process is more advanced in North America between Canada and the United States. Japan has also been investing quite heavily in some of its more advanced neighbours, but the degree of integration in the region is still quite low.

Within regional blocs, direct investment and trade are often complementary. Investment may lead to an internal division of labour within the same firm, whereby plants in different countries of a bloc collaborate in producing the same product, or else specialize to produce different goods for export to the entire bloc or beyond. *Between* regional blocs, there is less complementarity, and direct investment may lead to the replacement of trade by local production. Since the regional blocs are very large, local production facilities can be sufficiently large and complex to undertake most of the activities originally carried out at home by the parent company. The archetypal examples of this are Ford and General Motors whose European operations are largely self-contained, and the region imports very little from the American parent companies. Thus, within the regional blocs direct investment and trade are often complementary, while between such blocs they are more likely to be alternatives, so that outward investment may lead to a reduction in exports or inhibit their growth.

If these dynamics persist, we should expect the regional blocs of North America and Western Europe to consolidate still further with the large firms organizing a complex international division of labour within them. However, manufacturing trade between these blocs, which in most cases is already quite limited, may stagnate as direct investment becomes the main way of penetrating markets in the other bloc.

In the case of East Asia the picture is more complex because the region contains such a diversity of economies at different levels of development. Exports of sophisticated manufactures from East Asia will be constrained by the fact that many firms from this region will find it more profitable to serve the markets of Europe and North America by investing and producing locally. On the other hand, large-scale exports of labour-intensive products from the poorer countries of East Asia to Europe and North America are likely to continue and should even increase if the free trade commitments of the Uruguay Round are honoured. Within East Asia, regional economic ties will become closer under the combined impact of trade and investment flows. An important development here is the emergence of newly industrialized countries, such as Korea and Taiwan, as major investors in the region.

Whether similar regional dynamics emerge elsewhere in the developing world, such as in Latin America and Southern Africa, will to a large extent depend on how quickly lead economies, such as Brazil and South Africa, re-establish a robust growth dynamic.

In the literature on transnational corporations, a distinction is sometimes made between 'multi-domestic' industries in which competition in each country is essentially independent of competition in other countries, and 'global industries' in which a firm's competitive position in one country is significantly affected by its position in other countries.[5] This is a useful distinction, but it requires modification to take into account the rise of regional blocs. Within an integrated regional bloc, such as Western Europe today and North America in the future, the home market is no longer a single country, but the region as a whole, and the term 'domestic' must be reinterpreted accordingly. In the emerging world economy, a 'multi-domestic' industry will be one in which competition in each regional bloc is largely independent of competition in other regional blocs. The truly global industry will be one in which a firm's competitive position, even in huge regional blocs like North America and Western Europe, is significantly affected by its competitive position elsewhere. It is unclear how many industries will be truly global in this sense. In most industries, competition will certainly overstep purely national boundaries, but the regional dimension of such competition may often be more important than the global dimension.

SUMMARY AND OBSERVATIONS

The following remarks are partly a summary of what has been said and partly general observations.

- Manufacturing industry continues to be of central importance in advanced economies. Employment in this sector is falling, but production is increasing and, collectively, the advanced economies have an export surplus in their manufacturing trade with the rest of the world.
- A new international division of labour is emerging whereby the rich countries of the North export sophisticated manufactured goods to poorer countries of the South in return for traditional labour-intensive products. Moreover, some of the less-skilled stages of the manufacturing process, such as assembly, are being transferred to low-wage economies in the South.
- Transnational corporations are helping to shape the division of labour between North and South by integrating the latter into their global production chains as low-wage assemblers and suppliers. They are also a major force behind the emergence of regional trade blocs, especially in the North where the bulk of trade in sophisticated products occurs within three economic blocs: North America, Western Europe and East Asia. The volume of inter-bloc trade is constrained by the fact that many transnational corporations prefer to invest and produce locally in

other blocs instead of exporting from their home base. Thus, the rise of transnationals is encouraging certain types of global trade integration and discouraging others.

- Under the impact of transnational corporations, the advanced economies will coalesce into regional blocs whose trade with each other in physical products is modest. However, these various regional blocs will be closely linked through the intangible ties of finance, property, information, licensing and control.

- The existence of regional economic blocs creates the need for new forms of policy coordination, and may lead to the emergence of new regional political formations. The most extreme example is the European Union, where the dominant elites are seeking to create a federal superstate. Political integration is much less advanced in other parts of the world, where for the foreseeable future, regional policy coordination is likely to remain much looser than in Europe.

- Despite the modern growth of investment, there are few genuinely global firms. Even the largest firms typically produce the bulk of their output within the boundaries of a single country or regional bloc, and it will take many years for this situation to alter radically. And even where firms do spread their activities widely, they normally have a special relationship with some particular state which they hope will defend their global interests. For example, US firms were recently able to call on Washington to get better access to the European Union for their banana exports from Central America. A desire for muscle of this kind is a factor behind the current enthusiasm of large European firms for political integration in Europe.

- The extent to which regional blocs develop depends on what happens to the world economy as a whole. If there were a major world financial crisis, global trade might be severely fractured, and the members of existing economic blocs would be forced to rely on each other even more than at present. The political counterpart would be new forms of regional cooperation on such issues as external tariffs. These blocs would attract additional adherents seeking to avoid exclusion, while new blocs might also be formed as exposed countries banded together to defend themselves against global events. Similar developments occurred during the inter-war crisis, when regional and imperial economic ties acquired a new importance with the collapse of world trade.

- Even without such a major disruption, the trend towards regional economic integration looks set to continue, and the result is likely to be new forms of regional political cooperation. It is beyond the scope of this chapter to consider what these new forms, or their implications, might be. Suffice it to say that regional groupings may either obstruct or facilitate global cooperation, depending on how they relate to one another and what issues are at stake.

NOTES

1. This chapter draws heavily on Rowthorn (1997).
2. The issues covered in this section are discussed at length in Rowthorn and Wells (1987) and Rowthorn and Ramaswamy (1999).
3. Estimates given in Rowthorn and Ramaswamy (1999) suggest that a 1 per cent increase in relative productivity in manufacturing (as compared to services) will cause the relative output of manufactured goods to rise by approximately 0.4 per cent and relative employment in this sector to fall by 0.6 per cent. Subsequent estimates by the authors support the claim of Appelbaum and Schettkat (1999) that the demand for manufactured goods is becoming less elastic with respect to prices. This suggests that the negative impact productivity growth on manufacturing employment is now larger than in the past.
4. This is the approach taken by Dicken (1998) in the latest edition of his book on transnational corporations.
5. For an excellent discussion of this and many other related issues, see Dicken (1998).

REFERENCES

Appelbaum, E. and R. Schettkat (1999), 'Are prices unimportant? The changing structure of the industrialized economics', *Journal of Post Keynesian Economics*, **21** (3), Spring, 387–98.

Blades, D. (1987), 'Goods and services in OECD economies', *OECD Economic Studies*, 8, Spring, 159–84.

Brown, R. and De Anne Julius (1994), 'Is manufacturing still special in the world order?', in R. O'Brien (ed.), *Finance and the International Economy*, Oxford: Oxford University Press, pp. 6–20.

Dicken, P. (1998), *Global Shift*, 3rd edn, London: Paul Chapman.

Hymer, S. and R.E. Rowthorn (1970), 'Multinational corporations and international oligopoly: the non-American challenge', in C. Kindleberger (ed.), *The International Corporation*, Cambridge, MA: Harvard University Press, pp. 57–91.

Rowthorn, R.E. (1971), 'Imperialism in the 1970s – unity or rivalry?', *New Left Review*, 69, September, 31–54.

Rowthorn, R.E. (1997), 'Manufacturing in the world economy', *Economie Appliquée*, 4, 63–96.

Rowthorn, R.E. and R. Ramaswamy (1999), 'Growth, trade and de-industrialisation', *IMF Staff Papers*, **46** (4), March, 18–41, Washington, DC: IMF.

Rowthorn, R.E. and J.R. Wells (1987), *De-industrialisation and Foreign Trade*, Cambridge: Cambridge University Press.

Servan-Schreiber, J.-J. (1967), *Le Défi Americain* (The American Challenge), Paris: Editions de Noel.

Wood, A. (1994), *North–South Trade, Employment and Inequality: Changing Fortunes in a Skill-driven World*, Oxford: Oxford University Press.

9. The evolution of Japanese capitalism under global competition

Makoto Noguchi

INTRODUCTION

In the 1980s, the world marvelled at the strength of the Japanese management system. Japanese firms quickly recovered from the oil crises of the 1970s, and they adapted themselves promptly and flexibly to a rapid appreciation of the yen in the latter half of the 1980s. However, as a result of subsequent and radically altered circumstances, the structural fragility of Japanese capitalism has been revealed. Hence, in the 1990s, the reputation of the Japanese economy in the world has been reversed.

Why did the Japanese model of capitalism, at its heyday in the 1970s and 1980s, suffer from such a subsequent decline? Why did Japanese capitalism fail to cope with great changes in the global economy? Why did its international competitiveness deteriorate so dramatically? In what direction will it now evolve? These questions are important for their own sake. Clear explanations must precede adequate discussions of economic policy and institutional reform. This chapter situates the analysis of the Japanese economy in the conflictual dynamics of differentiation and homogenization, found in the institutional diversification and synchronized transformation of the capitalist world.

WHAT WAS THE SECRET OF JAPANESE STRENGTH?

The contrast between the Japanese and the US economies in the 1980s could not be more dramatic. In that decade the US economy fell into debt, accumulating huge budget and trade deficits. In contrast, the Japanese economy strengthened its position as a creditor, with cumulative export surpluses brought in by its superior competitiveness in export markets. During the first half of the 1980s, the high interest rate policy in the USA, designed to curb inflation, caused the dollar to appreciate and contributed to the Japanese export drive.

Nevertheless, the secret of Japanese strength was not the undervaluation of its currency. If this were true then the success story of Japanese firms would have ended immediately after the rapid depreciation of the dollar after 1985 – several years earlier than it actually ended. In fact, the predominant factor that reinforced the competitiveness of Japanese manufactured products on world markets was a microelectronic revolution in that industry. The widespread adoption of advanced microelectronic technology in manufacturing, combined with the Japanese management system, made it possible to achieve a considerable rise in productivity and a flexible responsiveness of production to a change or diversity in demand, especially in the machinery industry.

The strength of the Japanese production system must be discussed in the context of the dramatic reversal of the debtor–creditor relationship between Japan and the United States in the 1980s. To explore the secret of its strength, it is necessary to reveal the characteristics of the Japanese production system that were the foundation of its export competitiveness during the 1980s.

There are several principal reasons why Japanese firms established an advantage over their European and American competitors. First, key elements of the Japanese system, which had been built up during the post-war, high-growth period, played a crucial role during the 1980s in enhancing the flexibility of production in the main export sectors. These were largely assembly-type industries, such as electrical appliances, electronic products and automobiles. Furthermore, Japanese firms made the most of the fruits of innovations in microelectronics as a technological foundation of flexibility. In competing advanced industrial countries, in order to get rid of relatively sclerotic mass production systems and adjust production to more capricious and diversified global demands, most firms had little choice but to emulate the Japanese in pursuing flexibility as a base for competitiveness.

These intertwining factors largely account for the success of Japanese firms during the 1980s, but each of them is different in origin, dimension and inherent logic. To explain further why the inherited flexibility of the Japanese economic system was not sufficient to cope with the changes in the international economic environment in the 1990s, it is necessary to give careful consideration to all these factors. It also has to be asked whether in the altered circumstances of the 1990s these explanations still hold good. But first we must address the explanations of the post-war strength of the Japanese production system.

IN WHAT SENSE WAS THE JAPANESE CORPORATE SYSTEM EFFICIENT?

From the methodological standpoint of comparative institutional analysis, Masahiko Aoki has offered a persuasive explanation of the relative efficiency of Japanese corporate organizations (Aoki, 1988, 1995; Aoki and Okuno, 1996). According to his view, the Japanese economic system consists of a set of complementary institutions – within the firm, among firms, between firms and banks, and between firms and the government. These institutions are different from the Anglo-American type, which rely to a larger extent upon the efficacy of market adjustments. However, in different ways, both the Japanese and the Anglo-American systems contain mechanisms to cope with uncertain and asymmetrical information.

The question of institutional complementarities is important. If an institution that is part of the Japanese system is replaced by a Western-type counterpart, it will not immediately lead to the transformation of the Japanese system into another system, and it may detract from the efficiency of the system as a whole. Aoki argues that the key institutions that make up the Japanese system, are as follows:

1. institutionalized incentives to develop contextual skills that facilitate the sharing of knowledge among workers in a production team;
2. systems of centralized personnel administration to check and reconcile the decisions devolved to team supervisors;
3. subcontracting systems through which diverse components are efficiently supplied 'just-in-time' and through which subcontractors cooperate closely with prime contracting firms in product development or design;
4. a system of main banks that plays a part in monitoring management and bearing the risks of its affiliated companies; and
5. a state bureaucracy intervening to coordinate the diverse interests of economic agents by adopting *ad hoc* policies contingent upon the situation.

Aoki argues that an effective complementarity between these institutions enables the Japanese economic system to respond with some flexibility to changes in the economic environment.

While the conventional view of the firm presupposes that the centralized, vertical coordination exemplified within the Anglo-American firm is essential, Aoki's comparative institutional analysis seeks to show that the Japanese firm is another efficient system built on the basis of knowledge sharing at the shop floor. It is a system founded upon decentralized, horizontal coordination. This 'ideal type' represents the Japanese economic system in the high-growth period when it brought its institutional complementarity into full play.

The model, however, is not adequate to explain the outstanding perform-ance of Japanese firms during the 1980s, because this was precisely when the aforementioned institutional complementarities began to disintegrate. In the 1980s the main bank system began to exhibit severe problems. At the same time, the Japanese state bureaucracy failed to fulfil its role of absorbing the diverse interests of pressure groups. Public finances had become constrained in an attempt to deal with the legacy of the lavish spending in the 1970s. Moreover, in the latter half of the 1980s, Japanese firms achieved a global relocation of their production that caused some rifts among their domestic subcontracting relations.

Thus the improvement of Japan's international competitive advantage, and the dramatic reversal of the debtor–creditor relationship between Japan and the United States in the 1980s, happened just as the institutional comple-mentarity of the Japanese system was weakening and on the edge of collapse. This extra dimension to the historical explanation restricts the explanatory scope of Aoki's model.

But the crucial problem of Aoki's theory lies in a more fundamental methodological issue. This concerns the conceptualization of non-market behaviour. In a way, Aoki's research has similarities with those of main-stream economists who have also failed to develop adequate conceptual tools to deal with non-market phenomena. These include: quasi-markets within firms (which are different from true markets) and those inter-firm relations (such as so-called 'relational exchange') that differ substantially in character and outcome from open market trading. In contrast to mainstream approaches, Aoki at least considers how differing institutional schemes are compatible with specific, non-market relations. Nevertheless, in its understanding of the history and institutions of capitalism his theory has some problems common to new institutionalists.

A corporate system evolves in a specific direction under the pressure of structural changes resulting from the historical development of the capital-ist world. Being integrated in the world system, advanced capitalist countries come under some pressure to conform to world historical development. They emulate institutional patterns found elsewhere. Therefore, beyond the diversity that lies in the geographical location and the cultural tradition of each country, it is to be expected that institutions in the advanced countries would have some common structural features. These common institutions do not necessarily lead to an efficient allocation of resources. In contrast, the new institutionalists, including Aoki himself, consider efficiency to be an essential explanatory factor in the evolution of economic systems. Ad-mittedly, some institutions may be allocatively efficient. Others may function as stabilizing anchors for a system, or as levers of change, or as fetters to hinder progress.

To be sure, Aoki does not regard an institution as a competent resource allocator that simply takes the place of a market. He fully accepts the possibility that one institution, inferior to another in terms of allocative efficiency, may be adopted by an accident of history. In his view, institutional evolution is path dependent, in the sense that the initial conditions and subsequent path of historical evolution may prevent one institution from evolving into a superior, alternative form. Even if an existing institution is suboptimal, it can have 'self re-enforcing' qualities. Strategic complementarities can ensure that the payoffs that players may gain by following the majority are more lucrative to them than those they gain by not following them.

For example, in Japan a type of knowledge-sharing system was formed not only in the assembly-type industry, but also in some other sectors, like the chemical and information industries; although in terms of informational efficiency a more functionally differentiated system would have been more suitable. The reason why this seemingly irrational phenomenon happened is that the Japanese system was self re-enforcing, on the basis of its interlocking complementarities.

In Aoki's explanation, the existence of a specific institution is seen as the stable equilibrium of a game, resulting from individual rational calculation, even if rationality is bounded. But the role that institutions play in the world history of capitalism consists in regulating individual choices through the exertion of immanent power or authority. It is by stimulating, distorting or hindering individual behaviour that the institution exercises influence on the historical evolution of society. According to this view, and in contrast to Aoki, the institution is not simply an equilibrium formed by individual choices and behaviour, but pervasive and durable social relations that govern individual behaviour and also gradually transform themselves in response to events.

Aoki's comparative institutional analysis and theory of the Japanese system falls into the pitfall of methodological individualism that it was keen to avoid. The interpretation of the question of efficiency makes a big difference to the understanding of the Japanese system. It is unacceptable to consider the efficiency of the firm, apart from the particular social context within which it appears. For instance, whether a knowledge-sharing type of intra-firm organization is efficient or not, depends, for example, on the available technology, the pattern of industrial relations and distribution of power in society at large.

DIFFERENTIATED LABOUR AND DIFFERENTIATED DEMAND

The view that institutional differences in various advanced industrial countries led to disparities in macroeconomic performance has become more prevalent in recent years. There are strong structural grounds for this view.

In many developed economies, the engine of sustained post-war growth was the durable-goods industry. A crucial linkage in this machine was the harmonized growth of productivity and consumption.[1] In general terms, this sustained growth mechanism was found in several advanced countries and proved to be compatible with several institutional arrangements, both inside and outside the firm.

But the post-war regime of sustained accumulation collapsed after the oil crisis of 1973. Near full employment had enhanced trade union strength and made the workforce difficult to control. On top of this, the rising cost of energy forced major price and budgetary changes on the developed economies. The decline in growth itself exacerbated the problems by heightening the distributive conflict between capital and labour.

The collapse of sustained accumulation ended the fortuitous link connecting productivity growth and increasing effective demand. Faced with inflationary costs, firms changed their strategy. Instead of the virtuous circle of rising wages and rising productivity, they sought to keep down wages and to raise productivity by adopting state-of-the-art electronic and robotic technologies.

However, the decline of the mass production system that was the technological basis of the post-war regime of accumulation had an unequal impact upon the advanced industrial countries. Differences in national economic institutions, particularly differences among countries in their systems for security of employment and wage determination, seemed to account for the disparities in macroeconomic performance.

These institutional differences had emerged during or before the period of sustained growth mechanism. When each country had to adjust itself to changing circumstances, particularly the global transformation from mass production to flexible production, national institutional differences and peculiarities accounted for differing degrees of adaptability. In some countries, conventional practices admitted a flexible response to change, coping more quickly with problems and anticipating the direction of structural change. In other countries the outcome was different. They responded less flexibly, less quickly and less alertly because of their less-adaptable institutions.

In many countries after the mid-1970s there was a slowdown in productivity growth. Even when a rise in labour productivity did occur, it was typically unaccompanied by a stable growth in output or employment. Thus firms could not rely on extending their markets by mass production and mass merchandising. Instead, to gain a competitive advantage, the segmentation and differentiation of limited markets became crucial. Firms were forced to respond more flexibly to varied and capricious buyer demands, rather than simply to sell more and seek economies of scale.

This change in the relationship between productivity growth and demand formation corresponded closely to a change in the structure of income distribution. This, in turn, reflected a change in labour relations. During the second half of the 1970s, advanced industrial countries were inflicted with what was known as stagflation. The distributive adjustment between labour productivity and wages, or between wages and profits, lost its elasticity, and the pressure of an impending wage–price spiral restricted the freedom of discretionary economic policies within extremely narrow limits. In the meantime, at the firm and industry levels the efforts towards restructuring were continued in order that the corporate system might recover its elasticity in distributive adjustment and regain its profitability. Many firms introduced new developments in microelectronic technology into the labour process, and replaced regular workers with part-timers or temporary workers. This tendency grew further during the 1980s when inflation was drastically reduced, so that macroeconomic conditions further assisted the elasticity of real wages relative to productivity. The introduction of new production techniques, accelerated by the progress of information technology, not only resulted in the further segmentation of workers into the regular and the temporary. It also contributed to the polarization of workers into the skilled and the unskilled, by replacing a traditional type of skilled or semi-skilled work with simple work on the one hand and producing a new type of skill on the other which demanded higher, specialized education. Furthermore, a hysteresis effect hindered mobility in the labour market, fixing the distinction between the employed and the unemployed. A greater disparity of earnings arose between those who rode on a wave of development in the new industries and those who failed to do so. In this way, the economic conditions of workers were differentiated, multi-stratified and polarized.

The shift from mass production to multi-product, small-batch production became the trend in the 1980s. A remarkable change occurred in the demand conditions that governed the behaviour of individual firms. The differentiation of the economic conditions of workers was reflected in the multi-stratification of income structure, which transformed market structure from mass markets for standard products into subdivided markets for differentiated products. In short, the differentiation of demand corresponded to the differentiation of labour. Furthermore, demand was volatile as well as various, for differentiated demand in itself underwent incessant variation or fluctuation under the influence of structural changes in the whole industry.

No attempt to explain the strength of the Japanese production system is worthwhile without consideration of the global and historical background. In the 1980s, when the macroeconomic relationship linking a rise in productivity to an increase of quantity demanded was weakened, a firm's chances of competitive advantage rested on its ability to respond flexibly to the varied and capricious demands of multi-stratified households. The flexibility of labour management that was specific to the Japanese system was fitted for these historical conditions.

HALFWAY BETWEEN MASS PRODUCTION AND MULTI-PRODUCT PRODUCTION

Why did the new, differentiated structure of demand favour the Japanese production system? As noted above, Aoki's comparative institutional analysis sees the flexibility of the Japanese system as resulting from its capacity to share knowledge, between labour and management and among firms. This enhances its responsiveness to change. However, adaptability should not be evaluated simply in terms of informational efficiency. Structural changes require that the role of power or control exercised to cope with dilemmas or conflicts should be appreciated properly. Power is especially significant in changing circumstances – less so in equilibrium where opposing forces cancel each other.

Futurologists such as Alvin Toffler (1990) spread optimistic views on the information society and the effects of the microelectronic revolution. Many people believed that computerization would lead to production-to-order and as a result consumers would be able to get their favourite goods manufactured in a short time according to designated specifications. But the adoption of flexible production techniques such as flexible manufacturing system (FMS) could not ensure such outcomes in an efficient manner. Flexible manufacturing technology did not itself evolve as a means of automatically controlling diversified production in response to varied demand. Instead, firms were caught in the dilemma of diversifying their products at the cost of efficiency or making an effort to produce large batches of more standardized products at the cost of flexibility.

The production system that resulted from this trade-off between flexibility and efficiency can be described neither as mass production nor as multi-product, small-batch production. I would call it semi-rigid, medium-batch production.[2] The Japanese corporate system was capable of tackling the dilemma. Other advanced capitalist countries shared the problem but the Japanese system had a uniquely flexible response.

In the Japanese production system, a worker's job is not clearly specialized. A worker can be involved in various tasks as a member of a particular team that is responsible for the coordination of different operations. This characteristic relates closely to the flexibility of the Japanese corporate system. Facilitated by the flexible mobilization of workers within the team, Japanese firms eagerly introduced flexible manufacturing technology into the labour process.[3] The adoption of flexible manufacturing technology is inevitably accompanied by changes in the type and structure of jobs. In a production system where the demarcation between jobs is more vague and workers' skills are made more malleable through job rotation, the reorganization of job structure tends to bring about less friction or conflict. That was certainly true of the Japanese system.

According to Aoki's insight, unless semi-independent coordination at the shop floor can be complemented by centralized personnel administration, the Japanese type of corporate system does not work effectively. But a relationship between the one and the other should not be interpreted in the sense of a static duality. When firms have to alter the existing job classification in order to adapt to technological change or market diversification, they find that it involves a shift in the power relationships among stakeholders. In the Japanese production system, where jobs are not finely divided, management can wield centralized power to mobilize labour in a firm-wide manner, without being entangled in stubborn conflicts over alterations in job demarcation, even if a change in job structure necessitates personnel rearrangement beyond the range of coordination of a work team. Ordinary coordination rests mainly on semi-independent judgement or decisions at the shop-floor level, whereas organizational adjustment to structural change is enforced through management's intensified control over personnel administration. Such a quick conversion from more decentralized coordination to more centralized control of intra-firm labour utilization characterized the flexible responsiveness of the Japanese system to changes in technology and market conditions.

This peculiarity of the Japanese management system helped deal with the dilemmas of semi-rigid, medium-batch production. Yet it was a system in which Japanese firms got deeply trapped, as a result of the introduction of flexible manufacturing technology into the labour process.

The trade-off between flexibility and efficiency in flexible production has the following sources. On the one hand, mechanical and over-automated responses to diversified demand run into technological difficulties. On the other hand, there are high costs of coordination for a production system involving frequent changes in its multiple production processes. Because flexible-manufacturing technology left some key operations unautomated, the adjustments in flexible production fell to labour management. Malleable labour rather than specialized labour (or job integration rather than job demarcation) counted heavily for firms that had to make a changeover from one production to another quite frequently. This flexible mobilization of labour at low cost enabled Japanese firms to make up for a lack of technological flexibility and cut down costs of coordination for diversification. These conditions gave some competitive advantage to the Japanese production system.

What is more important, the sharing of knowledge within the team brought greater individual identification with the organization. In Aoki's research, this aspect of the Japanese type of labour mobilization does not receive due consideration. The experience of collective involvement in the labour process, through job rotation, instilled in the minds of Japanese workers the idea that all were jointly responsible for their work. This created a powerful combination of labour initiative and capital control. This helped firms to relocate and retrain their workers, or even extract intensified and overtime labour from them. As an outcome of their own collective involvement, workers tended to accept labour mobilization under centralized control.[4] This involvement in the labour process can be reinterpreted in terms of 'loyalty'. When firms cannot control workers either through mechanization or by means of incentive wages, they can resort to engendering loyalty in their employees (see Akerlof, 1982, p. 60). During the 1980s there were historical conditions under which Japanese firms could gain workers' loyalty. The closed system of intra-firm labour mobilization encouraged Japanese workers in their loyalty, while the dilemma of semi-rigid medium-batch production spurred Japanese firms to enhance it.

In contrast, the Anglo-American type of corporate system is less suited to the mobilization of labour in such a manner. In such a system, specialized workers are given a more rigid job demarcation, and information on the coordination of the production system tends to be concentrated in top management, without being shared with workers. During the 1980s, American firms were also faced with the necessity of organizational adjustment, in response to a growing tendency towards diversification in technology and market conditions. American firms responded chiefly by mobilizing fixed capital through the markets for corporate control. Mergers, take-overs and buyouts played a key part in the Anglo-American style of adjustment. But this way of restructuring a corporate system was not necessarily effective in handling the dilemma of flexible production.

Such a difference between the Japanese and Anglo-American systems of corporate control led to a disparity in performance in the 1980s. The disparity arose under the historical conditions that obliged firms to adjust from rigid mass to flexible production.

NETWORK-TYPE PRODUCTION AND THE FUTURE OF THE JAPANESE SYSTEM

In the 1990s, the macroeconomic performance of Japanese capitalism suddenly deteriorated. The 'bubble' boom collapsed at the beginning of the 1990s, bringing about numerous bad or doubtful debts. This was a contributory cause.[5] But, more importantly, systems of globally networked production had emerged, rivalling the practices of semi-rigid, medium-batch production. This development jeopardized the former comparative advantages enjoyed by the Japanese production system.

Typical of the difficulties that confronted Japanese firms in the 1990s were cost disadvantages suffered by personal computer manufacturers. NEC, the biggest manufacturer in the Japanese computer industry, had long held a monopolistic position in the domestic personal computer market. In the 1990s, facing keen competition from abroad, it lost a considerable share of its domestic market. Most personal computers built by Japanese manufacturers for domestic needs had specific hardware features that did not conform to de facto worldwide standards. Computer and network technologies made rapid progress. While the market for other durable goods had almost been saturated in advanced industrial countries, personal computers and other related electronic products showed great promise as the new mass-produced consumer durables of the future. In this growing market, IBM and compatible personal computers became the standard, threatening to drive the Japanese differentiated model out of the market by force of lower prices and wider software and hardware compatibility. Standardization (based on modularization of components) and mass production of computers enabled manufacturers to greatly reduce costs of production. Accordingly, price competition from foreign manufacturers became so fierce that domestic computer markets could not be protected against compatible computers by product differentiation. The sharp decline in NEC's market share signalled a new emerging pattern of competition. Firms competed in cost terms. Falling prices decisively undermined the foundation of Japanese flexible production system because it became more difficult for firms to compensate for their inefficiency in flexible production with high value added to differentiated products.

The diffusion of compatible computers revived the mass production of standardized products, although to a limited extent. But it was not a mere re-emergence of what was before. Today's mass producers disperse their production sites around the world to the most profitable locations, and integrate them efficiently into a network. Their choice of production sites is fluid. As soon as a local economic environment deteriorates and threatens profitability, investments are withdrawn and relocated. In addition, a firm's competitiveness on world markets depends also upon its ability to win a de facto standard. Once a firm wins a de facto standard, it becomes a mass producer overnight. This type of mass production is now prevalent in the computer industry.

The new type of mass production system is based on the intensive use of global networks. The rapid technological progress in the manufacture and use of computers has itself opened and enhanced such networks. As a result, a cumulative relationship is established between an increase in availability of the network on the one hand, and a rise in demand for personal computers and related products on the other. Not only in the manufacturing sector but also in distribution, finance and consumer life, intensive utilization of the network has helped to induce innovation. New commodities associated with the use of computer networks have been developed. In turn, increased consumption of these new products or services supplied by the information industry has enhanced availability of the network, and, in consequence, other new opportunities for innovation have opened up.

Nevertheless, the emerging cumulative relationship faces a market limit set by the inequitable distribution of the increasing returns from technical progress. The new mass production faces the barrier of widening income inequality. During the 1990s, the globalization of capital has brought unskilled workers into bitter competition with low-wage workers in developing countries, and has strengthened the 1980s' tendency towards the polarization between differentiated classes of labour. Today innovative firms, represented by Intel or Microsoft, often win 'runaway victories' in competition for new markets, and keep the lion's share of increasing returns. The new dynamics of increasing returns have a strong bias towards concentrating wealth in the hands of a few. They have not yet established a firm base for steady demand formation essential to the ongoing cumulative relationship.

It makes a big difference to the Japanese system as to how it adjusts to globally networked production. As noted above, the Japanese system showed its flexibility mainly in intra-firm labour mobilization, which was essential for semi-rigid, medium-batch production prevalent in the assembly-type industry. The multi-skilled flexibility of the Japanese worker presupposes centralized control of labour mobilization. Centralized control of labour mobilization is more effective within a corporate system whose boundary is fixed, than in integrating labour through the market in an open corporate framework where the boundary of the firm is much more mobile. This feature of Japanese corporate organization is not fitted for a globally networked production system.

Today, transnational corporations have a physical presence in many countries, but their investment in the local economy (and any withdrawal from it) is very sensitive to business conditions. Often they may even lack their own factory. Acting as a sort of merchant capitalist, they organize and reorganize a global network of enterprises flexibly in response to the changing worldwide demands. In such a case, the decentralized utilization of labour through external labour markets offers quick access to productive factors scattered throughout the world. It is difficult for a Japanese firm to transform itself into such a global network without reorganizing its closed labour mobilization system into an outwardly-open labour utilization system.

It is often remarked that the Anglo-American production system, with its decentralized system of labour utilization, is regaining its vigour by using advances in information and communications technology. This impression is, to some extent, founded upon recent developments in industry. In advanced industrial countries the centre of development in industry is shifting from conventional consumer durable goods to computers and other related electronic products. These growing sectors have revealed a dynamic of increasing returns, due to greater availability of the network opened up by new technological progress.

However, predictions that these developments will lead all diverse economic systems to converge into one Anglo-American type, vastly oversimplify matters. Conventional durable goods, in which the Japanese system can still display its strength, have become promising commodities for growing markets in developing countries. In some industrial sectors of the modern world economy, advanced industrial countries are no longer the powerhouses of manufacturing. Huge foreign direct investment has accelerated the industrialization of Asia. Some countries have rapidly joined the second tier (Malaysia, Indonesia and Thailand), behind the successful first-tier Asian industrial economies. Protected for a long time against foreign competition, and still groping for an alternative way to industrialization, the Chinese economy has opened its potential mass market to the capitalist world and forced the pace of economic development. Although financial fragility (due to speculative investment) since 1997 has cast a cloud over the Asian market, in the near future these countries promise to achieve a consumption revolution similar to the one experienced in the advanced industrial countries. These circumstances afford Japanese firms a good chance of finding their way into conventional durable-goods markets in Asia.[6]

In these markets, Japanese firms must compete with the newly industrialized Asian economies. What matters in this competition is the ability to transplant a system of centralized labour mobilization into the local economies. Herein lie some looming problems. In low-wage countries, it is difficult for Japanese firms to procure the multi-skilled labour requisite for intra-firm labour mobilization because training for multi-skilling is costly and takes much time. The use of low-wage labour in developing countries is difficult to reconcile with the transfer of a Japanese-style production system (technology transfer). If instead Japanese firms export finished products that are manufactured by Japanese high-wage workers, from production of components to their assembly, it impairs the international competitiveness of Japanese firms.

Japanese firms are inclined to adopt an eclectic response to this dilemma. On the one hand, they relocate only low-technology sectors abroad which depend mainly upon low-wage workers for unskilled labour, and on the other they keep high-technology sectors at home in which high wages are expected to have a stimulating effect on a worker's effort.[7] Also, deindustrialization in the home country, which results from production transfer abroad, presents a problem of how to coordinate two separate organizations that have differentiated functionally into a manufacturing division abroad and a non-manufacturing administrative (or research and development) division at home. This problem obliges Japanese firms to modify their organizations, from intra-firm knowledge sharing to a functionally differentiated type of knowledge utilization. It is also closely connected with a macroeconomic problem of how to enhance efficiency in domestic tertiary sectors.

What happens if local subcontractors emerge in the second-tier Asian economies, or in China? Given different cultural backgrounds, the Japanese parent contractor may face the difficulty of sharing skill and knowledge with the local subcontractor. Since the subcontracting relationship is the main vehicle to extend centralized control of labour mobilization through inter-corporate relations, this cultural friction restricts Japanese firms from introducing the full Japanese model of production into the local economy. It goes without saying that similar frictions can arise also between management and labour, and inside the Japanese-based local parent company itself. The modern globalization of capital demonstrates that a production system is not a mere physical combination of mechanical components, but also an institutional combination of cultural elements.

CONCLUSION

In what direction a capitalist economic system evolves depends largely upon three conditions: first, the pattern and character of technological development in commodity production; second, the social relations regulating capitalist enterprise; and, third, the dynamic relationship between production of and demand for commodities. In this context, where is Japanese capitalism heading?

During the period of sustained growth, the cumulative relationship that linked productivity growth to demand formation through reasonable income distribution was firmly established. Mass consumption kept pace with mass production. The large-scale production of standardized durable goods brought about dynamic, rather than static, increasing returns, which formed the foundation of the long post-war boom. In the 1980s, by contrast, the quasi-cumulative relationship between a diversification of production and a growth in demand for diverse high-value-added products masked the trade-off between flexibility and efficiency inherent in semi-rigid, medium-batch production.

Examining these distinct patterns of development, it is clear that there is no fixed pattern in the macrodynamics of Japanese capitalism. The near future will not change this. Manufacturing firms in advanced industrial countries, including Japanese firms, have relocated their productive capital over their borders, particularly to low-wage countries. Many transnational corporations are competing to achieve cost competitiveness by integrating, using computer networks, their globally located production sites. This global competition has brought the Japanese system under great pressure to transform itself, from home and abroad. Some Japanese firms, under the pressure of price competition, have groped for an effective way to transform their domestic closed system into a globally networked system. On the other hand, a transfer of production from Japan to abroad, involves firms attempting to transplant a Japanese-style system into a local economy. Such an attempt poses to Japanese firms a problem of institutional or cultural friction with a different business climate.

A solution is required. Japanese firms with large investments in developing countries face the challenge of harmonizing heterogeneous institutions, so as to ensure compatibility with stable development both at home and in the local economies. There are two possible directions in which the Japanese firm can evolve. One is towards a globally networked system. The other involves a harmonized compound of heterogeneous organizations. Neither option is yet within sight. What can be concluded is that the Japanese system, even if it meets the challenges, will take a long time to evolve into a new system and to establish another dynamic pattern of growth.

NOTES

1. A Marxian explanation of post-war growth in terms of 'anticipated production of relative surplus-value' (Noguchi, 1990, pp. 90–94) is much the same as what French *régulationnists* call the Fordist regime of accumulation. The idea of a sustained accumulation mechanism also derives inspiration from the economic theories of Nicholas Kaldor, and the additional influences of Antonio Gramsci and Michel Aglietta. It could also be described as a Kaldorian regime.
2. For the concept of a trade-off between flexibility and efficiency, see Ayres and Miller (1981). Noguchi (1996, pp. 79–87) reformulates this engineering concept into a socioeconomic one. Upon it he founds a new concept of 'semi-rigid medium-batch production'. This denotes a production system that embodies the dilemma of whether to diversify at the cost of efficiency, or to mass produce with much loss of flexibility.
3. The term 'mobilization' has two senses. One is to make mobile, and the other is to organize

towards a specific use. The Japanese system is orientated towards mobilization of labour; on the other hand, as discussed later, the American system leans towards mobilization of fixed capital.

4. This issue concerning Japanese workers' loyalty to the company they work for is associated with a theme Burawoy (1979) discusses. In the capitalist labour process, 'an element of spontaneous content combines with coercion to shape productive activities'; and institutions that 'mystify the productive status of workers' grow from this combination (pp. xii, 25). Suzuki (1994) also addresses a similar issue.

5. Noguchi (1998, ch. 5) includes summarized explanations on the domestic growth mechanism which led to the 'bubble' boom and its collapse.

6. There is a long-term problem whether limits on natural resources allow worldwide economic development to persist indefinitely. This chapter puts aside this long-term problem, and focuses on capital accumulation in the near future.

7. The disparity in the technological levels of firms has considerable influence on their choice between low-wage labour and high-wage labour. High-technology firms have great potential for damage due to shirking, and therefore show a strong tendency to employ high-wage labour (Ramaswamy and Rowthorn, 1991).

REFERENCES

Akerlof, G.A. (1983), 'Loyalty filters', *American Economic Review*, **73**, March, 54–63.

Aoki, M. (1988), *Information, Incentives and Bargaining in the Japanese Economy*, Cambridge: Cambridge University Press.

Aoki, M. (1995), *Keizai System no Sinka to Tayōsei* (Evolution of economic systems and their plurality), Tokyo: Tōyō Keizai Shinpō-sha.

Aoki, M. and M. Okuno (1996), *Keizai System no Hikaku Seido Bunseki* (Comparative institutional analysis: a new approach to economic systems), Tokyo: Tokyodaigaku Shuppan-kai.

Ayres, R.U. and S. Miller (1981), 'Robotics, CAM and industrial productivity', *National Productivity Review*, **1**, 42–60.

Burawoy, M. (1979), *Manufacturing Consent*, Chicago: University of Chicago Press.

Noguchi, M. (1990), *Gendai Shihonshugi to Yūkōjyuyō no Riron* (Modern capitalism and theories of effective demand), Tokyo: Shakai Hyōron-sha.

Noguchi, M. (1996), 'Jyōhō-ka to Keizai Shakai no Dōtai' (Diffusion of information technology and the dynamics of contemporary capitalist societies), in M. Itoh and Y. Okamoto (eds), *Jyohou Kakumei to Shijyoukeizai System* (Information revolution and market economic systems), Tokyo: Fujitsu Books, pp. 61–97.

Noguchi, M. (1998), 'Global competition and the Japanese model of capitalism', *Journal of the Faculty of International Studies*, Bunkyo University, **8**, 175–97.

Ramaswamy, R. and R.E. Rowthorn (1991), 'Efficiency wages and wage dispersion', *Economica*, **58**, 501–14.

Suzuki, R. (1994), *Nihon-teki Seisan System to Kigyō Shakai* (The Japanese production system and corporate society), Sapporo: Hokkaidōdaigaku Tosho Kankō-kai.

Toffler, Alvin (1990), *Powershift: Knowledge, Wealth and Violence at the Edge of the 21st Century*, New York: Bantam Books.

10. From bureaucratic capitalism to transnational capitalism: an intermediate theory

Nobuharu Yokokawa*

INTRODUCTION

In *Capital*, Karl Marx described the maxim of the capitalist as: 'Accumulate, accumulate! That is Moses and the prophets!' (1976, p. 742). This is no less true today, as it was in the nineteenth century. Only those firms that successfully accumulate capital can survive in the competitive process. In the twentieth century, the accumulation of capital became not only the private goal of capitalists but also the public goal of nations. Nations competed among each other for higher international economic and political status. The development of universal suffrage made full employment and the improvement of living conditions a political obligation. Furthermore, the existence of a rival mode of production in the form of a centrally planned socialist economy also helped to make the more rapid growth of each economy a national objective. The nation states came to resemble large corporations seeking ever-faster growth for their survival.

Marx called the compelling and self-regulating nature of capital accumulation 'the law of value'. The sections that follow illustrate the importance of an intermediate type of theory, between abstract theory and concrete analysis, to examine the law of value in various historical capitalist world systems. The law of value is examined in bureaucratic capitalism, which was established in the mid-twentieth century. The possible formation of a transnational capitalism since the 1990s is also discussed.

THE LAW OF VALUE AND INTERMEDIATE THEORY

As Marx explained, the existence of labour power as a commodity is the precondition for the capitalist mode of production, and the re-commodification of labour power is the prerequisite for capitalist social reproduction. The law of value is expressed in the competition between capitals for the highest rate of profit. It equalizes the rates of profit by adjusting the supply of and demand for commodities. The market mechanism may work well for commodities themselves produced under capitalist conditions, but the law cannot be applied directly to commodities, such as labour power, that are not themselves produced under capitalist conditions. Under capitalism, labour power is produced in the family and this institution is not essentially profit seeking. In some circumstances, there can be shortages or surpluses of labour power. Non-capitalist commodities require different mechanisms. Marx explained that capital accumulation regulated the wage rate and the demand for and supply of labour power through cyclical crises. Thus the law of value integrates the coordinating mechanisms in commodity, labour and financial markets, and describes the self-regulating nature of the capitalist economy.

Marx developed his analysis on the basis of his experience of mid-nineteenth-century British capitalism. The study of British industrial capitalism helped Marx to formulate a general theory of capitalism, but on the other hand it induced him to believe that all capitalist economies would follow the pattern of British capitalist development.

At the end of the nineteenth century, the new developments in the German and US economies transformed the capitalist economy into a new form. These developments led to doctrinal controversies, such as Eduard Bernstein's (1917) critique of Marx's long-run theory of capital accumulation. Marx's followers attempted to build a new theoretical framework, which included Rudolf Hilferding's *Finance Capital* (1980) and Vladimir Illych Lenin's *Imperialism* (1996). These works investigated new historical phenomena such as the monopoly system, the new relationship between banks and industry, modified business cycles, and new roles for economic policies. As a theoretical foundation for analysis of these new phenomena, both Lenin and Hilferding chose the more general notion of the materialist conception of history rather than the detailed economic theory set out in *Capital*. They developed intermediate-level theories between general theory and concrete historical analysis, examining the specific mechanism of capital accumulation at a particular stage of development of the capitalist world system.

The further development of the capitalist economy generated even more problems for Marx's one-level analysis. For example, when Marx's theory was applied to the industrialization of Japan in the 1930s, it was very difficult to determine whether the Japanese economy was a capitalist one or a pre-capitalist one, since it displayed many differences from the pure capitalist economy. In this controversy, Kozo Uno (1980) proposed a three-level analysis of the capitalist economy to solve these dilemmas between theory and history. The first level comprised the basic principles. The next level developed a 'stages theory of world capitalist development' which involved the concrete examination of the historical development of the leading industries, together with their main policies. At the third level of research, individual capitalist economies in their concrete historical situation were analysed. Although Uno's three-level analysis has theoretical and historical limitations, it is still a good starting point for development of multilayered analysis of the capitalist economy.

The basic theory describes the self-regulating character of capital accumulation, or the law of value, as if it continues for ever. Abstraction from particular historical developments gives logical clarity to the basic theory common to all capitalist economies. The law of value works at all stages of development of the capitalist economy with supporting social institutions. In a transitional period, when the social institutions that supported capital accumulation in the previous era have been destroyed and new social institutions have yet to be established, capital accumulation is fragile and never allows for full employment. Therefore the law of value is partially restrained in a transition period.

The intermediate theory explains the historical development of the capitalist world system by analysing systemic impurities and openness together with other historical determinants. The reproduction of labour power or of the family, of non-capitalist firms, and of states are the most important systemic impurities. Labour power is an important source of variation in the system. There are many ways to commodify labour power in the circulation process and many ways of subsuming labour power in the capitalist labour process. These differences can determine the specific character of each stage of the capitalist economy. Openness is another feature that should be considered when investigating the capitalist economy in more concrete terms. International financial systems and international trade structures are the two most important topics in the discussion of openness. The capital accumulation mechanism, combining coordination mechanism in commodity, labour and financial markets, shows the more concrete law of value for each stage of the capitalist world system.

In this chapter I build the most basic part of the intermediate theory in bureaucratic capitalism, paying special attention to the international financial system; however, it does not do away with the concrete analysis of the capitalist economy. There are marked common features among contemporary economies, since catching up is achieved within the shared framework of a capitalist world system. This is why an intermediate theory is necessary. However, the catching-up process does not induce all economies to converge on the same type, since all the evolutionary forms of capitalist economy contain specific core, semi-periphery and periphery relations. Moreover, path dependence of capitalist evolution makes each economy unique. These emergent characteristics require a third-level, concrete analysis.

THE INTERNATIONAL FINANCIAL SYSTEM

Historically, there were two periods when the law of value functioned fully: mid-nineteenth-century Britain and the Golden Age after the Second World War. The former, which I call market capitalism, is characterized by private ownership, entrepreneurial control, free competition, small non-interventionist states, and the gold standard system. The latter, which I call bureaucratic capitalism, since both firms and governments were well structured by bureaucratic systems (Chandler, 1988, p. 49), was characterized by joint-stock companies, managerial controls, oligopolistic competition, interventionist states and the Bretton Woods system. Marx's law of value shows the accumulation mechanism of market capitalism. The accumulation structure in bureaucratic capitalism is different from that in market capitalism. Nevertheless, demand for and supply of labour power was regulated automatically through the accumulation of capital in the Golden Age. In those periods, all the essential financial arrangements for a stable international system were present. In the transitional periods, the international institutions that supported capital accumulation had disappeared and new international institutions had yet to be established. As a result, the accumulation of capital was fragile and the law of value was restrained.

Following Mica Panic (1988), it is possible to distinguish between: (a) structural surplus economies, which are most dynamic and their current balances show a surplus even at full employment; (b) structural deficit economies, including developing economies and declining economies, where their current balances show a deficit at full employment; and (c) subsistence economies where economies lag behind the development of the capitalist world system, and current balances show either a surplus or a deficit. In order to keep the international economy stable and to ensure the rapid accumulation of capital, money capital must be transferred from structural surplus economies to structural deficit ones: only then will the self-regulating mechanism of capitalist economy work. We may examine the history of the international financial system in terms of efficiency in settling the balance of payments, using the following three criteria. What institution coordinates the system? What assets are chosen as the international means of payments? What are the rules for the creation of assets, a monetary system or a credit system? We also examine the efficiency of the capital flow in the system.

International financial systems can be broadly classified as either monetary systems or credit systems. In a monetary system the original purpose of economic transactions was the accumulation of gold, in mercantilist mode. Marx applied the concept of a monetary system to cases where gold payment is accepted as the only means to settle debt. Even in an early stage of capitalist development, rapid economic growth was not possible within a system based on commodity money such as gold, whose supply was restricted and could not be controlled easily. This induced the development of the credit system. In a credit system, instead of gold, credit money such as bills of exchange and banknotes circulate as means of payment in the network of credit transactions. In domestic trade, the credit system is developed and completed when central banknotes eventually replace local banknotes with the development of the national economy, acquiring the nature of fiat money under national laws. Similar developments of credit money can be observed in international trade. For example, merchants of the dominant economy usually granted credit to capitalists in other economies. The bills of exchange of the dominant economy were endorsed by the bankers of that economy and circulated in international trade as means of payment. Those bills of exchange were backed by the central bank notes of the economy. In the case of international trade the credit system may not be completed, since the central bank notes may not be reinforced by international law, and the final settlement of debts requires gold as the world money. The more international debts are settled by credit money, the more the international financial system acquires the character of a credit system. The more the international financial system requires gold, the more it acquires the character of a monetary system.

The Gold Standard System

In the 1870–1914 period, interdependence among capitalist economies increased with the expansion of industrialization in the world, and with the expansion of specialization to take advantage of scale of economy. British capital shifted investment from industry to the monetary sector, and its financial sector played a dominant role in international finance (Panic, 1992, p. 93). In this process, the classical gold standard system developed into a credit system. Although Britain chose gold to settle the international debt, it was necessary only to reinforce confidence in British credit money as an international means of payment. Other nations followed Britain and adopted the gold standard at fixed exchange rates to make trade and capital import with Britain easier (p. 66). The City was the most important money and capital market in the world, and it was there that many economies kept bank accounts and raised trade loans (p. 22). British bills of exchange circulated as a means of payment in international trades. Most debts and credits were cancelled out on bank accounts in the City; only the balance was settled by the Bank of England notes. Thus the expansion of international trade was mostly catered to by British credit money.

Under the international gold standard, Britain coordinated international capital flows efficiently. When prosperity started, the American economy attracted long-term capital from Britain, while the German economy attracted short-term capital from many economies. The prosperity of the US and German economies boosted international trade. When these economies suffered from short-term exchange problems, Britain played a critical coordinating role (Eichengreen, 1992, p. 66). The Bank of England could attract short-term capital from all over the world by raising the bank rate, and it loaned this capital to these economies to solve their short-term exchange problems (Panic, 1992, p. 76). All other central banks followed suit and raised their discount rates. In this sense, the Bank of England was the de facto lender of last resort and the central bank of the capitalist world system (Kindleberger, 1993, p. 70).

The Gold Exchange System

After the First World War, the USA became the largest and dominant economy in the world. But it could not coordinate the international financial system efficiently. Although gold, US dollars, and British pounds were chosen as the international means of payment in the gold exchange system, the international monetary system deteriorated from a credit system to a monetary system. The first cause was the decline of the British economy. Britain suspended the gold standard in 1914, and it took eleven years for her to return to it. The relative decline of her economy changed Britain's status in the world economy from the most advanced surplus economy to a deficit economy, which undermined confidence in Britain's currency and reduced the attractiveness of her financial assets. As a result, the acceptability of British bills of exchange as the international means of payment declined. Second, although only the USA could have taken over Britain's role, in contrast to Britain, which managed to play a coordinating role with the smallest gold reserve among advanced nations (Eichengreen, 1992, p. 49), the USA could not perform this role even with the largest gold reserve in the world, because its money supply was regulated to iron out the domestic business cycle. When the US economy expanded and the money supply was increased, the American monetary authority tightened credit without paying sufficient attention to international economies. Since higher American interest rates drew gold from all over the world, all other central banks had to raise discount rates to protect their gold reserve. The decline of the credit system ultimately increased the need for gold, and the growth of international trade was limited by the supply of gold.

In this monetary system, the efficiency of international capital flow deteriorated severely. Although European economic recovery depended on capital imports from the USA, poor trade growth due to gold strain did not allow enough trade surpluses for the repayment of debt. As a result, the accumulation of debt made the European economy extremely vulnerable to American monetary policy (Hobsbawm, 1994, pp. 91, 97). In the late 1920s, in spite of the fact that the USA was the main structural surplus economy, its stock market boom attracted short-term capital from all over the world. The US monetary authority tightened credit in order to curtail bubbles in the stock market, which further cut US foreign lending. Since the European economy depended on US capital exports, central banks in Europe had to tighten credit in order to reduce the gold outflow, which exerted a strong downward pressure on the real economy. When confidence in the US stock market finally collapsed in 1929, US demand for foreign commodities and US foreign lending were further reduced, causing further severe foreign exchange problems throughout the world.

The Bretton Woods System

The Bretton Woods system was a credit system designed in 1944 to relax the external constraints imposed by the gold exchange standard on national economies. Although it was more advanced than the gold standard system in its formal international cooperation, it was never managed supranationally as intended. It was the commitment of the USA as the dominant economy that sustained the Bretton Wood system (Panic, 1988, p. 280). However, the USA blocked John Maynard Keynes's proposal to create an international clearing union and international money. Instead, the US dollar, fixed at the rate of 35 dollars per gold ounce, was chosen as the key currency. All member countries were obliged to fix their exchange rates to the dollar. In the new managed currency system, the US Federal Reserve banks could supply US dollars in response to their needs.

In the Bretton Woods system, the United States coordinated international capital flows efficiently. Up to the 1960s, the highly productive US economy achieved a huge balance of payments surplus. Much of this surplus was transferred to Europe and Japan as government loans and capital investment. These funds were invested in these economies partly in order to expand their production and increase their demand for US products. The smooth expansion of international trade under the free and multilateral trade system (GATT), and the abundant availability of the international means of payment, accelerated the growth of international trade and helped debtor nations to service and repay their debts.

THE ACCUMULATION STRUCTURE OF BUREAUCRATIC CAPITALISM: THE 1950s AND 1960s

There were four characteristics to the accumulation of capital in the Golden Age: the bureaucratic government structure, the existence of dynamic economies of scale, the acceleration principle, and the capital/labour accord.

Bureaucratic Government Structure

In many countries in wartime, the capitalist mode of production was constrained by government central planning. However, there were differences in the degree of this regulation, which were reflected in the evolution of postwar bureaucratic capitalism (Chandler, 1988; Kawamura, 1995; Aoki, 1996; Okazaki and Okuno-Fujiwara, 1999).

At one pole, the US government controlled the economy through the well-established oligopolistic market mechanism. In 1942, when war needs replaced consumer markets as the determinant of end products, the War Production Board attempted to allocate scarce materials by the use of priorities. However, this system was entirely ineffective. Only when the Controlled Materials Plan tied the allocation of metals and other strategic components into the forecasting procedures developed by General Motors and other large corporations in the summer of 1942, did it start to work (Chandler, 1988, pp. 240–41).

At the other pole, the Japanese war economy was strongly influenced by socialist central planning. Since Japan's oligopoly structure was too immature to manage the national economy, the government's central planning mobilized both means of production and workers directly by commands issued in quantitative terms and directed from the top downwards. Although profit-orientated factors were incorporated into the command-type planned economic system in 1943 (Okazaki and Okuno-Fujiwara, 1999, pp. 24–9); the government could not halt the dramatic decline in production (Aoki, 1996, p. 239).

With the return of peace the USA favoured indirect control of the economy. The War Production Board was disbanded, and market demand again became the basic criterion for decisions concerning the allocation of resources and the coordination of flows (Chandler, 1988, p. 241). Keynesian macroeconomic policy was sophisticated, and formed the mainstream market-led bureaucratic economy. Fiscal policy stabilized the price level in order to prevent a deflationary spiral in the competitive sector. Monetary policy to prevent a bank crisis was strengthened by such regulations as central bank control and supervision over banks and such remedies as account insurance and lender of last resort. To counter an international eclectic flow of hot money, monetary authorities controlled exchange by adopting real demand principles.

In contrast to the USA, Japan favoured direct intervention. From the beginning of 1946 onwards, the government reinforced economic controls and pursued recovery by means of a planned economic system (Okazaki and Okuno-Fujiwara, 1999, p. 31). As Aoki has argued, the reconstructed government-led bureaucratic capitalism 'started to work in the high growth period of the 1950s and 1960s, only when it was found to fit with an evolutionary tendency that had been taking place in the private sector' (Aoki, 1996, p. 235). The resolution of *Zaibatsu* and newly developing *Keiretsu* effectively decentralized the oligopolistic structure, and allowed the government to perform a coordinating role.

Dynamic Economies of Scale

In structural deficit economies, in the first two post-war decades, total factor productivity growth was proportional to investment, giving rise to dynamic economies of scale. This favourable relation between investment and total factor productivity growth can be explained by the following two phenomena. First, these economies were benefiting from catching-up effects. Many economies introduced new technology from the upper side of production, which reduced the prices of the means of production. Therefore, productivity growth was realized without increasing the organic composition of capital. Second, the post-war accumulation process was realized as industrialization. For many economies, manufacturing was the engine of capital accumulation, where dynamic economy of scale works better than in other sectors.

Acceleration Principle

In this period, the oligopolistic firms increased investment in proportion to the increase in utilization, a phenomenon called the acceleration principle. With abundant relative surplus labour and an expanding market, planned excess capacity was an essential condition for securing a market share. Otherwise, when the demand for the commodity expanded, other firms supplied the demand, and the firm would lose its share. Taking the economy of scale into consideration, the lost share was difficult to recover, and, in the worst case, firms were driven out of the market.

Capital/Labour Accord

The experience of the Great Depression and the war economy strongly influenced post-war capital/labour relations. In order to boost wartime productivity, the scientific management method was adopted on an unprecedented scale in the USA, while teamwork in which random events were handled collectively became dominant in Japan (Aoki, 1996, p. 241). After the Second World War, workers accepted the introduction of these more productive methods in exchange for relatively long and secure employment contracts with productivity-indexed money wages.

THE LAW OF VALUE IN BUREAUCRATIC CAPITALISM

The Formal Model of Capital Accumulation

Let us build a formal structuralist macroeconomic model to investigate the significance of the accumulation structure in bureaucratic capitalism. In this formal model, we integrate a Kaleckian capital accumulation model below full capacity and a Kaldorian accumulation model at full capacity following Rowthorn (1981). Take the capacity utilization rate u on the x-axis, and the rate of profit r on the y-axis as in Figures 10.1 and 10.2. The profit curve, which shows equilibrium on the supply side, is given by the following equations. The net rate of profit r is given by the following equation normalized by fixed capital K:

$$r = (R/K) - (D/K) - (T/K), \tag{10.1}$$

where R is the gross profits, D is depreciation and T is the tax. Let us denote the national income by Y, the full utilization national income by $\underline{Y}$, the full utilization capital coefficient by $\underline{k}$. Since $R/K = (R/Y)(Y/\underline{Y})(\underline{Y}/K)$, the profit curve is defined thus:

$$r = (p/\underline{k})u - d - t, \tag{10.2a}$$

where p is the share of profit (R/Y) determined externally by the degree of monopoly, $d = D/K$, and $t = T/K$. When u rises, r also rises because the fixed capital K is used more efficiently. Let us suppose that the gap between supply and demand is covered by quantity adjustment under full utilization (Kaleckian adjustment), and by price adjustment at full utilization (Kaldorian adjustment). At full utilization, the price level may rise, and the rate of profit is given by the following equation:

$$r \geq (p/\underline{k})u - d - t. \tag{10.2b}$$

The profit curve has a positive slope of $p/\underline{k}$ below full capacity and is vertical at full capacity itself.

The realization curve, which shows the equilibrium of saving and investment, is given by the following equations. Let us suppose that workers do not save and that a constant fraction s_r is saved from the net profits. The net saving normalized by the fixed capital g^s is given by the following equation:

$$\text{Saving function: } g^s = s_r r - b - x, \tag{10.3}$$

where b is the budget deficit and x the net export, both normalized by the fixed capital.

We suppose that the current rate of profit and the capacity utilization influence investment. We denote the investment propensity to the rate of profit by i_r, and that to the utilization rate by i_u. The ratio of investment to the fixed capital g^i is given by the following equation

$$\text{Investment function: } g^i = i_0 + i_r r + i_u u, \tag{10.4}$$

where i_0 is the absolute term of investment.

The realization curve is obtained from (10.3), (10.4) and the equilibrium condition ($g^i = g^s$):

$$r = [i_u/(s_r - i_r)]u + (i_0 + b + x)/(s_r - i_r). \tag{10.5}$$

The economy must lie on the profit curve and the realization curve is in equilibrium. The stability of the equilibrium depends on the relative size of s_r to i_r. 'If saving propensity is very low ($s_r < i_r$) no stable equilibrium is possible'. When the saving propensity is very high, as in structural surplus economies, and the realization curve has a positive slope but is less steep than

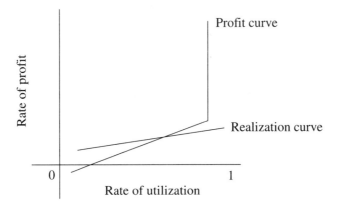

Figure 10.1   Structural surplus economies

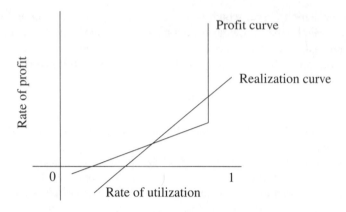

Figure 10.2   Structural deficit economies

the profit curve ($i_r + i_u k/p < s_r$), 'all equilibrium is stable' (Figure 10.1). When the saving propensity is moderately high, as in structural deficit economies, and the realization curve is steeper than the sloping part of the profits curve ($i_r < s_r < i_r + i_u k/p$), equilibrium is stable at full capacity and unstable below full capacity (Figure 10.2) (Rowthorn, 1982, pp. 20–21).

Changes in parameters concerned with savings and investment (i_u, s_r, i_r, b, and x) shift the slope and position of the realization curve. For example, larger i_u, i_r, b, x and smaller s_r, shift the realization curve upwards, which 'will increase the equilibrium rate of profit and cause the economy to grow faster' (ibid., p. 22).

Changes in parameters concerned with the cost structure of firms (p, k, d, t) shift the profits curve. For example, larger k, d, t and smaller p increase the costs of firms and initially reduce the rate of profit. In the case of a stable economy, since $i_r < s_r$, this reduction in profits will cause excess demand. At full capacity, firms will raise their prices and the economy will return to its previous equilibrium. Below full capacity, firms respond to greater demand by producing more output. 'If there is no accelerator effect ($i_u = 0$), expansion will come to a halt once profits have reached their old level … if the accelerator effect is positive ($i_u > 0$) … both profits and investment will be higher in the new equilibrium than they were in the old' (ibid., pp. 24–5).

The Law of Value in Bureaucratic Capitalism

We may now describe the accumulation mechanism in bureaucratic capitalism. Prosperity started mainly when increased investment and consumption shifted the realization curve upwards and raised both employment and the rate of profit. As prosperity increased, firms maximized investment, utilizing credit in order to take advantage of the dynamic economy of scale, which further increased investment demand. At full capacity utilization, a Kaldorian profit-led accumulation mechanism came into operation. The increase of investment raised the price level, which increased profits with sticky money wages. Workers tolerated higher prices because an increase in investment boosted the demand for labour, and the increased productivity made possible by the dynamic scale of the economy eventually increased real wages.

The most significant difference displayed by the new managed currency system was the self-sustainability of savings and investment at any investment level. In the case of the gold standard system, the supply of currency was limited by the gold reserve. In the new managed currency system, there was no such external constraint. The central banks could create currency to meet the liquidity needs of the expanding domestic economy. As far as the domestic credit system was concerned, investment continued limitlessly.

Acceleration of capital accumulation and eventual breakdown took different forms according to the levels of savings. In moderately high-saving economies, or in structural deficit economies, the economy reached equilibrium at full capacity utilization with the help of capital inflow, and often overaccumulated at the end of prosperity with expansionary monetary policy. As long as the country kept the rate of inflation equal to or less than the US rate of inflation, solvency was ensured. But once the credit creation accelerated inflation beyond that level, the balance of payments was degraded. When the exchange rate dropped below the predetermined rate, the IMF fixed rate system forced the economy to tighten credit. In high-saving economies, or in structural surplus economies, both equilibria below full capacity and at full capacity are stable. Hyman Minsky's (1982) financial instability theory applies here to explain the limiting of investment by financial market psychology. The demand price of investment was determined by expected profit flow divided by present interest rate. As long as the demand prices of investment exceeded the supply prices of investment, investment continued. Once the financial market suspected that the supply prices of investment were higher than the demand prices due to higher wage costs, investment stopped.

In all economies, reduction of investment triggered depression, which created Keynesian unemployment, which re-established labour discipline. However, depression was a temporary problem. In the depression period a Kaleckian wage-led accumulation mechanism operated. Sticky money wages and lower price level pushed up real wages. Increased real wages and government spending raised aggregate demand, shifting the profit curve down. Firms responded to this increased demand by stepping up output. As a result of the acceleration principle, the increase of demand more than compensated for the increase of wages, and both the rate of utilization and the rate of profit rose. Then the prosperity began again.

Thus, the capitalist economy recovered its self-regulating nature, or the law of value, coordinating commodity, labour, and money and capital markets with endogenous business cycles.

DECLINE OF BUREAUCRATIC CAPITALISM: THE 1970s AND 1980s

Decline of the Bretton Woods System

In their later stages, both 'the gold standard system' and 'the Bretton Woods system' were characterized by growing uncertainty, flights of short-term capital and concern about the adequacy of the leading countries' reserves (Panic, 1988, p. 182). The reasons for this were quite similar: (a) the dominant country's relatively slow productivity growth, (b) its inability to sustain structural surplus, (c) concern about the adequacy of its reserve, and (d) its incapacity to stabilize the system. In the Bretton Woods system, long-lasting high capital accumulation changed relative productivity between countries. Productivity growth in Japan and the former West Germany, thanks to higher accumulation rate, catching-up effects and a newly formed bureaucratic system, was faster than in the USA, and thereby decreased the relative strength of US trade. In spite of the decline of its trade surplus, the USA could not decrease both capital export and government deficit in order to keep its dominant status in the world economy and stabilize the domestic economy. The result was an increased US deficit and an increased supply of US dollars which undermined confidence in the US dollar and heightened concern about the US gold reserve and the USA had to stop conversion in 1971. At the same time, the disproportional development of productivity made it difficult for countries with relatively slower productivity growth to maintain the fixed exchange, and this induced the international financial system to return to the floating exchange rate system. Thus the Bretton Woods system was abandoned.

Conflicting Capital/Labour Relations

Long-lasting high capital accumulation also changed coordinated capital/labour relations into conflictual capital/labour relations. The first problem was slow productivity growth. Productivity growth was the key factor in the success of the post-war capital/labour accord, since firms could pay higher real wages and secure capital accumulation only with steady productivity growth. First, the mass production method had reached saturation in many advanced countries by the early 1970s, with a reduction of the catch-up effect. Further productivity growth required expensive investment in plants and equipment. Second, the relative laggardiness of productivity growth in the service sector forced deindustrialization (Rowthorn and Wells, 1987). Productivity growth in the service sector was difficult with the available technology. The second problem was the structural overaccumulation of capital. The growth of output is equal to the growth of employed labour power plus the growth of total factor productivity. With declining productivity growth, the growth of output increased demand for labour and eventually exhausted the available industrial reserve army. The creation of unemployment by cyclical depression slowed the absorption of the industrial reserve army but could not reverse this tendency. Labour then became militant, and wage bargaining changed from Keynesian with sticky money wages to Marxist with sticky real wages (Epstein and Schor, 1990, p. 130).

In this environment, a Kaldorian accumulation mechanism could not work, because, when firms increased investment at full capacity operation, the prices of products rose but the increase in wages squeezed profits. Once depression started, recovery from depression by the Kaleckian accumulation mechanism also became difficult. First, increased competition between capital required that idle fixed capital had to be kept to a minimum. As represented by the lean production system, information technology was adapted to keep idle productive and circulating capital to a minimum. Second, conflictual capital/labour relations made capital cautious of increased employment. As a result, the positive effect of demand by increased real wages on investment became less than before.

With the destruction of the social institutions that coordinated both international and domestic economies, the macro performance of the economy stagnated. After 1973 the unemployment rates of advanced nations never dropped to their respective average levels in the 1960s (Dicken, 1998, p. 432). Economic fluctuations became more severe, and the economy did not recover automatically. Thus the law of value has been partially restrained since the 1970s.

THE FORMATION OF TRANSNATIONAL CAPITALISM: THE 1990s AND BEYOND

Without a complementary combination of capital/labour relations and production method, accumulation of capital cannot restart. There were three successful attempts to re-establish labour discipline in the 1980s. Centralized bargaining in corporatist nations rehabilitated cooperative relations, and workers agreed to reduce wages in order to safeguard employment. Decentralized bargaining in Anglo-American economies subdued the power of organized labour, and restrained wages stimulated capital accumulation. In-between, Japanese mini-corporatism combined labour loyalty and the flexible production system. Only the Japanese economy successfully combined a new capital/labour relationship with a new production method in the 1980s and understandably was the most successful. The market-led international financial system, information technology and globalization changed this picture, however. In this new environment, some economies fared better: East Asian economies by the early half of the 1990s, and the US economy in the 1990s. These experiences show that a newly evolved form of capitalism such as transnational capitalism is emerging.

Transnational Enterprises and the Market-led International Monetary System

The international financial system after 1985 has many similarities with the 1930s, yet the breakdown of the Bretton Woods system has not led to international financial disintegration (Hirst and Thompson, 1996, p. 130; Panic, 1988, p. 184). It was effectively replaced by a market-led international financial system which is more similar to the gold standard system than to the other two systems: (a) in its coordinating institutions, (b) in its method of coordination, and (c) in its means of payment. But it is quite different in the stability of the international capital flow.

International interdependence underwent exceptional development after the 1950s, especially at the hands of the transnational enterprises which developed a network of credit systems in the form of the euromarket. It was their need to minimize uncertainty and to preserve the international credit system under ineffective government action that induced the phenomenal growth of the euromarket as an alternative international financial system. The euromarket chose the dollar, with the yen and the euro in supporting roles as the standard, since these were the currencies of the main players. However, these assets were more accounting units than means of payments, since most debts were settled on bank accounts in the euromarket.

There are important differences between the gold standard system and this market-led international financial system in the volatility and efficiency of capital flow. In the process of globalization, countries have liberalized capital flow, with the result that the financial portfolios of firms are internationalized both in the advanced and developing countries. At the same time they have stopped insulating economies against exchange rate pressure by disciplining them in terms of their domestic economic policies. Although the euromarket has facilitated both the financing of short-term imbalances and the adjustment of long-term disequilibria, these are essentially short-term loans, which have increasingly caused a mismatch with long-term demand. These developments have made economies extremely vulnerable to short-term capital flows both in advanced and developing economies. Especially, the Asian crises in the latter half of the 1990s showed that the market-led international monetary system did 'a poor job of discriminating between good and bad risks' (Rodrik, 1999, p. 90).

Transnational Enterprises and Foreign Direct Investment

Just as the declining period of market capitalism was characterized by a strong increase in international finance and factor movements and restriction in trade, so the declining period of bureaucratic capitalism is characterized by the sudden increase in foreign direct investment (FDI) relative to exports (Panic, 1988, pp. 166–7; Hirst and Thompson, 1996, pp. 54–5). As an increase in capital export helped the industrialization of the US and German economies, so FDI helped the industrialization of East Asian economies, but, more importantly, it also increased regional integration among developed economies. I distinguish here between two kinds of FDI: one based on resources and the other based on a division of labour between equals (see Rowthorn, Chapter 8 in this volume). The former is traditional and is based on differences in resources, especially cheap labour. Since replica factories are exported to developing countries, this process itself does not involve any development of total factor productivity. The latter is based on the development of a division of labour among equals which has hitherto been limited to the margins of an economy. In a technical context, these are normal evolutionary features of the economy of scale. The further development of modern technology requires a wider market and a wider division of labour than a national economy can afford. The development of the second kind of FDI enables new combinations of forces of production and relations of production integrating regions in the form of transnational capitalism.

Transnational Capitalism

The present market-led international financial system has allowed only the US economy to shift to transnational capitalism. The US economy, which combined decentralized capital/labour relations with open network production in the North American economic bloc, was the most successful economy in the 1990s. There were several reasons for this success. First, the market-orientated nature of the US transnational enterprise was best suited to the market-led international monetary system. Second, the US economy demolished the labour unions, and there was no strong opposing power. Third, US transnational enterprises were most advanced in standardization and modular production, which made the introduction of open network production possible.

In contrast to the US economy, since 1991 the Japanese government-led economy has been suffering from the worst depression in its post-war history, due to three problems related to increasing complexity and openness. In Japan, the state played an essential role in the process of transformation to bureaucratic capitalism, creating the consensus for change that made Japanese economy the most efficient and developed economy in the world. But at the same time it became too complex for a centralized body to coordinate its numerous operations, especially in times of rapid or unforeseen changes after 1985. First, financial deregulation and globalization in the 1980s cramped government-led governance without suitable alternatives, which caused an excess bubble and the subsequent difficulty in liquidating bad debts. Second, the Japanese economy avoided deindustrialization by achieving huge manufacturing exports. After 1985, the growth of FDI exceeded the growth of exports, which eventually reduced domestic manufacturing production, resulting in unemployment in the industrial sector. Third, in the 1970s the Liberal Democratic Party was confident with conflict management, and achieved a successful economic recovery. A more open environment coupled with a change of the electoral system towards proportional representation in 1983 and 1994 confused economic policy, and governments lost confidence. Japanese debt deflation was triggered by tight monetary policy in 1991. Although the Japanese economy recovered briefly in 1996, a higher consumption tax killed economic recovery in 1997.

The new trend to re-regulation, however, may allow developments of other combinations of transnational capitalism. Now the necessity of a formal arrangement to mitigate volatility of the market-led international financial system is widely discussed (Hirst and Thompson, 1996, p. 197). Among possible formal arrangements, the formation (or continuance) of the regional credit system seems to be the most promising. First, reconstruction of a dominant economic model may be difficult, because the USA has lost its dominant status and neither Japan nor the European Union (EU) is likely to replace it. Second, it is also difficult for a supranational institution to coordinate the international financial system under the present complex nature of the economy and rapid technical changes. Third, regional credit systems fit with transnational capitalism, since the multilayered character of transnational enterprise works better with multilayered coordination. Property rights or the ownership of a transnational enterprise often belong to its mother nation, while management, production and marketing are organized at regional transnational levels. For transnational enterprises, the region is not limited to the region where the mother nation belongs either. The multilayered nature of transnational enterprises requires global, regional, national and local coordination.

In all likelihood, the North American bloc will be most successful in creating a regional credit system in the form of a regional dominant economic model, because of the global dominance of the US economy. In the EU, the rivalry between leading nations and the strong monetary character of its monetary union may slow down economic growth and widen productivity gaps among member nations, as the gold exchange standard did. The formation of the East Asian bloc is undoubtedly the most difficult among the three leading economic regions. FDI in this bloc has been mainly the first kind, and intra-industry trade has just started to develop between Japan and its more advanced neighbours such as South Korea and Taiwan. Only when multilayered formal arrangements have been made among divergent government-led economies, and their productivity has sufficiently developed, will the combination of forces and relations of production in the form of transnational capitalism become possible.

NOTE

* The author is grateful to Bob Rowthorn, Geoff Hodgson, Makoto Itoh, Makoto Noguchi, Gary Dymski, Mica Panic, Ugo Pagano and Michael Best for discussions and comments.

REFERENCES

Aoki, M. (1996), 'Unintended fit: organizational evolution and government design of institutions in Japan', in M. Aoki, K. Hyung-ki and M. Okuno-Fujiwara (eds), *The Role of Government in East Asian Economic Development, Comparative Institutional Analysis*, Oxford: Clarendon Press, pp. 231–53.

Bernstein, E. (1917), *Sozialdemokratische Volkerpolitik*, Leipzig: Verlag Naturwissenschaften.

Chandler, Alfred (1988), *The Essential Alfred Chandler: Essays Toward a Historical Theory of a Big Business*, ed. T. McCraw, Cambridge, MA: Harvard Business School Press.

Dicken, P. (1998), *Global Shift: Transforming the World Economy*, 3rd edn, London: Paul Chapman.

Eichengreen, B. (1992), *Golden Fetters: The Gold Standard and the Great Depression, 1919–1939*, Oxford: Oxford University Press.

Epstein, G. and J. Schor (1990), 'Macro policy in the rise and fall of the Golden Age', in S. Marglin and J. Schor (eds) (1990), *The Golden Age of Capitalism*, Oxford: Clarendon, pp. 126–52.

Hilferding, R. (1980), *Finance Capital*, London: Routledge.

Hirst, P. and G. Thompson (1996), *Globalization in Question*, Cambridge: Polity Press.

Hobsbawm, E. (1994), *Age of Extremes: The Short Twentieth Century, 1914–1991*, Cambridge: Polity Press.

Kawamura, T. (1995), *Formation of Pax-Americana*, Tokyo: Touyou-keizai-shinpousya (in Japanese).

Kindleberger, C.P. (1993), *A Financial History of Western Europe*, Oxford: Oxford University Press.

Lenin, V.I. (1996), *Imperialism: The Highest Stage of Capitalism*, London: Pluto.

Marx, Karl (1976), *Capital*, vol. 1, translated by Ben Fowkes from the fourth German edition of 1890, Harmondsworth: Pelican.

Minsky, H.P. (1982), *Can It Happen Again?*, New York: M.E. Sharpe.

Okazaki, T. and M. Okuno-Fujiwara (1999), 'Japanese's present-day economic system and its historical origins', in T. Okazaki and M. Okuno-Fujiwara (eds), *The Japanese Economic System and its Historical Origin*, Oxford: Oxford University Press.

Panic, M. (1988), *National Management of the International Economy*, London: Macmillan.

Panic, M. (1992), *European Monetary Union: Lessons from the Classical Gold Standard*, London: Macmillan.

Rodrik, D. (1999), *The New Global Economy and Developing Countries: Making Openness Work*, Baltimore, MD: Johns Hopkins University Press.

Rowthorn, Robert E. (1981), *Demand, Real Wages and Economic Growth*, London: Thames Papers in Political Economy – Thames Polytechnic and North East London Polytechnic.

Rowthorn, R.E. and J.R. Wells (1987), *De-industrialisation and Foreign Trade*, Cambridge: Cambridge University Press.

Uno, K. (1980), *Principles of Political Economy*, translated by Thomas T. Sekine, Brighton: Harvester.

11. The evolutionary spiral of capitalism: globalization and neo-liberalism

Makoto Itoh

INTRODUCTION

The globalization of the modern capitalist economy is widely acknowledged. More and more firms, products, financial assets and workers are being drawn into the global whirlpool of competitive markets. Capitalism has become increasingly competitive on a global scale.

Repeated economic crises since 1973 have prompted the restructuring of capitalist economies. As a result, capitalist firms have extended and strengthened their global competitive activities. These achievements have been facilitated by new, microelectronic-based information technologies. At the same time, neo-liberal policy beliefs in the harmonious efficiency of freely competitive market have prevailed. The collapse of Soviet-type central planning reinforced the faith of the neo-liberals, and seemed to mark the final victory over socialism (Fukuyama, 1992). It is widely believed that the globalization of capitalism involves the extension of a self-regulating and efficient economic order.

Yet we have a world with economic instability and polarized wealth and income. Especially when looked at over the broad span of history, neo-liberal triumphalism is somewhat tempered by a sense of disillusionment and confusion.

Ironically, several neo-liberals have acknowledged that Marx was the prophet of capitalist globalization. The year 1998 was the 150th anniversary of the publication of the *Communist Manifesto*. The authors of the *Manifesto* had pointed out that the growth of bourgeois society had 'given a cosmopolitan character to production and consumption in every country' (Marx and Engels, 1998, p. 39). They also emphasized that the strong growth of the capitalist economy itself created the potential for self-destructive commercial crises.

Recent world history has many illustrations of such crises. World financial markets are vulnerable and unstable. The Japanese financial bubble has burst. There have been devastating monetary crises in other Asian countries and in

Russia. Brazil rocks precariously on the edge. Could these events burst the overinflated bubble on the US stock market, and lead to a world economic crisis?

The evolution of capitalism is non-linear. It is rather a complex spiral process, moving in alternate directions, in turn interwoven with political interventions, communal human relations and socialist movements. This chapter re-examines the nature of the capitalist world system from a contemporary point of view, and reconsiders the significance of current globalization of capitalist economies in the light of its historical process of evolution.

THE EVOLUTION OF THE CAPITALIST WORLD SYSTEM

From World Empires to the Capitalist World Economy

According to Immanuel Wallerstein (1974, 1983), there have been two kinds of world system in human history: world empires and the capitalist world economy. Modern capitalism appeared through 'the long 16th century' as a new type of European world system, by replacing the preceding world empires. While the world empires were integrated by political and military power, the capitalist world system formed a global system of division of labour mainly by means of the self-regulating market order.

Indeed, capitalism anarchically promoted the market-orientated system of division of labour, starting from the expansion of the world market after the discovery of the new continent and the circumnavigation of the earth. Capitalism was thus originally grounded upon the global market economy.

However, the forms of market economy such as commodity, money and (merchant and usurer) capital were not original to the modern capitalist age. They originally appeared in a very ancient age of human history. They sprang and grew, as Marx (1976, p. 182) pointed out, as inter-social economic relations. When a communal society came into contact with another society, there were basically two options; either it could conquer by force, or it could trade by treating products as commodities. All the world empires actually included heterogeneous communal social organizations at various levels in different local areas, and contained horizontal inter-social trades more or less as a subsystem of integration beside the vertical imperial political and military power. The horizontal trading relations in the forms of market economy were qualitatively different from both the major organizational political orders of the empires and of the intra-social communal social relations. Therefore, excessive growth of the market economy could undermine both the imperial and the communal social orders. Mainly for this reason, the growth of the market economy was restricted in many pre-modern societies.

Modern capitalism developed the market as a means of global integration. Beginning in Western Europe, the old feudal hierarchical and communal orders were undermined. At the heart of capitalism, labour power became a commodity and a generalized commodity economy emerged; commodities were produced by means of commodities. The development of agricultural production, navigation technology, the woollen industry, the cotton industry, steam power, and iron and steel, were all driving forces in the intensive and extensive expansion of the capitalist system.

Unlike pre-modern societies, capitalism was organized on the basis of the market. It could therefore utilize the emerging world market as its stepping stone. The development of capitalism meant the development of free trade, both domestically and internationally. The market economy had some independence from the political and communal social orders. Consequently, liberal ideological notions of individual freedom, of private property rights derived from individual labour, and of equal human rights, prevailed. These ideologies were opposed to feudal discrimination and religious authority. The idea sprang up of a free, competitive, market economy, as the natural means to the realization of an efficient and harmonious economic life. Such assertions permeate the social sciences, from classical political economy to neoclassical economics. Neo-liberalism has found its strength in the endurance of the market, and in its modern extension and reinvigoration, in the form of the global market economy of today.

The Roles of Political Power and Communal Human Relations

While capitalism is grounded on the free, competitive, market economy, it has not dissolved all the political power and communal human relations outside of the market order.

In the transitory long process of dissolving the feudal societies and shaping modern capitalist societies, powerful mercantilist nation states were built up and played an important role as midwife. Even absolutist political and military powers were used protectively to promote the growth of monopolistic foreign trade and commercial activity as a main source of wealth of nations. Domestically, political power served as a backup for violent deprivation of cultivating land from peasants in the enclosure movements typical in the UK, resulting in the creation of proletarian workers for capitalist enterprises. However, with the development of a self-regulating commercial society, absolutist regal political power from above became unnecessary or burdensome, and was abandoned by bourgeois revolutions ideologically demanding freedom, equality and human rights for citizens. The civil revolutions, however, did not immediately stop violent governance and exploitation of colonies, and violent slave hunting in Africa as an important external source of profit making.

Even after the stormy stage of mercantilism, full of exhaustive wars, Pax Britannica in the stage of liberalism in the nineteenth century was actually maintained by British naval hegemony in addition to her industrial hegemony. Advanced capitalist countries still maintained if not increased their colonial territories, and utilized slave labour in plantations such as in the USA. Thus, the world capitalist system did not homogenize various societies throughout the world, but contained diversified heterogeneous social relations. It was substantially uneven or unequal in geographical development, and had re-course to politico-military power as a subsystem for integration beside the global market. This was symmetrical with the world empires where commer-cial activities served as a subsystem to the main politico-military order for integration.

At the same time, the political and administrative mechanism of the state remained so as to maintain and supplement the functions of the capitalistic market order within the central capitalist societies. The Poor Law and the Factory Legislation in the UK exemplify this. A free, competitive, market economy would not necessarily realize a harmonious economic life but would often endanger the maintenance and reproduction of human beings without such political regulations. The inherent instability in the capitalistic market economy also required political attempts to avoid or mitigate the self-destruc-tive financial crises after speculative booms and bubbles. A typical example is the 1844 Bank Act and its repeated suspension at the peaks of subsequent money crises. After more than a century of evolution of capitalism, the threat of collapse in the monetary and financial system, the nexus rerun of the capitalistic market economy, still reappears in the contemporary world on a large scale, and enforces emergency political rescue operations, against the liberal or neo-liberal creed. The competitive free capitalistic market system cannot be a harmonious natural order of liberty to *laissez-faire*.

Direct human social relations outside the market order also remain or originate in various ways within the capitalist firm. Although based upon transactions in the labour market, capitalist firms generally organize their managerial systems in basically a top-down despotic order. After the pur-chase of labour power as a commodity, it is duly the purchaser's right to decide how to utilize its use value in workplaces. Against oppressive capital-ist management, trade unions grew as communal and friendly associations, so as to defend workers' interest in workplaces and to strengthen the bargaining power of workers. In many workplaces, even without trade unions, the sense of horizontal associate mutual assistance has grown steadily among workers. These horizontal communal human relations are always combined, some-times create conflicts, but sometimes work together cooperatively with the vertical managerial order within capitalist firms. In the Japanese style of management, for example, the small-group, communal human relations of the workplace, as well as the communal sense of cooperation among all the workers in each company, are deliberately fermented as a strong basis for increasing efficiency and flexibility for technological changes. It is hard to judge and rather dubious to claim that this sense of cooperation and loyal attitudes among Japanese company workers is directly based upon Japanese family culture, especially as Japanese family culture itself has already become highly deconstructed by increasing individualism. Also the Japanese style cannot be almighty for managerial success, for it sometimes delays necessary adjustment of employment. It is still clearly the case that a key factor for the success or failure of Japanese capitalist firms, particularly in a hard depressive period like the 1990s, involves how to organize labour management by reshaping both vertical and horizontal human relationships within firms. Under the same capitalistic market order, this aspect much diversifies the social life of workers in different stages or various countries through the evolution of capitalism.

Reproduction of the labour force has to be performed not just by purchase of necessary means of consumption, but also with the support of cooperative human gender relationships in the form of family. With the evolution of capitalism, historical changes have certainly occurred in family life and gender relations, according to the changes in women's position in employment. A fixed model of the typical family in a capitalist economy is not generally definable. Nevertheless, capitalism has always relied on family relationships between a man and a woman, or between parents and children to supplement market principles for generational reproduction of labour power, survival of unemployed, and care of elderly persons. There also exist various forms of communal relations in some social life, such as in consumer cooperation, political or religious associations.

Evolutionary Changes in the History of Capitalism

Thus, while the capitalist world economy has been formed in the main by the self-regulating market order, it actually contains two other kinds of subsystems of integration of human economic life; one is political and military power, and the other is communal human relationships. Even capital itself contained such a subsystem of integration within its managerial organization.

The Marxist approach has always noted that capital has organized social human relationships into a special historic form of production on the basis of the forms of market economy. The formula of historical materialism served as 'a guiding thread' for this approach (Marx, 1970, Preface). From this point of view, it must always be important to see how concrete development in productive power in changing leading industries has caused changes in the relationships of production between capital and labour. The corresponding changes in supplementary politico-military order or economic policies, and the roles of communal human relationships outside of the market order are also quite important to characterize the evolutionary stages of capitalist development. In contrast, the basic forms of market economy, such as commodity, money and capital, would not essentially change by themselves, although their functions would change in the process of historical evolution of capitalism.

Especially in analysing the evolution of advanced capitalist countries, an approach focusing on the historical changes in capitalistic relations of production is mostly relevant. This applies to major works in the French *régulationnist* approach and the US radical theory of the social structure of accumulation.[1] However, this type of approach is methodologically insufficient when applied to the global economy. In most peripheral countries, the capitalistic relations of production are partly formed in urban cities. The socioeconomic issues in these countries are closely related to the unequal working of the global division of labour in the structural context of centre–periphery in the evolution of capitalist world system. The economic difficulties of peasants and other small family businesses at the periphery of the capitalist economic system are quite important. The Japanese Uno school has thus underlined the importance of agricultural problems in the stages theory of capitalist development as well as in more concrete empirical analyses of the world economy.[2]

At the same time, the historical evolution of monetary and financial systems must also be both important and interesting. Although the historical features of monetary and financial systems are certainly related to the changes in the relations of production in leading industries, they have a degree of independence as a sort of economic superstructure. Flexible expandability of monetary and financial systems, their instability, and political or administrative attempts for their control are surely to be studied as an essential aspect of the evolution of capitalism. Especially where the features of business fluctuations and the workings of self-destructive crises and depressions are concerned, this topic must be of the utmost importance (Itoh and Lapavitsas, 1999).

These contemporary concerns must inevitably be considered when deciding which key aspects should be focused on in studying the evolution of capitalist world history.

THE HISTORIC RESTRICTION OF THE FREE MARKET

The evolution of capitalism is like a spiral. It did not proceed one-sidedly towards a free competitive world market to reach contemporary global mega-competition. The historical evolution of capitalism from mercantilism to

Pax-Britannica liberalism, up to the 1870s, clearly showed a trend towards a more and more freely competitive market order. However, for about a century from the late nineteenth century, the capitalist world system took a spiral course and reversed the trend. Free market competition was restricted in the following ways.

With the development of heavy industries, giant joint-stock companies grew larger and larger. They tended to form monopolistic organizations so as to avoid cut-throat competition and tried to earn monopolistic profit by controlling the prices of their products.

In heavy industries, experienced strong male workers were essential and were employed together in large workplaces. Consequently, trade unions developed rapidly among them as well as among the increasing number of workers in the public sector. They attempted to restrict free competition in the labour market so as to defend workers' class interests. Based upon the growth of labour movements, the socialist movements for social conscious organization of economies beyond anarchical capitalism could also grow. Eventually they realized the Russian Revolution via the historical crisis of the First World War, and the Soviet type of socialism was formed. This demonstrated that the evolution of capitalism might turn into its revolution.

In accord with these trends the economic roles of nation states were greatly reintensified. Imperialist colonial and tariff policies were restrengthened to suit the economic interests of monopolistic firms. This turn of the spiral has been described as neo-mercantilism. New social policies to cope with labour and agricultural problems emerged. Their effect was to enlarge the national support for imperialism and to defend the capitalist order against socialism. Two imperialist world wars required large-scale state intervention in the market economy and the mobilization of national economic power. Subsequently, with the Cold War, the military–industrial complex continued to exist to a large extent. To cope with unemployment, the New Deal and Keynesianism emerged. Social democratic, welfare state policies were promoted. These developments also favoured the growth of trade unions especially in public sectors.

The increasing economic role of the state did not necessarily reduce the role of the market. However, the increased state intervention meant that the workings of free markets were subject to social control and that the ideology of liberalism was rejected in one way or another.

Soviet-type socialism, without free markets, emerged, and then spread after the Second World War. At its height it covered about 30 per cent of the land area on Earth and embraced 35 per cent of the global population. The capitalist world market system seemed seriously challenged by the remarkable growth of this contrasting politico-economic order. Up to the 1970s, within both core and peripheral countries, some socialist and revolutionary movements gained strength. These developments were used to justify enhanced military and intelligence powers for the capitalist states.

Thus the basic historical trend of the capitalist world system to expand its competitive market order throughout the world was actually restricted and reversed to a certain degree for about a century. The market vitality of the capitalist world system was seemingly undermined. The economic and territorial growth of socialist countries was a serious challenge. Just as in the mercantilist period the capitalist world system was born with the state power acting as its midwife, twentieth-century capitalism seemed to be withering away with reintensified state intervention in various ways.

THE REVITALIZATION OF THE COMPETITIVE MARKET ORDER

After the Second World War, the Bretton Woods international monetary system integrated managed currencies with fixed exchange rates. It provided a stable, Keynesian framework for the capitalist world system. The success of Keynesianism in 1945–73 was, however, largely due to both the Fordist regime of accumulation, where real wages were raised in line with increases in productivity, and a series of favourable conditions for capital accumulation. Among these were the US industrial hegemony to sustain the core basis of the Bretton Woods international monetary system, and the availability of technological frontiers as well as relatively cheap primary products and labour power for advanced capitalist countries (Itoh, 1990). Without these basic conditions, Keynesian policies could no longer be effective but rather promoted the inflationary crisis and stagflation after 1973, and eventually had to be abandoned.

Actually, the Bretton Woods international monetary system collapsed when the USA lost her industrial hegemony in international trade and became unable to maintain convertibility of dollar into gold. With the transition of the international monetary system to floating exchange rates, instability strongly re-emerged. Simultaneously in advanced capitalist countries, towards the end of high economic growth, there was an overaccumulation of capital in relation to relatively inflexible supplies of labour power and primary products. In the early 1970s this caused a profit squeeze and a subsequent destructive inflationary crisis and stagflation.

In the USA, these events were followed in the 1980s by monetarist policies and extremely high rates of interest due to the crowding-out effect under Reaganomics. The increased disparity in the interest rates among nations and wide fluctuations in the exchange rates led to a huge increase in international speculative trading of currencies, securities and derivatives. Huge financial bubbles swelled successively in Japan and then neighbouring Asian countries among others. In the 1990s the Japanese and then the surrounding Asian bubbles burst and caused serious damage to these economies. Although the US economy has enjoyed a strong recovery in the meanwhile, the overvalued market in stocks has created speculation concerning the possibility of another Wall Street crash.

Through these phases of crisis and depression after 1973, capitalist firms have attempted to survive by introducing more and more sophisticated, microelectronic-based information technologies. With the wide-ranging impact of this information revolution, capitalism reversed gear and began to remove its restrictions on competitive markets. Accordingly, there has been a global revitalization of the competitive market order. The following five points are relevant:

1. By restructuring and introducing microelectronic-based automation systems, in both factories and offices, capitalist firms have raised labour productivity. Flexible production has made possible the manufacture, by the same automated production line, of multiple versions of cars, electric appliances, clothing and so on, tailored to an individualistic consumer market. Market competition is not confined to price but extends to model type and quality.

   Microelectronic-based information technologies have also increased the flexibility to relocate manufacturing and business sites, and thus restrengthen global competition across borders. Accordingly, regional economic development has become more uneven, as the most rapidly growing tertiary sectors – such as finance, trading and other services – tend to concentrate their activities in big business centres. Financial markets have also become widely globalized, with intensified competition across different financial areas and sectors.

2. As microelectronic-based automation spread in factories, offices and shops, capitalist firms have been able to dispense with some skilled and experienced workers, and have increased flexible forms of irregular employment such as homeworkers, part-timers, seasonal workers and temporary workers sometimes subcontracted from other companies. Some areas have witnessed the increasing employment of cheap and sometimes illegal foreign workers. The increasing international mobility of the labour force is one of key features of the globalization of the market economy.

   Partly as a result of these trends, trade unions have suffered from a decline of influence in the organization. The labour market has become more competitive and flexible. Capitalist firms are able to choose different types of workers in combination so as to economize operational costs. Unlike the 'Fordist' 1950s and 1960s, more recently trade unions have successively failed to raise the real wages, despite increased labour productivity. Many workers have suffered a decline in real wages. The inequality of income distribution has widened.

3. In reaction to the failure of Keynesianism in solving prolonged stagflation and cumulative fiscal crises, the economic role of the state has been reduced. Since the beginning of the 1980s, neo-liberalism has eclipsed Keynesianism and has become the dominant policy stance in the capitalist world. Accordingly, privatization, deregulation and freer market competition have been promoted globally. Neo-liberalism stands against trade unionism, social democracy and socialism. State expenditures on welfare, education and medical services have suffered in many countries.

4. Corresponding to these changes, the globalization of the capitalist market economy has increased. Capitalism is restoring its vitality by coming back to its original mother sea of the world market. Modern globalization involves the use of microelectronic-based information technologies, the multinationalization of capitalist firms and increased speculative flows of money and finance throughout the world. National states have increasingly become unable to regulate the flow of multinational capital. Against multinational capital, the powers of the nation state are relatively weak. Globalization is also used as a further excuse for deregulation, tax reduction and the opening of the market economy.

5. While the capitalist economies reacted to the economic crises with new policies, the Soviet-type economies, with their ossified state and party bureaucracies, could not manage to change either their industrial technologies or their economic structures in the face of economic stagnation. This impasse led finally to the dissolution of these regimes in Eastern Europe and the USSR. In the 1990s the countries of the former Soviet bloc set out to establish a capitalist market economy. In contrast, China has maintained Communist Party leadership. It is experimenting with a socialist market economy, and has achieved a high rate of economic growth since 1978. Vietnam and Cuba are following this experiment. Their markets have gradually been opened up to multinational capital. In sum, these changes in the former centrally planned economies have clearly re-extended the global space for multinational capitalist firms to invest and trade.

The strong tide of contemporary capitalist globalization – with its heightened competition and neo-liberal ideology – is thus not a simple linear extrapolation in the historical evolution of capitalism. It signifies a spiral-like historical reversal, after a century with various attempts to regulate the competitive market, alongside the socialist bid to construct planned economies without a free market. Arising from the depth of its historical crisis, capitalism is restoring the competitive vitality of the global market economy. Correspondingly, individualism and market freedom – rather than a concern for economic equality and social cohesion for the mass of working people – have become the dominant ideology in the world.

CONCLUSION: PROBLEMS AND POSSIBILITIES

Problems of the Current World Order

The recent turn in capitalist evolution is not without its problems and anxieties. First, the former belief in the ability of capitalist nation states to improve the economic life of the people has largely disappeared. Although Keynesianism seemed quite effective in the past, it has failed to prevent depression and unemployment since 1973. The increased multinational activity of capital and the rapid growth in speculative international financial flows have undermined the ability of national states to manage their economies. Hence capitalist states have a crisis of credibility concerning their ability to manage their own economies in the future.

Second, the post-1973 crisis of capitalist economies did not serve to benefit socialism as an alternative path for the future. On the contrary, Soviet-type socialism also fell into economic stagnation and crisis. Its social systems were revealed as economically inflexible to changes in industrial technologies for consumer goods and politically repressive and corrupt. Since the Soviet Union was widely regarded as a representative model of socialism, its collapse in 1991, following the revolutions in Eastern Europe in 1989, spread disillusion for socialism as a whole. Despite its economic success, the Chinese model is not yet challenging economic life in the advanced capitalist countries.

Third, neo-liberalism could not avoid its own problems. The revitalized competitive capitalist world market is far from realizing a harmonious, stable and rational economic order. On the contrary, it is rather widening the economic inequality between the rich employers and the workers, between the centre in the advanced countries and the poor periphery in the South. It has also deepened the global ecological crisis, and has increased wasteful speculative instability in world markets. In Eastern Europe and Russia, neo-liberal shock therapy has clearly failed to revive these economies and has finally been abandoned.

Nevertheless, neo-liberalism sustains its ideological appeal through its fundamentalist and unfalsifiable belief in the efficacy of markets. Any failures are put down to the incompleteness or non-existence of perfect, transparent, competitive markets. However, real-world markets can never be so pure. Armed with such excuses, any neo-liberal government can exempt itself from responsibility for any failures, no matter how disastrous.

In the name of market principles and globalization, neo-liberalism has changed working conditions in favour of capitalist firms. In the face of deepening budget crises, marginal income tax rates and corporation tax rates have been reduced for the wealthy while the tax burden for the mass of working people has been increased typically through increases in consumer taxes. Former welfare states have returned an increasing part of the costs of medical care and child education to individuals.

All this risks serious damage to the social fabric and morale. While the gains of speculators in modern casino-capitalism are praised by neo-liberal ideology, the wealth created from industry and labour is undervalued. In this climate of speculative individualism, moneymaking criminals permeate both businesses and governments, all over the world. Trust and confidence in leaders and politicians are lost.

We are thus witnessing multilayered uncertainties and disillusions in the old ideologies of Keynesianism, social democracy, Soviet socialism and even neo-liberalism.

Possibilities for Evolutionary Progress

In the face of these problems, what possibilities are there for historical progress? We can sketch out the following incomplete agenda.

First is the possibility of arms reduction or disarmament. The old pretexts for maintaining military forces so as to keep empires and colonial territories or as a defence against Communism have now gone. In 1980, the Brand Report estimated that the total cost for a 10-year aid programme for supplying necessary minimum foods and sanitation to developing countries was less than half the world military expenditure in a single year (Kidron and Smith, 1983, Figure 24). If realized, the peace dividend could help the budgetary crises of rich countries and mitigate the serious problems of the poor in developing countries.

Second on the agenda is the possibility of a restructuring of the world political and economic order. Will the globalization of capitalist economies be followed by a homogenization and integration of political power, or create more room for a variety of political power structures? The possibility for an enhanced role for the United Nations and other international cooperative organizations emerges. However, the idea of forming a unified world government still seems unrealistic in a world full of diverse cultures and countries.

The historic experiment of integration within the European Union is likely to proceed, although with uneven success and some resultant dissatisfaction among people in member countries. The EU political leaders may be able to construct a new agenda for social democracy, and thus limit the influence of global neo-liberalism. By contrast, in North America, NAFTA (North American Free Trade Agreement) is much less likely to follow this road. Economic and political integration in Asia, South America and Africa faces even greater difficulties. Despite some initial steps in this direction, including discussions concerning a common market in East Asia, substantial integration in these regions is unlikely to be achieved in the foreseeable future. While economic globalization is undermining the power of the national state, a viable alternative political structure of integration, including the possibility of a number of regional blocs, has not yet emerged on a world scale.

The capitalist market economy can be combined with a variety of forms of government and units of political power. In the long, evolutionary history of the capitalist world system, we have observed absolute monarchy, restricted democracy, imperialism, fascism, despotism and liberal democracy. The liberal democratic state, alongside competitive markets, is therefore not necessarily the destined natural order for the capitalist world system. Economic globalization may not homogenize but rather may maintain a diversity of politico-economic orders in the world.

Another key issue for the twenty-first century is how to stabilize the international monetary system. The introduction of floating exchange rates in 1973 was in accord with neo-liberal belief in the rational harmonious efficiency of the competitive free market. The outcome has been to greatly increase the potential instability of economic life throughout the world. The destructive potential of monetary and financial instability must be marked down as a serious failure for neo-liberalism.

What are the alternatives? Some have suggested a return to the gold standard. However, this would enforce too strict a restriction of the supply of money and credit to be popular. The Hayekian theory of free banking is more in accord with the current neo-liberal fundamentalism. It seems to match the potential growth of global electronic money. However, it is deeply misled by a belief in the harmonious rationality of free markets. Furthermore, to establish free banking and abolish central banks will require strong political intervention. If implemented, it would further exacerbate inflation, speculation and financial crises (Itoh and Lapavitsas 1999, pp. 204–5).

Global Keynesianism with an integrated world central bank would not be a realistic option in view of the current diversity of politico-economic orders in the world. By contrast, regional monetary integration, such as within the EU, is a much more realistic programme. It would help to stabilize international monetary issues at least within the EU. Once the euro grows as a reliable and stable key currency, then wider international cooperation to stabilize the speculative trading of exchange rates, either by political intervention in the exchange market or by means of taxes, would become easier and more feasible. The idea of a 'Tobin tax' has attracted international attention as a possible policy to limit speculative trading in foreign currencies. It involves the setting up of a low rate of tax on each purchase of a foreign currency. This would not substantially hamper real needs for transactions or travel, but would establish prohibitively heavy costs for frequent speculative trading in currencies.[3] Ironically, the role of neo-liberalism in causing financial instability has helped to revive international and cooperative proposals for the control of money.

A fourth issue concerns the future of socialism as a potential alternative to the capitalist market economy. Capitalism can only survive by incorporating and regenerating, as it has long done, various communal human relations at several social levels. Most of countersystemic social movements, such as trade unions, cooperatives, feminism, ecologism, dissident political groups and parties, rest more or less on such communal human cooperation relatively independent from the individualistic market order. These movements provide the basis for the continuous rebirth of new ideas and movements for socialism. There remain indeed many different models of socialism for the future.[4]

The evolutionary spiral of capitalism will proceed in the twenty-first century. Experiences from Eastern Europe in 1989 to the Philippines in 1986 show that relatively peaceful change can take place when workers and citizens stand up and demand it. The problems in the current capitalist world system suggest that the current turn towards neo-liberalism with globalization can be reversed. The evolutionary spiral may turn yet again.

NOTES

1. The French *régulation* school was initiated by Aglietta (1981) and its characteristics are summarized typically in Boyer (1986). Gordon et al. (1982) present the representative approach of the American radical theory of the social structure of accumulation.
2. This methodological position was presented by Uno (1962, 1971) and applied by Albritton (1991).
3. See Tobin (1978) and Dornbusch (1997) for arguments in favour of this policy.
4. Attempts to reconcile socialist ideas with the market can take various forms, including the actually existing case of the Chinese market economy (Bardhan and Roemer, 1993; Itoh, 1995).

REFERENCES

Aglietta, M. (1981), *A Theory of Capitalist Regulation*, translated by D. Fernbach, London: New Left Books.

Albritton, R. (1991), *A Japanese Approach to Stages of Capitalist Development*, London: Macmillan.

Bardhan, P.K. and J.E. Roemer (eds) (1993), *Market Socialism*, New York and Oxford: Oxford University Press.

Boyer, R. (1986), *La Théorie de la Régulation: Une analyse critique* (Regulation theory: a critical analysis), Paris: Edition La Découverte.

Dornbusch, R. (1997), 'Cross-border payments taxes and alternative capital account regimes', in *International and Financial Issues for the 1990s*, vol.V, New York: United Nations.

Fukuyama, F. (1992), *The End of History and the Last Man*, 2 vols, translated by S. Watanabe, Tokyo: Mikasa-shobo.

Gordon, D.M., R. Edwards and M. Reich (1982), *Segmented Work, Divided Workers*, Cambridge: Cambridge University Press.

Itoh, M. (1990), *The World Economic Crisis and Japanese Capitalism*, London: Macmillan, and New York: St Martin's Press.

Itoh, M. (1995), *Political Economy for Socialism*, London: Macmillan, and New York: St Martin's Press.

Itoh, M. and C. Lapavitsas (1999), *Political Economy of Money and Finance*, London: Macmillan, and New York: St Martin's Press.

Kidron, M. and D. Smith (1983), *The War Atlas*, London: Pluto.

Marx, K. (1970), *A Contribution to the Critique of Political Economy*, translated by S.W. Ryazanskaya from the edition of 1859, Moscow: Progress Publishers.

Marx, K. (1976), *Capital*, vol. I, translated by B. Fowkes, Harmondsworth: Penguin Books.

Marx, K. and F. Engels (1998), *The Communist Manifesto*, translated by S. Moore from the edition of 1848, London: Verso.

Tobin, J. (1978), 'A proposal for international monetary reform', *Eastern Economic Journal*, 4, July–October, 153–9.

Uno, K. (1962), *Methodology of Political Economy*, in Japanese, Tokyo: University of Tokyo Press.

Uno, K. (1971), *Types of Economic Policy*, in Japanese, Tokyo: Koubundo.

Wallerstein, I. (1974), *The Modern World System*, New York: Academic Press.

Wallerstein, I. (1983), *Historical Capitalism*, London: Verso.

Index